Rise Above Bullying

Rise Above Bullying

Empower and Advocate for Your Child

Nancy E. Willard

Published by John Wiley & Sons, Inc., Hoboken, New Jersey.
Published simultaneously in Canada.

Limit of Liability/Disclaimer of Warranty
While the publisher and author have used their best efforts in preparing this book, they make no representations or warranties with respect to the accuracy or completeness of the contents of this book and specifically disclaim any implied warranties of merchantability or fitness for a particular purpose. No warranty may be created or extended by sales representatives or written sales materials. The advice and strategies contained herein may not be suitable for your situation. You should consult with a professional where appropriate. Further, readers should be aware that websites listed in this work may have changed or disappeared between when this work was written and when it is read. Neither the publisher nor authors shall be liable for any loss of profit or any other commercial damages, including but not limited to special, incidental, consequential, or other damages.

For general information on our other products and services or for technical support, please contact our Customer Care Department within the United States at (800) 762-2974, outside the United States at (317) 572-3993 or fax (317) 572-4002.

Wiley also publishes its books in a variety of electronic formats. Some content that appears in print may not be available in electronic formats. For more information about Wiley products, visit our web site at www.wiley.com.

Library of Congress Cataloging-in-Publication Data
Names: Willard, Nancy E., author. | John Wiley & Sons, publisher.
Title: Rise above bullying : empower and advocate for your child / Nancy E.
    Willard.
Description: Hoboken, New Jersey : Wiley, [2025] | Includes bibliographical
    references and index.
Identifiers: LCCN 2024041119 (print) | LCCN 2024041120 (ebook) | ISBN
    9781394282562 (paperback) | ISBN 9781394282586 (adobe pdf) | ISBN
    9781394282579 (epub)
Subjects: LCSH: Bullying–Prevention. | Parenting.
Classification: LCC BF637.B85 W533 2025 (print) | LCC BF637.B85 (ebook) |
    DDC 302.34/3–dc23/eng/20241023
LC record available at https://lccn.loc.gov/2024041119
LC ebook record available at https://lccn.loc.gov/2024041120

Cover Design: Wiley
Cover Image: © FG Trade Latin/Getty Images

Set in 9.5/12.5pt STIXTwoText by Straive, Pondicherry, India
SKY10090439_110924

Contents

Introduction

My daughter has a learning disability which makes her life a living hell every day at school. She is insulted almost daily by the other students and even her teacher. Yep, that's right. My daughter is in a classroom with 35 students who are 9 years old. She is unable to follow instructions because she has other things going on in her brain. That's why she has a learning problem. The other students insult and joke about her. The teacher laughs when this happens. She has meltdowns almost every day.

My question is this: Should I give up on public school? Should I stop sending her because she is a disruption to other students? Should I keep my mouth shut when she comes home to tell me, "The teacher does not like me mom." Year after year! That is my question. What do I do? I am up against people who think they know the answer to everything. What the heck can I do? Can someone tell me? Do I walk away and allow this to continue or do I search for one ounce of hope that the system is not broken and that my child will not be broken by it. Feeling really sad.

This was a post made by a parent on social media. Does this describe your anguish and frustration because your child is being broken – constantly being treated badly by other students at school? Is a school staff member being hurtful to your child or do staff ignore situations where your child is being treated badly?

If so, then you are the parent this book has been written for. *Rise Above Bullying: Empower and Advocate for Your Child* will provide you with insight and guidance to both better empower your child to be a Thriver even though they are being treated badly and to insist that the school take the steps necessary to stop the hurtful behavior and remedy the harm to your child.

The way in which schools are addressing bullying is not achieving success in far too many situations. Your response to this statement is likely "Duh, that is the problem we are facing."

Rise Above Bullying: Empower and Advocate for Your Child, First Edition. Nancy E. Willard.
© 2025 John Wiley & Sons, Inc. Published 2025 by John Wiley & Sons, Inc.

A huge concern is that too many school leaders appear to think they are handling these situations effectively. If there is news coverage on concerns of bullying, you can pretty much count on a school leader with the school or district saying, "Bullying in any form is unacceptable. We take reports of bullying very seriously and have policies and procedures in place to address such behavior." This is what the Owasso Public Schools stated after the death of Nex Benedict.[1] But, if students are asked, they will say quite clearly that they do not report because whenever they have, nothing was done. As Nex Benedict said when she was asked about whether she reported being bullied to the school, "I did not really see the point to it." Her classmates also told news reporters that they do not report being bullied or, if they do, nothing happens.

The approach that schools are directed to use to address bullying is grounded in the myth that students who are being treated badly will report to the school and the intervention by the school will be effective. The vast majority of bullied students do not ask for help from their school. Many students do not think that the way the school will respond will make things better. They have legitimate fears that reporting to the school could make things worse. Research supports the concerns held by students.

However, it is important that you understand that your child's principal is doing what they have been directed to do. Principals and school staff want all students to feel safe, welcomed, and respected. Principals are "following the book." The problem is the requirements and guidance in "the book." At the heart of the problem are the anti-bullying statutes that are in every state. These statutes call for a rules-and-punishment, disciplinary-code approach to bullying. This approach is entirely ineffective.

Telling students what the rules are does not effectively stop hurtful behavior, especially when school staff are not present – even when they are – if their hurtful acts are routinely ignored. The vast majority of bullied students do not generally report. When they do, this most often either does not resolve the situation or makes things worse. Most bullying is persistent hurtful behavior that is verbal or relationship aggression which occurs in a subtle and covert manner. This behavior does not meet the "substantial disruption" standard most principals apply to the question of whether an accused student violated the policy. Principals are directed under state statute to address bullying by imposing disciplinary consequences. They have also been told to stop suspending students. In too many states, there are requirements that schools make an annual report

1 Alfonseca, K. (2024). Students walk out over nonbinary student Nex Benedict's death, anti-LGBTQ bullying in Oklahoma. ABC News, February 26. https://abcnews.go.com/US/ student-walkout-owasso-high-school-oklahoma-nonbinary-student-nex-benedict-death/ story?id=107546201 (accessed 1 August 2024).

of bullying incidents. This has resulted in way too many principals deciding that reported incidents are "not bullying."

There is also a stereotype that the students who engage in bullying are at high risk in other ways. These students may be considered "hurt people hurting people." There are some students in schools who are both treated badly and excluded and are also aggressive. These students are not the primary source of bullying. Students who engage in bullying are more often socially skilled students who are considered "popular" and "cool." They are hurtful in order to achieve dominance and social status. They are often considered to be leaders in the school and are compliant to school staff. The odds of principals imposing disciplinary consequence on these students are slim to none.

The increased contention in our society appears to be generating an even greater level of bullying in our schools. However, on the positive side, it does appear that many students have greater commitment to social justice than their elders. We are seeing many situations of wonderful students standing up for the rights and well-being of others.

What you will learn in *Rise Above Bullying: Empower and Advocate for Your Child* includes insight into:

- Those who are bullied and the harms.
- Those who are hurtful, including both students and staff.
- Why what schools are doing is not working.
- Youth development, trauma, and post-traumatic growth.
- Powerful strategies to empower your child and increase their happiness and resilience.
- How your child can use these empowerment and resilience strategies in situations where someone is being hurtful to them, they have been hurtful to someone, in close relationships, when using social media, and in situations where they witness someone else being treated badly.
- Federal civil rights protections against harassment and bullying and how to obtain such protections for your child, even if your child is not currently considered within a class of students who are protected by these laws.
- How you can document the concerns of what is happening to your child and the harmful impact. How you can effectively proceed either individually or with a group of parents of bullied students to insist that your child's school stop the bullying, remedy the harm to those who have been bullied, correct aspects of the school environment that are contributing to the concern, and monitor to ensure a positive outcome for all involved students.

Rise Above Bullying: Empower and Advocate for Your Child is written for parents. The term "parent" means any person acting in a caregiving capacity for a child.

This book is also appropriate for those who work with young people and families in a counseling or advocacy relationship. This could include counselors, parent advocates, professionals who work with advocacy groups, youth faith leaders, and others who are in a supportive role with young people and their families. This book will also hopefully be of interest to school principals, counselors, social workers, psychologists, and nurses.

The legal aspects I will be discussing are grounded in US law. However, many of the principles and some of the protections will be applicable in other countries.

The objective of *Rise Above Bullying: Empower and Advocate for Your Child* is to help you to support your child in being resilient when things get tough and empowered to achieve success in their life. When your child is resilient, they can "bounce back" from difficult experiences and are able to feel happy and be successful – even though they have faced such challenges. They can learn from any bad things that have happened. They can then use what they learned to live a more happy and successful life. Becoming empowered is a process of becoming strong and confident, especially being able to control their life and make decisions in a responsible manner.

Being resilient is being like a dandelion. Even a sidewalk or bunch of rocks cannot stop a dandelion from growing and blooming. Providing the insight to support you in empowering your child to be a beautiful, growing, and blooming dandelion is the purpose of this book.

The Positively Powerful strategies set forth in Chapter 5 of *Rise Above Bullying: Empower and Advocate for Your Child* have been demonstrated through social science research to be effective in increasing the resilience and empowerment of both youth and adults, including those who have experienced adversities. Much of this insight comes from a field of study called "positive psychology." Positive psychology is a scientific approach to studying how people think, feel, and behave, with a focus on how they build strengths. Positive psychology focuses on such things as happiness, confidence, well-being, and compassion.

Please do not use the term "victim" in reference to your child. Calling your child a "victim" may cause them to think of themselves as a victim, with all of the powerlessness that this term conveys. My focus in this book is to provide you with guidance on how to empower your child to reduce the potential risk that they will be treated badly, effectively respond if they are, and engage in follow-up actions so that the hurtful way they have been treated does not harm their heart and soul. My goal is that your child is not a "victim," not even a "survivor." My goal is that your child become a "Thriver" – a person who experienced challenging times who shows growth because of the experience and is thriving, successful, happy, and making a positive contribution to others.

Taylor Swift was bullied as a teen. This is comment she provided to a fan who had said she was being bullied demonstrates the voice of a Thriver:

> (Y)ou will always be criticized and teased and bullied for things that make you different, but usually those things will be what set you apart. The things that set you apart from the pack, the things that you once thought were your weaknesses will someday become your strengths. So if they say you are weird or annoying or strange or too this or not enough that, maybe it's because you threaten them. Maybe you threaten them because you are not the norm. And if you are not the norm, give yourself a standing ovation.[2]

My goal in writing this book is to provide insight to parents, and those who support parents, to support all young people, especially those who are being treated badly by peers, to become empowered and a "Thriver."

While we are on the topic of words and definitions, please do not call students who are hurtful "bullies." Bullying is behavior – behavior that we hope can be changed. When young people, or anyone else, is called "a bully," this is name calling. This is not helpful to resolving these concerns.

The other important objective of this book is to provide you with the insight necessary for you to be able to effectively advocate for your child. When these hurtful situations are more serious or are persistent, which means that your child is unable to get this hurtful treatment to stop, your child's school must intervene. Far too often, schools do not intervene effectively.

The approach that schools have been directed to use under state anti-bullying statutes will not result in a positive outcome. The requirements placed on schools under the federal civil rights laws hold a much greater promise for a resolution. If your child is being persistently bullied and this has been going on for some time, it is probable that your child has developed mental health concerns and there has been an interference with your child's ability to learn and participate in school activities. Assuming this is the case, then your child receives protections under one of the federal civil rights laws, Section 504. Section 504 also requires that bullying of a student be addressed by a team of knowledgeable staff members.

A bit about my path. I went through school as "Weirdo Willard." I became a special education teacher of students who had emotional and behavioral challenges. Then, I became an attorney and did work in the area of computer law. As schools began to implement more technology, I shifted to become an educational

---

2 Strecker, E. (2015). Read Taylor Swift's sweet message to bullied fan. *Billboard*, January 27.

technology consultant. Then, in the early 1990s, as the internet came into society and schools, my focus shifted to digital safety.

In 2007, my book on cyberbullying, *Cyberbullying and Cyber Threats: Responding to the Challenge on Online Cruelty, Threats, and Distress* was published.[3] As I was writing this book, I was confronted with a problem. Based on what I saw happening online, the information being provided to educators about those who bully was inaccurate and the directives set forth under state statutes were flat not going to work. The greatest source of bullying is not "at risk" students. The greatest source of bullying is socially skilled, compliant students who are being hurtful to achieve dominance and social status. These students are highly unlikely to ever be punished for their hurtful actions. The rules-and-punishment, disciplinary-code approach is never going to be effective in addressing bullying either in schools or online.

The rules-and-punishment disciplinary approach focuses on these efforts:

- **Make rules against bullying.** Students do not always follow rules, especially if they are not enforced or they are not being directly supervised. Schools are not making rules for social media sites.
- **Tell students to report.** The overwhelming majority of students do not report when they are being bullied because they know that this will not resolve the problem and could very well make things worse.
- **Investigate.** When responding pursuant to the disciplinary code, the principal's sole focus is on whether the accused student violated the rule and should be punished. There is generally not a sufficiently comprehensive investigation to support a comprehensive and effective intervention. Principals face major challenges investigating social media incidents.
- **Impose consequences.** Ample evidence documents that punishing students rarely results in positive behavior change. With the advent of social media, punishing a student raises additional concerns. It is entirely possible for the hurtful student and their supporters to engage in vicious, uncontrollable, anonymous social media retaliation.

In 2010, the Obama Administration launched greater efforts to address bullying. I decided to shift to a focus on all forms of bullying. Since this time, neither I, nor any other experts I know, have achieved much, if any, effectiveness in communicating about these concerns to school leaders. With the enactment of the Every Student Succeeds Act in 2015, the primary focus of school leaders has been on test scores. Further, they are following the dictates of their state statutes.

---

3 Willard, N. (2007). Cyberbullying and Cyber Threats: Responding to the Challenge on Online Cruelty, Threats, and Distress. Research Press.

More on why what school leaders are doing is not working is addressed in Chapter 3. Essentially, in US schools we have reached the point of "insanity" – as defined reportedly by Einstein. US schools are continuing to follow the same approach year after year, with absolutely zero evidence of effectiveness.

In 2015, I conducted a national survey of 1549 secondary students on bullying and hurtful behavior.[4] Students were asked questions about hurtful incidents, the impact, reporting, and effectiveness of a school response. This survey also included what are called "positive social norms questions," that asked for students' values related to how students interact with peers. Data from this survey has been incorporated into the insight presented in this book. You can also review the full results online.

It is my hope that by empowering parents and others in their community who can be supportive advocates for parents and young people, we can ensure that all students feel safe, welcome, and respected in all schools.

The chapters in this book include:

- **Chapter 1. Those Who Are Bullied and the Harms.** This chapter will address those who are being bullied and the harms associated with being bullied. These harms are a form of trauma which can lead to long-lasting emotional challenges, academic failure, and challenges in maintaining positive relationships. Despite experiencing these challenging situations, bullied young people can become empowered and strong.
- **Chapter 2. Those Who Bully.** The students who are the greatest source of bullying are the socially skilled and popular students who are hurtful to gain dominance and social status. It also must be recognized that sometimes adults are hurtful to young people. This could include school staff, coaches, and other youth workers.
- **Chapter 3. Lack of Effectiveness of Anti-bullying Efforts.** Educators want students in their school to feel safe, welcome, and respected. The challenge is that the approach educators have been directed to use to address to bullying is not achieving positive outcomes. This chapter will provide insight into why these directives are not achieving positive outcomes and recommendations for strategies that will likely achieve better results.
- **Chapter 4. Youth Development, Trauma, Post-traumatic Growth.** Young people go through stages in development that relate to how their brain is developing. These stages include cognitive, moral, and identity development. Young people who are being bullied are experiencing trauma. This chapter will address

---

4 Willard, N.E. (2016). Embrace Civility student survey. Embrace Civility in the Digital Age. https://www.embracecivility.org/wp-content/uploadsnew/ECSSFullReportfull.pdf (accessed 1 August 2024).

how trauma impacts the brain and how those who have experienced trauma can achieve post-traumatic growth.

- **Chapter 5. Positively Powerful.** The longest chapter in this book will introduce seven Positively Powerful strategies that are grounded in research into positive psychology and resilience that can support your child in becoming empowered and resilient. These strategies include: Make Positive Connections; Reach Out to Be Kind; Build Your Strengths; Focus on the Good; Be Mindful; Keep Your Personal Power; and Think Things Through. Each of these strategies have two or three sub-strategies.
- **Chapter 6. Positively Powerful Strategies for Those Being Treated Badly.** The Positively Powerful strategies can be used by your child to both reduce the potential they are treated badly and improve their response if they are.
- **Chapter 7. Positively Powerful Strategies for Those Being Hurtful.** The Positively Powerful strategies can also support your child in reducing the potential they will be hurtful, avoiding impulsive retaliation, accepting personal responsibility for their hurtful behavior, and taking steps to remedy the harm if they were.
- **Chapter 8. Positively Powerful Strategies for Close Relationships.** Your child will form closer relationships with some special friends, and, when teens, will likely form dating relationships. The Positively Powerful strategies can support positive relationships and help your child in those inevitable situations where a relationship ends.
- **Chapter 9. Positively Powerful on Social Media.** The Positively Powerful strategies can also support your child in engaging in safe and responsible use of social media. There are also a number of strategies in this chapter: Do Not Let Them Tell You That You Are Not Good Enough; Think Before You Post; Keep Your Life in Balance; Connect Safely; Protect Your Face and Friends; Read with Your Eyes Open; and Embrace Digital Civility.
- **Chapter 10. Be a Powerfully Positive Helpful Ally and Leader.** In line with the objective that your child is able to become a Thriver, the next step your child may want to take is to become a helpful ally who supports others who are being treated badly or excluded. Your child may also want to move into a leadership position in their school to support an environment that is safe, welcoming, and respectful for all students.
- **Chapter 11. Federal Civil Rights Laws and Free Speech.** Under federal civil rights laws, schools are obligated to address hurtful behavior that is sufficiently serious, persistent, or pervasive so that it interferes with or limits a student's ability to learn and participate school activities, and is based on a student's race, color, national origin, sex, disability, or religion. This is called a "hostile environment." If there are concerns that this might be happening, a school must conduct a prompt, unbiased, comprehensive investigation. If a hostile

environment exists, the school must implement a comprehensive intervention that must include steps reasonably calculated to stop the harassment, remedy the harm to the target, correct the school environment, and monitor to ensure the problem has stopped. If your child is receiving services on an Individualized Education Plan (IEP) or Section 504, the school is required to engage the IEP or Section 504 team to develop this comprehensive plan. If, because of the bullying, your child is now experiencing mental health concerns and an interference in their learning, they should be placed on a Section 504 plan, even if the only accommodations addressed in the plan are those directed as resolving the bullying situation.

- **Chapter 12. Stop the Harm.** Stopping the harm will require that you effectively document what is happening to your child and pursue a complaint against the school under civil rights law, preferably under Section 504. You can file this complaint either as an individual or within a group of parents and students who are all experiencing bullying. This chapter also outlines the comprehensive intervention you should seek to obtain.

The Rise Above Bullying website has been established to support this book. The URL is https://rise-above-bullying.com. This website has additional resources for parents and advocates.

1

Those Who Are Bullied and the Harms

What Is "Bullying?"

> Anston is being treated really badly by some of the other students in his sixth grade class. They make fun of his glasses and his weight. They intentionally refuse to allow him to sit with them at lunch. This has been going on for months. Anston is becoming more and more depressed. His grades are dropping. He often stays home because of headaches. When he told his principal that he was being bullied, her response was, "This is not bullying. There is nothing I can do."

What is "bullying?" It will likely not surprise you to know that there is no clarity on the answer to this question. It will be helpful for you to know about the different definitions so that if you are told that what is happening to your child is "not bullying," you will be empowered to respond in an effective manner. These are the different definitions.

- **Academic definition.** Researchers consider "bullying" to be when someone intends to be hurtful to someone, this harm is repeated, and there is an "imbalance of power." Imbalance of power means that the hurtful person has greater social or physical power than the one they are treating badly. There is general agreement that bullying behaviors include these components and can involve physical aggression, verbal aggression, and relational aggression or social exclusion.[1]

---

[1] Hellström, L., Thornberg, R., and Espelage, D.L. (2021). Definitions of bullying. In: *Wiley Blackwell Handbook of Bullying: A Comprehensive and International Review of Research and Intervention* (ed. P.K. Smith and J. O'Higgins Norman), 2–21. Wiley Blackwell.

- **Statutory definitions.** In the United States, are 50 different state statutory definitions of what is called bullying or harassment, and sometimes intimidation.[2] A 2011 US Department of Education (USDOE) report on state statutes noted that the lack of consistency "contributes to confusion over how a specific incident should be treated."[3] You can see all of the different state statutory definitions at https://stopbullying.gov. Because these statutes require that school districts create anti-bullying policies, your state's statutory definition becomes part of the policy in your district's disciplinary code. When a principal tells you or your child that "this is not bullying," they are saying "this does not, in my opinion, meet the definition in our policy."

- **Discriminatory harassment.** The definition of "discriminatory harassment" or "harassment" comes from US federal civil rights laws. This is a definition provided by the USDOE Office for Civil Rights (OCR): "Harassment creates a hostile environment when the conduct is sufficiently severe, pervasive, or persistent so as to interfere with or limit a student's ability to participate in or benefit from the services, activities, or opportunities offered by a school. When such harassment is based on race, color, national origin, sex, or disability, it violates the civil rights laws that OCR enforces."[4]

- **International definitions.** Internationally, the term "bullying" is defined in different ways by different countries. There are cross-cultural differences in how hurtful behavior is expressed in different countries. There are also differences in perspectives associated with physical aggression, verbal aggression, and relational aggression or social exclusion.[5]

- **Terms or questions in surveys.** The term "bullying" is also used in surveys. These generally ask about hurtful acts. The CDC's Youth Risk Behavior Survey (YRBS) uses this definition: "Bullying is when 1 or more students tease, threaten, spread rumors about, hit, shove, or hurt another student over and over again. It is not bullying when 2 students of about the same strength or power argue or fight or tease each other in a friendly way."[6] Most of the surveys do not ask about seriousness, frequency, or harmful impact. This is a concern because

2 https://www.StopBullying.Gov/resources/laws (accessed 1 August 2024).

3 Stuart-Cassel, V., Bell, A., and Springer, J.F. (2011). Analysis of state bullying laws and policies. US Department of Education. https://files.eric.ed.gov/fulltext/ED527524.pdf (accessed 1 August 2024).

4 https://www2.ed.gov/about/offices/list/ocr/letters/colleague-201010.pdf (accessed 1 August 2024).

5 Smith, P.K., Robinson, S., and Slonje, R. (2012). The school bullying research program: why and how it has developed. In: *Wiley Blackwell Handbook of Bullying: A Comprehensive and International Review of Research and Intervention* (ed. P.K. Smith and J. O'Higgins Norman), 42–59. Wiley Blackwell.

6 https://www.cdc.gov/healthyyouth/data/yrbs/questionnaires.htm (accessed 1 August 2024).

the surveys do not distinguish between hurtful incidents that were resolved and those that are more serious or persistent.

- **Cyberbullying.** Cyberbullying is a newer form of hurtful behavior that is accomplished using digital technologies and social media. Because there is such a clear overlap between face-to-face bullying and cyberbullying, my recommendation would be a focus on the hurtful behavior, not the means by which this occurred.
- **What students think.** A student could complain they are being bullied based on one hurtful act that was not significantly serious – or serious or persistent hurtful incidents and situations that match any of the above definitions.

A document on bullying and cyberbullying was recently provided by the California School Board Association.[7] On page one, column one, the document references a recent California statute that addresses the need for a policy that prohibits discrimination, harassment, intimidation, and bullying based on specified protected class status. The state statute requires schools to address what should be considered discriminatory harassment, but under the state anti-bullying statute. These provisions are not in accord with the requirements under federal civil rights laws. On page one, column two, the document provides the academic definition. The difference between definitions is not addressed. On page two, the document references the California Healthy Kids Survey, which asks students about a range of hurtful acts which could or might not have been serious or persistent. This is a recipe for total confusion.

The perspective I share with school leaders is that we need to shift to a focus on empowering students to maintain positive relationships, reducing all forms of hurtful behavior, and ensuring both students and school staff can respond effectively to all incidents that involve hurtful behavior. Some of these may be more minor incidents that students should be able to resolve by themselves or with school staff assistance. Other more serious incidents will need to be resolved by a school team including the principal. All of these hurtful incidents cause some level of harm and can disrupt the environment.

If a student is experiencing someone being hurtful to them, they are unable to get this to stop, and this is causing them distress and an interference with their learning, should it really matter whether the hurtful acts meet the district's policy on "bullying?"

7 Asch, A. (2023). School safety: bullying and cyberbullying. California School Boards Association. https://www.csba.org/-/media/CSBA/Files/GovernanceResources/EducationIssues/ConditionsofChildren/BullyingGovBrief-REPD_10-2023.ashx?la=en&rev=d409e63de5f641839230ee2dd9ae9ff9 (accessed 1 August 2024).

Students Who Are Bullied

In this section, I will describe two general profiles of the kinds of students who are bullied.

Bullied and Hurtful Students

> *Jacob has had a challenging life. He is living with his single mom, as his father is in prison. His mom struggles with ensuring the family has sufficient money and sometimes she drinks too much. Jacob has attention challenges, which interfere with his ability to focus while in school. Jacob is frequently excluded by other students in his class. They also often poke fun at his clothes and indicate that he smells. Jacob has begun to be aggressive to other students. He triggers and gets very upset. When he is upset he will lash out at anyone around him, especially those who are always poking fun at his clothing.*

Some students have both been bullied and excluded by others and they are also being hurtful. Sometimes, these students are called "bully-victims." This is backwards. The saying "hurt people hurt people" fully applies to these students. They are "victims" who are now also "bullies" – except I suggest not using these terms. It is imperative to address the hurtful way these students are being treated to support them in stopping their hurtful behavior.

This may be your child or a student who is being hurtful to your child. These students have generally been repeatedly denigrated and excluded by other students and sometimes by school staff. They may also often come from homes that have a high level of violence or neglect. This has impacted their ability to self-regulate. These young people tend to be unpopular, aggressive, easily angered, and have few friends.[8] They are very low on the school's social ladder – the most ostracized by peers.[9]

These students may engage in behaviors that encourage other students to be hurtful to them. They are generally impulsive and poor in regulating their

---

8 Kochel, K.P., Ladd, G.W., Bagwell, C.L., and Yabko, B.A. (2015). Bully/victim profiles' differential risk for worsening peer acceptance: the role of friendship. *Journal of Applied Developmental Psychology* 41: 38–45. Nansel, T.R., Overpeck, M.D., Pilla, R.S. et al. (2001). Bullying behaviors among US youth: prevalence and association with psychosocial adjustment. *Journal of the American Medical Association (JAMA)* 285 (16): 2094–2100. Juvonen, J., Graham, S., and Schuster, B. (2003). Bullying among young adolescents: the strong, the weak, and the troubled. *Pediatrics* 112 (6 Pt 1): 1231–1237.
9 Cook, C.R., Williams, K.R., Guerra, N.G. et al. (2010). Predictors of bullying and victimization in childhood and adolescence: a meta-analytic investigation. *School Psychology Quarterly* 25: 65. https://doi.org/10.1037/a0020149.

emotions.[10] Other students can subtly pick on them until they "snap" and become disruptive. Most school staff do not notice or they ignore the more minor hurtful acts directed at these students. Then, when they become disruptive, they are the ones who are disciplined.[11]

These students engage in "reactive aggression."[12] Reactive aggression is emotional and impulsive hurtful behavior. They impulsively react badly in response to something bad that has been happening to them.

Marginalized hurtful students are at high risk.[13] They have higher levels of depression, anxiety, eating disorders, substance abuse, and suicidal behavior.[14] They are less successful academically.[15] They are more likely to carry weapons to school to protect themselves.[16] They are less likely to graduate.[17] They have the highest rates of self-harm, plans for suicide, and attempted suicide.[18] They also have higher rates of serious criminal charges in adulthood.[19]

---

10 Juvonen, J., Graham, S., and Schuster, B. (2003). Bullying among young adolescents: the strong, the weak, and the troubled. *Pediatrics* 112 (6 Pt 1): 1231–1237.

11 Green, V.A. (2021). The role of teachers. In: *Wiley Blackwell Handbook of Bullying: A Comprehensive and International Review of Research and Intervention* (ed. P.K. Smith and J. O'Higgins Norman), 333–350. Wiley Blackwell.

12 Dodge, K.A. (1991). The structure and function of reactive and proactive aggression. *The Development and Treatment of Childhood Aggression* 16 (5): 201–218. https://doi.org/10.1111/j.1467-6494.2009.00610.x.

13 Gini, G. and Pozzoli, T. (2009). Association between bullying and psychosomatic problems: a meta-analysis. *Pediatrics* 123 (3): 1059–1065. Copeland, W.E., Wolke, D., Angold, A., and Costello, E.J. (2013). Adult psychiatric outcomes of bullying and being bullied by peers in childhood and adolescence. *JAMA Psychiatry* 70 (4): 419–426. Wolke, D. and Lereya, S.T. (2015). Long-term effects of bullying. *Archives of Disease in Childhood* 100 (9): 879–885. https://doi.org/10.1136/archdischild-2014-306667.

14 Juvonen, Graham, and Schuster, Bullying among young adolescentsKowalski, R.M. and Limber, S.P. (2013). Psychological, physical, and academic correlates of cyberbullying and traditional bullying. *The Journal of Adolescent Health* 53 (1 Suppl): S13–S20.

15 Glew, G.M., Fan, M.Y., Katon, W. et al. (2005). Bullying, psychosocial adjustment, and academic performance in elementary school. *Archives of Pediatrics & Adolescent Medicine* 159 (11): 1026–1031. Schwartz, D. (2000). Subtypes of victims and aggressors in children's peer groups. *Journal of Abnormal Child Psychology* 28: 181–192.

16 van Geel, M., Vedder, P., and Tanilon, J. (2014). Bullying and weapon carrying: a meta-analysis. *JAMA Pediatrics* 168 (8): 714–720. Klomek, A.B., Sourander, A., and Elonheimo, H. (2015). Bullying by peers in childhood and effects on psychopathology, suicidality, and criminality in adulthood. *Lancet Psychiatry* 2 (10): 930–941.

17 Wolke, D., Copeland, W.E., Angold, A., and Costello, E.J. (2013). Impact of bullying in childhood on adult health, wealth, crime, and social outcomes. *Psychological Science* 24 (10): 1958–1970. https://doi.org/10.1177/0956797613481608.

18 Ford, R., King, T., Priest, N., and Kavanagh, A. (2017). Bullying and mental health and suicidal behaviour among 14- to 15-year-olds in a representative sample of Australian children. *The Australian and New Zealand Journal of Psychiatry* 51 (9): 897–908.

19 Wolke, D., Copeland, W.E., Angold, A., and Costello, E.J. (2013). Impact of bullying in childhood on adult health, wealth, crime, and social outcomes. *Psychological Science* 24 (10): 1958–1970. https://doi.org/10.1177/0956797613481608.

These students are functioning at a high level of traumatic distress.[20] They have learned that their environments are unsafe. Their amygdala, their threat sensor, is always functioning at "on." They may also trigger and become upset or aggressive in response to situations that, from an outside perspective, appear to be relatively minor.

If your child is being treated badly and is also engaging in hurtful and disruptive behavior, the guidance set out in Chapter 5 provides recommendations to better support your child. Chapter 12 will provide you with guidance on how to document what is happening and the recommended steps to address this concern, which will require both support for your child and holding your child accountable for any harm they cause.

Bullied Students

> *Jessie is an autistic, non-binary high school student. They have challenges "acting normal" because their brain does not function in a way that supports them in doing so. Jessie has been bullied by other students since kindergarten, because they are thought of as "weird." Now that Jessie has changed their name, the students have realized why they are so different. The bullying and exclusion has increased. Jessie stopped reporting being bullied to the school. They learned long ago that this only made things worse. They were told to stop acting so strangely and the bullying would stop. The students would then call them a "snitch."*

Bullied students are those who are seriously or persistently treated badly by their peers. When students are asked by researchers to describe those who are bullied, they frequently refer to bullied students in a negative way.[21] They use terms such as "different," "odd," or "weird." Some students perceive that these students are not behaving as they "should." Therefore, they deserve to be treated in a hurtful manner. These "misfit" students disturb the status quo, which demands conformity to "normal."[22] They are on the lower levels of the school's "social ladder."

---

20 Woods, S. and White, E. (2005). The association between bullying behaviour, arousal levels and behaviour problems. *Journal of Adolescence* 28 (3): 381–395. Fanti, K.A. and Kimonis, E.R. (2013). Dimensions of juvenile psychopathy distinguish "bullies," "bully-victims," and "victims.". *Psychology of Violence* 3 (4): 396–409.

21 Thornberg, R. (2011). She's weird! – the social construction of bullying in school: a review of qualitative research, 2011. *Children & Society* 25 (4): 258–267.

22 Pouwels, J.L. and Garandeau, C.F. (2021). The role of the peer group and classroom factors in bullying behavior. In: *Wiley Blackwell Handbook of Bullying: A Comprehensive and International Review of Research and Intervention* (ed. P.K. Smith and J. O'Higgins Norman), 450–466. Wiley Blackwell.

Those students who engage in bullying strategically target students they know others do not support. This is less risky for them. Other students are less likely to step in to help these bullied students, because this could raise the risk of being targeted themselves or damage their reputation by standing up for a student who is considered "weird."

However, it is not always the case that lower social status students are the ones being treated badly by peers. Especially in the teen years, students at higher levels on the social ladder may also be bullied.[23] These students are those who the hurtful students perceive to be rivals or potential rivals. The involved students are at a relatively equivalent level of the school's social ladder. These students are treated badly by peers who are trying to obtain dominance, which will be discussed in Chapter 2. Often, these are situations that relate to romantic relationships and dating.

> *Amber is a freshman in high school. She gets good grades, is a member of a student leadership group, and she plays on the school's volleyball team. One day, she spent some time in the lunchroom talking to Burt. Lilah is also a freshman and is one of the top players on the volleyball team. She is very popular. She really likes Burt. After she saw Amber talking with Burt, she started attacking Amber. Mostly she posted hurtful stuff about Amber on social media. She also encouraged the other players to ignore her. Other students have started laughing at and avoiding Amber.*

Identity-based Bullying

Identity-based bullying is biased-based bullying that occurs because of the student's actual or perceived "identity" within a group or class of people who are marginalized within our society.[24] Marginalized identity groups include those who are considered a protected class under most civil rights laws. This generally includes race, color, national origin, religion, disabilities, and sexual minorities. Students within other identity groups may also be the subject of identity-based bullying. This includes students who are overweight, low income, or some other group of marginalized students.

Identity-based bullying may be serious or may be persistent minor incidents, the harms of which add up. These serious or persistent hurtful acts may be

---

23 Pouwels and Garandeau. The role of the peer group and classroom factors in bullying behavior.
24 Espelage, D.L. (2021). What do we know about identity-based bullying? Virtual Symposium: Understanding and Preventing Youth Hate Crimes and Identity-based Bullying. OJJDP. https://ojjdp.ojp.gov/programs/preventing-youth-hate-crimes-bullying-initiative (accessed 1 August 2024).

directed at one young person. Identity-based bullying also includes the pervasive or widespread targeting of many students within the entire identity group.

> *Zahra recently immigrated from Afghanistan. She is learning to speak English. She wears a hijab, which is considered sacred in her family and religion. She has been called a "terrorist" and asked if she was a member of the Taliban. Students try to pull off her hijab. One asked her, "Do you have any hair under there?" She has been told that she is not welcome in our country and to go back to where she came from. One of her teachers has trouble pronouncing her name and has decided to call her "Sarah."*

Identity-based bullying is recognized as causing greater harm than more general bullying.[25] The reason for this is that in addition to the actual experience of being treated badly, students who are bullied based on their membership in an identity group can have an ongoing expectation that they will always be treated badly because of "who they are."

Many students who are in minority identity groups also have concerns related to intergenerational trauma.[26] This will be discussed in Chapter 4. For sexual and gender minorities, the stress may also include the need to conceal their identity from those within their family, school, and/or community.

There is an overlap between identity-based bullying and hate crimes.[27] A hate crime is a criminal offense against a person or property motivated in whole or in part by the offender's bias against that person based on their race, ethnicity, national origin, religion, disability, sexual orientation, or gender identity.[28]

Hate crimes committed by young people look similar to adult hate crimes.[29] Most juvenile hate crimes are motivated by bias based on race or ethnicity. Almost

25 Flentje, A., Heck, N.C., Brennan, J.M., and Meyer, I.H. (2020). The relationship between minority stress and biological outcomes: a systematic review. *Journal of Behavioral Medicine* https://doi.org/10.1007/s10865-019-00120-6. Meyer, I.H. (2003). Prejudice, social stress, and mental health in lesbian, gay, and bisexual populations: conceptual issues and research evidence. *Psychological Bulletin* 129: 674–697. https://doi.org/10.1037/00332909.129.5.674.

26 Bhushan, D., Kotz, K., McCall, J., et al. (2020). Office of the California Surgeon General. Roadmap for Resilience: The California Surgeon General's Report on Adverse Childhood Experiences, Toxic Stress, and Health. Office of the California Surgeon General. doi: 10.48019/PEAM8812.

27 Jones, L.M, Mitchell, M., and Turner, H. (2021). Characteristics of hate crimes involving juveniles: findings from the National Hate Crime Investigations Study (NHCIS). Virtual Symposium: Understanding and Preventing Youth Hate Crimes and Identity-Based Bullying. OJJDP. https://ojjdp.ojp.gov/programs/preventing-youth-hate-crimes-bullying-initiative (accessed 1 August 2024).

28 Title 18, USC, Section 249, *Matthew Shepard and James Byrd, Jr., Hate Crimes Prevention Act.*

29 Jones, L.M, Mitchell, M., and Turner, H. (2021). Characteristics of hate crimes involving juveniles: findings from the National Hate Crime Investigations Study (NHCIS). Virtual Symposium: Understanding and Preventing Youth Hate Crimes and Identity-Based Bullying. OJJDP. https://ojjdp.ojp.gov/programs/preventing-youth-hate-crimes-bullying-initiative.

half of the hate crime cases involving juvenile suspects are incidents that happened at school or on school grounds.

Societal Values of the Local Community

There are regional differences in how identity-based bullying manifests in schools that relate to the values held by local community residents. Recently in the United States, intense battles have emerged in many states over the increased efforts of schools to achieve greater diversity, equity, and inclusion. Battles over these issues are raging in some communities, with angry parents accosting board members, school leaders, and teachers. These parents have children who are attending school in these communities, who may be bringing these values into the school.

If you live in a region or state where these battles have been raging, this is going to create greater difficulties in interacting with the school to achieve a resolution of the situation with your child. Hopefully not, but possibly, the principal or other leaders in your district may also hold attitudes that are biased. If information that your child has filed a complaint with the district becomes known, your child and your family could face retaliation from others in the community.

In Chapter 12, you will learn about strategies to document what is happening and the harmful impact on your child, and to file an effective complaint with your child's school. Your complaint will include a specific request to keep the fact that you or your child were the source of the complaint confidential.

If your child is a member of a minority identity group and other students within this minority group are also being bullied, my guidance is to not try to address this concern just from the perspective of your child. If you proceed to address these concerns as a group of families, hopefully with the support of an advocacy group, there is likely a lower potential for your child to be specifically identified and retaliated against. This is discussed more in Chapters 11 and 12.

Identities

The following are the different bases for identity-based bullying:

- **Race, ethnicity, religion, national origin.** Data related to the concern of race, ethnicity, or religious-based bullying can be complicated.[30] The basis and level of bullying of racial or religious minorities will be different depending on the racial or religious make-up of the school and community.[31]

---

30 Espelage. What do we know about identity-based bullying?
31 Kuldas, S., Dupont, M., and Foody, M. (2021). Ethnicity-based bullying: suggestions for future research on classroom ethnic composition. In: *Wiley Blackwell Handbook of Bullying: A Comprehensive and International Review of Research and Intervention* (ed. P.K. Smith and J. O'Higgins Norman), 252–272. Wiley Blackwell.

- **Newly immigrated.** Students who have newly immigrated have many times experienced trauma that led to their relocation, which could contribute to behavior that makes them more vulnerable to being bullied.[32] These students are also less likely to feel comfortable reporting this to the school due to their lack of comfort in their new community and school.
- **Indigenous youth.** In the United States, Native American students have both the highest rates of experiencing victimization in the form of threats or physical violence and the highest dropout rates when compared to other racial groups. In other countries, these hurtful dynamics between the majority society and Indigenous peoples also appears evident.[33]
- **Asian American.** A 2021 survey, found that 80% of Asian American teens had experienced bullying, both in person or online, and that they are significantly less likely to report bullying to an adult than non-Asian American teens.[34]
- **Religious minorities.** In the United States, religious minorities include members of minority religions such as Muslims, Sikhs, Hindus, and Jews. The Council on American–Islamic Relations reports that, over the last decade, 40–50% of Muslim students have consistently reported being bullied, nearly half reported feeling unsafe, unwelcome, or uncomfortable at school because of their Muslim identity, and 25% of students reported that an adult at their school made offensive comments or acted in a way that was offensive to Islam/Muslims.[35] Over 50% of Sikh children experienced school bullying.[36] The percentage increased to 67% for turbaned Sikh children. Each year, the Anti-Defamation League (ADL)

32 Fandrem, H., Strohmeier, D., Caravita, S.C.S., and Stefanek, E. (2021). Migration and bullying. In: *Wiley Blackwell Handbook of Bullying: A Comprehensive and International Review of Research and Intervention* (ed. P.K. Smith and J. O'Higgins Norman), 361–378. Wiley Blackwell.

33 National American Indian & Alaska Native School Mental Health Program (undated). Bullying & native youth. https://mhttcnetwork.org/wp-content/uploads/2021/11/Bullying-fact-sheet.pdf (accessed 1 August 2024); Campbell, E.M. and Smalling, S.E. (2013). American Indians and bullying in schools. *Journal of Indigenous Social Development* 2 (1): 1–15. http://hdl.handle.net/10125/29815. Allam, L. (2018). Indigenous children more likely to fear lack of safety, bullying and discrimination. *The Guardian*, October 11. https://www.theguardian.com/australia-news/2018/oct/11/indigenous-children-more-likely-to-fear-lack-of-safety-bullying-and-discrimination (accessed 1 August 2024).

34 Act To Change, ADMERASIA, and NextShark (2021). 2021 Asian American bullying survey report in partnership with Act To Change, ADMERASIA, and NextShark. https://acttochange.org/bullyingreport (accessed 1 August 2024).

35 Council on American–Islamic Relations (2024). CAIR-CA. 2023 bullying report. https://ca.cair.com/losangeles/publications/2023-annual-bullying-report/?eType=EmailBlastContent&eId=c41cc598-4752-461d-8272-8d127d133f1b (accessed 1 August 2024).

36 The Sikh Coalition (2014). "Go home, terrorist": a report on the bullying of Sikh American school children. March 1. https://www.sikhcoalition.org/documents/pdf/go-home-terrorist.pdf (accessed 1 August 2024).

tracks incidents of anti-Semitic harassment, vandalism, and assault in the United States. In 2022, the ADL found that there was a 36% increase from 2021.[37] Another study of middle and high schoolers in the United States demonstrated that 34.3% of Muslim students, 25% of Jewish students, and 23.1% of Hindu students reported they had been targeted at school because of their faith the last 30 days.[38]

- **Disabilities.** A new report from UNESCO, *Violence and Bullying in Educational Settings: The Experience of Children and Young People with Disabilities*, documented the nature of violence and bullying experienced by young people with disabilities in schools.[39] This assessment concluded that young people with disabilities are three to four times more likely to be victims of any type of violence in all settings. Within education systems throughout the world, students with disabilities have been found to experience substantially higher rates of peer bullying than those without disabilities. Students with emotional and behavioral challenges are more likely to be victimized than those with other disabilities. Students with disabilities also experience higher rates of physical violence at the hands of teachers, are more likely to be physically restrained or confined, and are also subjected to greater emotional and psychological violence from teachers than students without disabilities.

- **Sexual or gender minority status.** Sexual and gender minority students are extremely vulnerable to being bullied.[40] GLSEN's *2019 School Climate Report* revealed that 82% of LGBTQ+ students reported feeling unsafe in school because of at least one of their actual or perceived personal characteristics, 79% reported avoiding school functions or extracurricular activities because they felt unsafe or uncomfortable, 58% reported hearing homophobic remarks from teachers or other school staff and 72% reported hearing negative remarks about gender expression from teachers or other school staff, and almost all of the

---

37 Anti-Defamation League (2023). Audit of Antisemitic incidents 2022. https://www.adl.org/resources/report/audit-antisemitic-incidents-2022 (accessed 1 August 2024).

38 Hinduja, S. and Patchin, J.W. (2022). Bias-based cyberbullying among early adolescents: associations with cognitive and affective empathy. *The Journal of Early Adolescence* 02724316221088757.

39 United Nations Educational, Scientific and Cultural Organization (UNESCO) (2019). Violence and bullying in educational settings: the experience of children and young people with disabilities. https://unesdoc.unesco.org/ark:/48223/pf0000378061. See also O'Moore, M. and McGuire, L. (2021). Disablist bullying. In: *Wiley Blackwell Handbook of Bullying: A Comprehensive and International Review of Research and Intervention* (ed. P.K. Smith and J. O'Higgins Norman), 342–360. Wiley Blackwell.

40 Blaya, C. (2021). Bias bullying problems among school children: sexual and gender-based bullying, and intersectional considerations. In: *Wiley Blackwell Handbook of Bullying: A Comprehensive and International Review of Research and Intervention* (ed. P.K. Smith and J. O'Higgins Norman), 273–289. Wiley Blackwell.

students heard negative remarks about sexual identity or gender orientation and very few witnessed school staff step in to stop this.[41] In addition, 76% experienced in-person verbal harassment and 31% were physically harassed. Only 35% of these students reported the harassment to the school and, of those who reported, 60% said staff did nothing in response. Most did not report because they did not think staff would do anything. These students may be living in families where their sexual or gender minority status will not be accepted. They cannot risk reporting any concerns of being treated badly to school leaders. These leaders could also be biased against them or could "out" them in a way that will lead to greater challenges, including within their family.

- **Groups that do not receive civil rights protections.** Students in all of the above sections are considered protected class students under US civil rights laws. These laws likely do not provide protections for all students who may experience identity-based bullying. This includes students who are overweight, obese, or have some other "undesirable" physical appearance; students who are in foster care; lower-income students, and those who are experiencing significant home adversities, such as parents who are incarcerated or engaged in drug or alcohol abuse.[42] In a study of students in middle and high school, both overweight and obese students were at increased risk of experiencing bullying.[43] They may also experience situations where school staff blame them for being targeted.[44] There is no easily available data for other groups of students. Chapters 11 and 12 will provide insight into a strategy to bring students within these groups under federal civil rights laws if a student is now experiencing mental health concerns and an interference with their learning.

Implicit Bias and Microaggressions

Ella is a black student who just had beautiful, colorful extensions in her hair. Amy came up to her at school and immediately reached out to play with her hair extensions, without asking permission. When Ella stepped back and tried

---

41 Kosciw, J.G., Clark, C.M., Truong, N.L., and Zongrone, A.D. (2020). *The 2019 National School Climate Survey: the experiences of lesbian, gay, bisexual, transgender, and queer youth in our nation's schools*. GLSEN.

42 There is, unfortunately, not sufficient research on the common identity-focused basis upon which students are treated badly in addition to protected classes. The recent report by National Academies of Sciences, Engineering, and Medicine did have an extensive section on concerns of students with obesity who experience bullying.

43 Waasdorp, T.E., Mehari, K., and Bradshaw, C.P. (2018). Obese and overweight youth: risk for experiencing bullying victimization and internalizing symptoms. *American Journal of Orthopsychiatry* 88 (4): 483–491. http://dx.doi.org/10.1037/ort0000294.

44 Gray, W.N., Kahhan, N.A., and Janicke, D.M. (2009). Peer victimization and pediatric obesity: a review of the literature. *Psychology in the Schools*. https://doi.org/10.1002/pits.20410.

to explain that she did not think it was respectful for Amy to just come up and touch her hair and she felt this was racist, Amy responded, "Well, I am color blind. I do not see colors."

Students who are members of marginalized identity groups also deal with concerns related to implicit bias and microaggressions. To start this discussion, it is helpful to consider three forms of bias or prejudice against those who are not members of the dominant group in society:

- **Explicit bias.** Explicit bias is a known negative attitude about a specific identity group.[45] Overt comments or behavior that demonstrate this explicit bias could be considered bullying or discriminatory harassment. These concerns are not the focus in this section, but are the focus of this book.

- **Implicit bias.** Implicit bias is an unconscious negative attitude against members of an identity group. Implicit bias is shaped by our life experiences. Implicit bias is developed through repeated reinforcement of stereotypes through media, families, schools, and communities.[46] The way people behave can be influenced by their implicit biases – but they are unaware they hold such biases.[47] Acts or statements that are not intended to cause harm, but do cause harm because of underlying identity issues, are sometimes referred to as microaggressions. However, the person who has said or done something that caused offense is not intending to be aggressive. It is important to distinguish between "intent" and "impact."

- **Institutional inequities.** Institutional inequities are the ways in which institutions or systems function that disadvantage marginalized identity groups.[48] Individuals within institutions who make decisions that result in inequities may make these decisions based on their personal explicit or implicit biases. Institutional inequities are a profound concern. These inequities have an extensive historical basis, which has resulted in profound inequities in our society. Schools absolutely have significant concerns related to institutional inequities, very frequently driven by the implicit biases of staff members and school board members.

---

45 Understanding bias: a resource guide. https://www.justice.gov/d9/fieldable-panel-panes/basic-panes/attachments/2021/09/29/understanding_bias_content.pdf (accessed 1 August 2024).
46 Staats, C., Capatosto, K., Wright, R.A., and Contractor, D. (2015). *State of the Science: Implicit Bias Review 2015*, 3e. Kirwan Institute for the Study of Race and Ethnicity, The Ohio State University.
47 Implicit bias. APA Dictionary of Psychology. https://www.apa.org/topics/implicit-bias (accessed 1 August 2024).
48 Authority. Oxford Reference.com. https://www.oxfordreference.com/display/10.1093/oi/authority.20110803095435710 (accessed 1 August 2024).

Implicit bias can influence behavior. Implicit bias is understood to be a cause of unintentional discriminatory acts. These implicit biases are in large part outside the conscious awareness of individuals.[49] Most people consider themselves moral and respectful people, not wanting to engage in hurtful behavior directed at others. While the intent of a person may not be to offend, the impact of their statement or actions may have been perceived to be offensive by another.

Complicated History of Focus on Microaggressions

Chester M. Pierce, an African American Harvard-trained psychiatrist, was the first to describe the concept of microaggressions in the 1960s. He defined microaggressions as "black–white racial interactions [that] are characterized by white put-downs, done in an automatic, preconscious, or unconscious fashion."[50] Note that his focus is on unconscious actions, not actions intending to cause harm. These are actions that are grounded in implicit bias.

Derald Wing Sue is another researcher in this area. He describes racial microaggressions as:

> Racial micro aggressions are brief and commonplace daily verbal, behavioral, or environmental indignities, whether intentional or unintentional, that communicate hostile, derogatory, or negative racial slights and insults toward people of color. Perpetrators of micro aggressions are often unaware that they engage in such communications when they interact with racial/ethnic minorities.[51]

Sue also stated:

> People who engage in microaggressions are ordinary folks who experience themselves as good, moral, decent individuals. Microaggressions occur because they are outside the level of conscious awareness of the perpetrator.[52]

You can see in these statements that the original definition of microaggressions involved unconscious, unintended hurtful statements or actions. Sue has created confusion by expanding the definition to include both intentional or unintentional, but he essentially acknowledges most of these are unintentional.

---

49 Greenwald, A.G., Dasgupta, N., Dovidio, J.F. et al. (2022). Implicit-bias remedies: treating discriminatory bias as a public-health problem. *Psychological Science in the Public Interest* 23 (1): 7–40.

50 Pierce, C.M. (1974). Psychiatric problems of the Black minority. In: *American Handbook of Psychiatry* (ed. S. Arieti), 512–523. Basic Books.

51 Sue, D.W., Capodilupo, C.M., Torino, G.C. et al. (2007). Racial micro aggressions in everyday life: implications for clinical practice. *The American Psychologist* 62 (4): 271–286. https://doi.org/10.1037/0003-066X.62.4.271. PMID: 17516773.

52 Desmond-Harris, J. (2015). What are microaggressions? Vox, February 16. https://www.vox.com/2015/2/16/8031073/what-are-microaggressions (accessed 1 August 2024).

Sue's work has been criticized by Scott Lilienfeld, who finds the concept of a microaggressions to be excessively fuzzy. As he stated:

> Yet despite the good intentions and passionate embrace of this idea, there is scant real-world evidence that micro aggressions is a legitimate psychological concept, that it represents unconscious (or implicit) prejudice, that intervention for it works, or even that alleged victims are seriously damaged by these under-the-radar acts.[53]

Lilienfeld certainly affirms that prejudice exists and can manifest as subtle snubs, slights, and insults directed at members of historically marginalized identity groups or through more overtly prejudicial statements or actions. However, he has noted that as a result of the work of some researchers, what has emerged in companies, universities, and in K-12 education settings are workshops on how to identify and avoid microaggressions. These workshops include disseminated lists of microaggressions to caution against expressing statements that might cause offense. Statements such as "Where are you from?," "America is a land of opportunity," or "I believe that the most qualified person should get the job" are considered by Sue and Monnica Williams, another researcher, to be microaggressions.[54]

Williams suggests that if 30% of people within an identity group find a statement to constitute a microaggression, then it should be considered a microaggression.[55] This is her arbitrary figure. Who gets to decide what statements are microaggressions? A study by Lilienfeld found that many of the microaggression statements identified by Sue and Williams are not perceived by most minorities as offensive.[56]

Another challenge relates to how discussions about microaggressions are being perceived by members of marginalized identity groups. A focus on implicit bias and microaggressions may make them feel more threatened and create the perception that they should always be on the lookout for signs of prejudice. Not only do they have to deal with situations of explicit bias and institutional inequities,

---

53 Lilienfeld, S.O. (2017). Microaggressions? Prejudice remains a huge social evil but evidence for harm caused by microaggression is incoherent, unscientific and weak. AEON. https://aeon.co/essays/why-a-moratorium-on-microaggressions-policies-is-needed.

54 Lilienfeld, S.O. (2017). Microaggressions: strong claims, inadequate evidence. *Perspectives on Psychological Science* 12: 138–169.

55 Williams, M.T. (2019). Microaggressions: clarification, evidence, and impact. *Perspectives on Psychological Science* 15: 3–26.

56 Lilienfeld, S.O. (2020). Microaggression research and application: clarifications, corrections, and common ground. *Perspectives on Psychological Science* 15 (1): 27–37. https://doi.org/10.1177/1745691619867117. Lilienfeld, S.O. (2017). Microaggressions? Prejudice remains a huge social evil but evidence for harm caused by micro aggressions is incoherent, unscientific and weak. *Aeon*, June. https://aeon.co/essays/why-a-moratorium-on-microaggressions-policies-is-needed (accessed 1 August 2024).

they also have to be on the lookout for unintentional hurtful acts – which are yet another reminder of the discrimination they face in our society.

While none of the research in the area has mentioned this, it is important to recognize the role a part of the brain called the hippocampus is playing. This will be discussed in Chapter 4. The hippocampus is where our life experiences are processed. These life experiences impact how we act and how we respond to new situations. Stored life experiences are guiding perceptions and emotions for everyone in the situation – both the person who says or does something that someone else finds offensive and the person who is feeling offended. Members of marginalized identity groups have plenty of challenging memories of hurtful life experiences stored in their hippocampus. It is not unreasonable that they may feel offended – even in situations when no offense was intended.

Ineffective Efforts to Change Implicit Bias

Another significant challenge in this area is that efforts to inform people about their implicit biases and to encourage positive change have not been effective. In 1998, Anthony Greenwald and colleagues developed an assessment that is said to measure implicit bias.[57] He has noted that an assessment of over 490 studies of anti-bias training in companies found that these trainings were ineffective in changing behavior.[58] Of significant concern, according to Greenwald, is that there are many consultants who are offering their services to institutions for "anti-bias training" when there are no research findings that demonstrate any significant effectiveness of such trainings. Many consultants are offering such services to schools.

In a recent article, Greenwald stated this:

> I see most implicit bias training as window dressing that looks good both internally to an organization and externally, as if you are concerned and trying to do something. But it can be deployed without actually achieving anything, which makes it in fact counterproductive.[59]

Greenwald suggested two strategies that can play a more effective role in undermining the damaging impact of implicit biases in companies and other institutions:

---

57 Greenwald, A.G., McGhee, D.E., and Schwartz, J.L.K. (1998). Measuring individual differences in implicit cognition: the Implicit Association Test. *Journal of Personality and Social Psychology* 74: 1464–1480.

58 Patrick Forscher Calvin, K. and Axt, L.J.R. (2019). A meta-analysis of procedures to change implicit measures. *Journal of Personality and Social Psychology*.

59 Mason, B. (2020). Making people aware of their implicit biases doesn't usually change minds. But here's what does work. PBS, June 10. https://www.pbs.org/newshour/nation/making-people-aware-of-their-implicit-biases-doesnt-usually-change-minds-but-heres-what-does-work (accessed 1 August 2024).

- **Preventive measures.** Preventive measures that make it less possible for people to act with implicit biases in a way that has discriminatory outcomes. A good example of this is when orchestras started using audition approaches that hid the identities of the people auditioning. This resulted in a significant increase in women players.
- **Maintaining a focus on data.** An analysis of the data of the company or school should reveal where inequities exist, how much of a challenge this is, and who should be responsible for implementing a remedy.

Implicit Bias in Schools

There are significant concerns about the role implicit bias plays in schools. It is absolutely clear from the data that the implicit biases of educators play a huge role in the institutional inequities that are negatively impacting students in minority identity groups. It might be hoped that teachers are supportive of all students and want the best for their students. However, recent studies have shown that teachers in the United States hold pro-white/anti-bias at the same level as the general population.[60]

The most obvious evidence of concerns about the role of implicit bias is the difference in the disciplinary rates between white and black students and students with disabilities.[61] Even when considering issues such as poverty, students who are black are suspended more often than students who are white for the same kinds of misbehavior. A focus on suspensions is important because this is a leading indicator of whether a student will drop out of school, and because out-of-school suspension increases their risk for future incarceration.

There is a myth that it is necessary to suspend the misbehaving students so the good students can learn. However, it appears that schools that have lower levels of suspensions have higher test scores.

Other research shows that teachers' implicit racial/ethnic biases are associated with the fact that white teachers have lower academic expectations of students of color.[62] Yet another study showed that there were larger racial disparities in test scores and suspensions in counties where larger number of teachers had both

60 Starck, J.G., Riddle, T., Sinclair, S., and Warikoo, N. (2020). Teachers are people too: examining the racial bias of teachers compared to other American adults. *Educational Researcher* 49 (4): 273–284. https://doi.org/10.3102/0013189x20912758.

61 Losen, D.J. and Gillespie, J. (2012). *Opportunities suspended: the disparate impact of disciplinary exclusion from school*. The Civil Rights Project/Proyecto Derechos Civiles: UCLA https://escholarship.org/uc/item/3g36n0c3 (accessed 1 August 2024).

62 Jacoby-Senghor, D.S., Sinclair, S., and Shelton, J.N. (2016). A lesson in bias: the relationship between implicit racial bias and performance in pedagogical contexts. *Journal of Experimental Social Psychology* 63. https://doi.org/10.1016/j.jesp.2015.10.010.

explicit and implicit anti-black biases.[63] Even when teachers believe they are being fair and are using a grading rubric, their implicit biases can lead to rating students negatively on the basis of gender, race, and assumed ability, even when achievements are equal.[64]

One study in this area focused on why black children are more likely to be expelled or disciplined in preschool than their white peers.[65] This study found that preschool teachers tend to complain more about children classified as black/Hispanic/poor and black/non-poor and identify their behavior as problematic compared to white/Hispanic/non-poor children. However, the researchers found no differences in patterns of misbehavior when the children were observed.

Many of these studies have focused on race, specifically black students. The concerns of excessive suspensions of students with disabilities have also been addressed. The focus on implicit bias concerns associated with the instruction of students who are neurodivergent or sexual minorities are also being expressed.[66]

Underlying these concerns are findings that are similar to those noted by Greenwald, which is that trainings in implicit bias do not seem to result in positive behavior change. Greenwald's encouragement for practices that can reduce the potential impact of the implicit biases held by school staff are appropriate. His recommendation for use of data to identify the concerns and harmful impact is of exceptional importance. In Chapter 12, you will note my recommendations for a Continuous Improvement Process to identify and address concerns about the school environment. The Continuous Improvement Process data analysis must reveal the concerns of inequities grounded in all forms of bias in every school, with a requirement to identify and implement strategies to address these concerns, with subsequent evaluation of effectiveness by the same data. It is essentially to hold schools accountable for making positive change.

---

63 van den Bergh, L., Denessen, E., Hornstra, L. et al. (2010). The implicit prejudiced attitudes of teachers: relations to teacher expectations and the ethnic achievement gap. *American Educational Research Journal* 47 (2): 497–527. https://doi.org/10.3102/0002831209353594; Chin, M.J., Quinn, D.M., Dhaliwal, T.K., and Lovison, V.S. (2020). Bias in the air: a nationwide exploration of teachers' implicit racial attitudes, aggregate bias, and student outcomes. *Educational Researcher* 49 (8): 566–578. https://doi.org/10.3102/0013189X20937240.

64 Parrekh, G., Brown, R.S., and Zheng, S. (2021). Learning skills, system equity, and implicit bias within Ontario. *Canada Educational Policy* 35 (3): 395–421.

65 Sabol, T.J., Kessler, C.L., Rogers, L.O. et al. (2022). A window into racial and socioeconomic status disparities in preschool disciplinary action using developmental methodology. *Annals of the New York Academy of Sciences* 1508: 1. https://doi.org/10.1111/nyas.14687.

66 Robertshaw, S. (2024). How educators' implicit bias stifles neurodivergent learners. Attitude, May 21. https://www.additudemag.com/implicit-bias-educators-learning-differences (accessed 1 August 2024); Marks, M.J. and Amodei, M.L. (2023). Implicit gender bias in the classroom: memories from K-12 education. *Journal of Research Initiatives* 7: 2.

Respectful Dialogue

The increased activities in schools related to diversity, equity, and inclusion have been interpreted by some as intending to shame white students and families for their privilege. People do not like to be blamed for systemic inequities in society that they had absolutely nothing to do with creating. At this point in time, everything has gotten very political, which is not helping anyone.

Systemic inequities have been a part of our society essentially for forever. Significant progress has been made to address these inequities. More work is absolutely essential. Because we have not yet accomplished what we need to accomplish, we do not know how to effectively do this. Some of the approaches may be effective. Others may be ineffective or even harmful. Respectful dialogue about these concerns would be a preferred way to accomplish this, rather than angry parents protesting at school board meetings.

Consider the recommendations made by Lilienfeld:

> So, what to do? Although the [micro aggression research] is presently highly problematic, we should not throw the baby out with the bathwater. Subtle prejudice undeniably exists, and a certain proportion of what are now misleadingly termed "micro aggressions" probably reflect such prejudice. If we could reconceptualise most micro aggressions as inadvertent cultural and racial slights, we'd all be better off. The micro aggressions culture prevalent on many campuses and in many businesses makes just about everyone feel threatened, and could amp up already simmering racial tensions. This culture often makes minority individuals feel that they should be on the lookout for mild signs of prejudice, and that they need to walk on eggshells. Distributing lists of "forbidden" phrases to campus administrators or faculty members, or mandating micro aggressions training for employees, are unlikely to be helpful. A time-out on these ill-advised programmes is long overdue.
>
> Yes, many majority individuals say unintentionally offensive things to minority individuals from time to time, often because they are careless or oblivious, or because they are simply unaware of these individual's past racial and cultural experiences. Microaggressions should be the start of an open dialogue, not the end. Telling someone: "What you just said is a racist microaggression. You offended me and you have to stop" is unlikely to lead to a productive two-way conversation. In contrast, it could be a fruitful entry-point into a difficult but mutually enlightening discussion to say: "You probably did not mean this, but what you said bothered me. Maybe we are both misunderstanding each other. I realise that we are coming from different places. Let us talk."[67]

---

67 Lilienfeld, Microaggressions?

The challenge in the situations when someone has engaged in unintentional actions or statements that cause offense is that the person who is offended is the only one who recognizes this. The person who said or did something that another perceived as offensive did not intend to cause harm and does not have the insight into the fact that this is what happened. This, then, will require the person who is offended to take one of two actions:

- Decide that the situation is not sufficiently serious for them to do anything.
- Decide that they would like to reach out to the person who said or did something that caused them offense and bring their concerns to this person's attention.

This is essentially a version of the Serenity Prayer – to "serenely accept the things I cannot change, the courage to change the things I can, and the wisdom to know the difference." I make this statement full well knowing how many times a day members of marginalized identity groups take a deep breath and choose serenity, but harm has been done to their emotional well-being. In Chapter 5, I will provide some suggestions on how your child can respectfully reach out to someone who said or did something that did not appear to be intended to be hurtful, but was.

My Thoughts

These are my thoughts on how we might be able to proceed in addressing these issues in a way that could potentially be less contentious:

- Significant efforts need to be made to address the institutional inequities that exist in our society, including in schools. To address institutional inequities requires a focus on what the data are saying, the identification of how the institution functions to identify the underlying sources of those inequities, the identification and implementation of strategies to address these inequities, and proceeding with the understanding that the effectiveness of the institution's efforts will be measured by the data. It is for this reason that my strong recommendation is for parents and students within marginalized identity groups to strongly advocate for a data-based approach to address institutional inequities.
- It must be recognized that everyone has implicit unconscious biases gained through life experiences. This includes those who would be considered to be part of the dominant culture, as well as those who are in marginalized identity groups. These biases are wired into our brains. However, our brains can change.
- These implicit unconscious biases can have an impact in our saying or doing something that makes someone else feel offended or sad, even though this was not our intent. That person's implicit, unconscious bias, given their life experiences, has also shaped how they perceive our statement or action. Implicit biases are impacting both how someone says something and how it is received.

- To better address implicit bias, there is a need to increase respectful dialogue. It is understandable that people who are within marginalized identity groups may have concerns about speaking up if someone has said or done something that had a harmful impact on them. But that person is not going to know they have caused offense unless someone tells them. If they are approached in a calm and respectful manner and also given the opportunity to explain and to further the dialogue, this is likely to be a path that can lead to positive outcomes. When someone says or does something, grounded in their implicit biases, that someone else finds to be offensive, this presents a valuable "teachable moment." If the person who was offended, or a person who witnessed this, takes steps that seek to increase understanding and promote dialogue, this could provide a pathway to address the implicit biases that are interfering with positive society.

The Harms of Bullying

Jason is a middle school student. He has always been considered by other students to be "different" or "weird." Jason has been bullied since he entered kindergarten. Whenever he complained about this or a teacher witnessed this bullying, he was told that if he would just stop acting so strangely the other students would not treat him like they are. Jason had a friend through elementary school, Eileen. But as they entered middle school, Eileen was told by the other students that she should not hang out with Jason because the other students would also think she is "weird." So she told Jason that she could not hang out with him any more. That night, Jason took his life.

The harms caused by being bullied have been extensively and well documented. A recent commentary in *Pediatrics*, outlined these harms:

Bullying can have life-long health consequences. It has been associated with stress-related physical and mental health symptoms, including depression, anxiety, post traumatic stress, and suicidal ideation. When bullying is motivated by discrimination or an attack on someone's core identity (e.g., their sexual orientation), it can have especially harmful health consequences. The effects of bullying are not limited to the bullied. Bystanders who witness bullying may experience mental health consequences (e.g. distress) as well.[68]

---

68 Schuster, M.A. and Bogart, L.M. (2013). Did the ugly duckling have PTSD? Bullying, its effects, and the role of pediatricians. *Pediatrics* 131 (1): e288–e291.

A report by the American Educational Research Association, entitled *Prevention of Bullying in Schools, Colleges, and Universities: Research Report and Recommendations*, also provided an overview of concerns:

1) Bullied students experience higher rates of anxiety, depression, physical health problems, and social adjustment problems. These problems can persist into adulthood.
2) Bullying students become less engaged in school, and their grades and test scores decline.
3) In high schools where bullying and teasing are prevalent, the student body is less involved in school activities, performs lower on standardized tests, and has a lower graduation rate.
4) Students who engage in bullying are at elevated risk for poor school adjustment and delinquency. They are at increased risk for higher rates of criminal behavior and social maladjustment in adulthood.
5) Students who are bullied but also engage in bullying have more negative outcomes than students in bully-only or victim-only groups.
6) Cyberbullied students experience negative outcomes similar to those experienced by their traditional counterparts, including depression, poor academic performance, and problem behavior.[69]

A significant aspect related to the harms experienced by those who are bullied depends on the extent to which those targeted are defended by their peers. If they are defended by at least one classmate, students who are bullied appear to experience less distress.[70] This is why it is really important for schools to focus on strategies to increase the willingness of students to step in to help if they witness bullying.

Trauma

It is essential to "connect the dots" between experiencing being bullied and trauma. One study that looked at the connection between bullying and trauma symptoms found a high incidence of trauma symptoms among students who were

---

69 American Educational Research Association (2013). Prevention of bullying in schools, colleges, and universities: research report and recommendations. http://www.aera.net/newsroom/news/preventionofbullyingresearchreportandrecomm/tabid/14865/default.aspx, 9–10 (accessed 1 August 2024).
70 Sainio, M., Veenstra, R., Huitsing, G., and Salmivalli, C. (2011). Victims and their defenders: a dyadic approach. *International Journal of Behavioral Development* 35 (2): 144–151. https://doi.org/10.1177/0165025410378068.

bullied. The more frequently they were bullied, the worse the symptoms.[71] The students with the worst trauma symptoms were the ones who both engaged in and were bullied.

The National Child Traumatic Stress Network (NCTSN) describes two forms of trauma.[72]

- **Acute trauma.** Acute traumatic events involve experiencing, witnessing, or a threat of a serious injury to yourself or another.
- **Chronic stress.** Chronic traumatic situations that occur repeatedly over periods of time. This also is called "toxic stress."

Bullying situations could involve acute trauma, chronic stress, or both. The term "serious" bullying is connected with what would be considered an acute traumatic incident. "Persistent" bullying is a situation of chronic or toxic stress.

The standards for trauma under the new American Psychiatric Association's *Diagnostic and Statistical Manual of Mental Disorders, Fifth Edition* (DSM-5) focus on major traumatic events, unfortunately not on chronic or complex traumatic situations.[73] However, it is very helpful to consider the four diagnostic symptom clusters outlined in DSM-5. These are:

> Re-experiencing covers spontaneous memories of the traumatic event, recurrent dreams related to it, flashbacks or other intense or prolonged psychological distress. Avoidance refers to distressing memories, thoughts, feelings or external reminders of the event. Negative cognitions and mood represents myriad feelings, from a persistent and distorted sense of blame of self or others, to estrangement from others or markedly diminished interest in activities, to an inability to remember key aspects of the event. Finally, arousal is marked by aggressive, reckless, or self-destructive behavior, sleep disturbances, hyper-vigilance, or related problems.[74]

The trauma symptoms outlined in DSM-5 closely match the reported symptoms of students who are bullied. In Chapter 12, you will find a Documentation Guide to document the harmful incidents and the harmful impact on your child. The questions related to the harmful emotional impact on your child are in accord with the symptoms outlined in DSM-5.

---

71 Idsoe, T., Dyregrov, A., and Idsoe, E.C. (2012). Bullying and PTSD symptoms. *Journal of Abnormal Child Psychology* 40: 901–911. http://www.uis.no/news/being-bullied-can-cause-trauma-symptoms-article62673-8865.html (accessed 1 August 2024).
72 National Child Traumatic Stress Network. About Child Trauma. https://www.nctsn.org/what-is-child-trauma/about-child-trauma (accessed 1 August 2024).
73 American Psychiatric Publishing (2013). Posttraumatic stress disorder. http://www.dsm5.org/Documents/PTSDpercent20Factpercent20Sheet.pdf (accessed 1 August 2024).
74 American Psychiatric Publishing. Posttraumatic stress disorder.

Academic Performance and Absences

It is widely recognized that maintaining a positive school climate is critical component for supporting student academic achievement.[75] Schools that have a high level of bullying have lower achievement scores. If your child is being bullied, this is highly likely to be having a damaging impact on their academic success. If many students in the school are being bullied, this will result in lower academic progress for the school. Schools focus so much attention on learning objectives and test scores. They would have higher levels of achievement if they would focus on improving the feelings of safety and belonging of their students.

School absences and avoidance are also a major concern. If your child is being bullied, there is a significant risk that they will try to be absent from school.[76] One study examined the impact that bullying had on fear of attending school and school avoidance.[77] This study found that bullied students were six times more likely to report fear at school and school avoidance than their non-bullied peers.

The Cyberbully Research Center conducted a survey of approximately 5,700 middle and high school students in the United States. They asked if they had stayed home from school at any time during the last school year because they were being bullied at school or online. The responses showed that: 18.5%, about 4,750,000 students, skipped school at some point in the last year because they were bullied at school; 10%, about 2,750,000 students, stayed home because of cyberbullying; approximately 2%, over 500,000 students, said they stayed home many times due to bullying at school; 1.2%, or 300,000 students, stayed home many times because of cyberbullying. Based on these numbers, approximately 5.4 million students skip school at some point in the year due to bullying or cyberbullying and over 530,000 students skip school many times.

There is a significant focus at this time on addressing concerns of school absenteeism. USDOE released a report entitled *Chronic Absenteeism in the Nation's Schools*.[78] There are two major factors that relate to students being absent. One is

75 Huang, F.L., Eklund, K., and Cornell, D.G. (2017). Authoritative school climate, number of parents at home, and academic achievement. *School Psychology Quarterly* 32 (4): 480–496.
O'Brien, N. (2021). School factors with a focus on boarding schools. In: *Wiley Blackwell Handbook of Bullying: A Comprehensive and International Review of Research and Intervention* (ed. P.K. Smith and J. O'Higgins Norman), 467–484. Wiley Blackwell.
76 Havik, T., Bru, E., and Ertesvag, S.K. (2015). School factors associated with school refusal-and truancy-related reasons for school non-attendance. *Social Psychology of Education* 18 (2): 221–240.
77 Vidourek, R.A., King, K.A., and Merianos, A.L. (2016). School bullying and student trauma: fear and avoidance associated with victimization. *Journal of Prevention & Intervention in the Community* 44 (2): 121–129.
78 USDOE (2019). Chronic absenteeism in the nation's schools: a hidden educational crisis. https://www2.ed.gov/datastory/chronicabsenteeism.html (accessed 1 August 2024).

that there are significant problems in the home. The other is that students do not feel they are safe, welcome, and respected in school – because they are being bullied. Curiously, despite the data that shows black, Hispanic, Native American, and Pacific islander students, and students of two or more races having greater absences, the word "bullying" does not appear in the report.

> My own story fits in this section. I was bullied as "Weirdo Willard" throughout junior high school. I had contracted mononucleosis. This disease saved me. If I did not want to go to school, I put the bulb of the thermometer against a light bulb to give the appearance of a mild fever. Seeing this, my mom let me stay home. I missed 31 days of school. The school wanted to hold me back, but my grades were okay. I had essentially been homeschooling myself with the textbooks. I was dropped out of Honor Society.

Suicide and Self Harm

There is a clear association between bullying and engaging in suicidal behavior, including self-harm.[79] It is known that suicide behavior involves many factors. However, persistent bullying can create higher risk of suicidal thoughts and behavior. A serious or significant bullying incident can trigger suicidal behavior.

A study that looked at the results of 47 other studies found that being targeted by bullying, engaging in bullying, and both being targeted and hurtful were all associated with increased experiences of suicidal thoughts and suicidal behavior.[80] Those who are both bullied and are being hurtful have the greatest risk.

Self-harming behavior is when people intentionally hurt themselves when the immediate objective is not to lead to death.[81] This includes cutting or burning their body. Both being bullied and being hurtful increases the risk of teens and young adults engaging in these self-harming behaviors.[82]

While being bullied is a well-documented factor in youth suicide, students who have engaged in bullying should never be blamed for a decision of a young person

79 Suicide Prevention Resource Center (2011). Suicide and bullying: issue brief. https://sprc. org/wp-content/uploads/2023/01/Suicide_Bullying_Issue_Brief-2.pdf (accessed 1 August 2024).
80 Holt, M.K., Vivolo-Kantor, A.M., Polanin, J.R. et al. (2015). Bullying and suicidal ideation and behaviors: a meta-analysis. *Pediatrics* 135: e496–e509. https://doi.org/10.1542/peds.2014-1864.
81 Nock, M.K., Joiner, T.E. Jr., Gordon, K.H. et al. (2006). Non-suicidal self-injury among adolescents: diagnostic correlates and relation to suicide attempts. *Psychiatry Research* 144: 65–72. https://doi.org/10.1016/j.psychres.2006.05.010.
82 Heerde, J.A. and Hemphill, S.A. (2018). Are bullying perpetration and victimization associated with adolescent deliberate self-harm? A meta-analysis. *Archives of Suicide Research* 23: 353–381. https://doi.org/10.1080/13811118.2018.1472690.

to take their life.[83] Blaming tragic incidents on students who engaged in bullying ignores the multiple factors, can increase copy-cat behavior, and unfairly blames students for what are overall school climate concerns.

What should be considered, however, is whether the school knew the student was being persistently bullied and failed to effectively intervene. The feelings of hopelessness and helplessness of students who are experiencing persistent bullying and know from experience that there is no way to get this stopped by asking for help can be profound.

School Violence

There is a clearly established connection between bullying and school violence. When students are bullied, they appear to be more likely to bring a weapon to defend themselves. Like suicide, students engaging in school violence is a situation that involves many factors.

In one study, researchers found that high school kids who had been bullied in the past year were more likely to carry a weapon to school.[84] The study also looked at other actions that could make a student feel unsafe. This included students who had been threatened or injured with a weapon, had been in a physical fight, had their property stolen or damaged, or had missed school because they felt unsafe. With each additional reported concern, the percentage of students who brought a weapon to school increased.

A comprehensive study of school shootings by the US Secret Service (USSS) and USDOE demonstrated that almost three-quarters of the attackers felt persecuted, bullied, threatened, attacked, or injured by others prior to the incident.[85] In some of these cases, being bullied appeared to have a significant impact on the shooter and appeared to have been a factor in the decision to attack at the school.[86] Students who engage in school shootings or other forms of violence do

---

83 Robinson, I. (2018). I tried to befriend Nikolas Cruz. He still killed my friends. *New York Times*, March 27. https://www.nytimes.com/2018/03/27/opinion/nikolas-cruz-shooting-florida.html (accessed 1 August 2024).

84 Pham, T.B., Schapiro, L.E., John, M., and Adesman, A. (2017). Weapon carrying among victims of bullying. *Pediatrics* 140 (6): e20170353. https://doi.org/10.1542/peds.2017-0353. PMID: 29180461.

85 Vossekuil, B., Fein, R.A., Reddy, M. et al. (2004). The final report and findings of the Safe School Initiative: implications for the prevention of school attacks in the United States. US Secret Service and US Department of Education. https://www2.ed.gov/admins/lead/safety/preventingattacksreport.pdf (accessed 1 August 2024).

86 Vossekuil et al. The final report and findings of the Safe School Initiative.

not fit into one singular profile. There are always multiple factors involved in these situations.[87]

If your child is being bullied and you maintain guns or other weapons in your house, it is exceptionally important that they are kept in secure storage location that your child is unable to access. Often decisions to take one's life or take a gun to school are made in an impulsive manner. The last thing you want is for your emotionally distressed child to be able to access a gun.

87 National Threat Assessment Center (2018). Enhancing School Safety Using a Threat Assessment Model: An Operational Guide for Preventing Targeted School Violence. U.S. Department of Homeland Security. Secret Service https://www.secretservice.gov/data/protection/ntac/USSS_NTAC_Enhancing_School_Safety_Guide_7.11.18.pdf (accessed 1 August 2024).

2

Those Who Bully

Most insight provided to educators describes students who engage in bullying as having significant other challenges – essentially describing them as "maladjusted youth." This is an inaccurate stereotype. The students who are the greatest source of bullying are socially competent students who are being hurtful to achieve dominance and social status. Sometimes, what might be considered "bullying" is students who are being hurtful in retaliation because others have been hurtful to them. There are also significant concerns associated with school staff who are hurtful to students. This chapter will address these concerns.

The Quest for Dominance and Social Status

In Chapter 1, those students who are both bullied and also engage in reactive hurtful acts were described. These kinds of hurtful students can indeed be aggressive to other students. However, they are not the greatest source of bullying in schools.

The greatest source of bullying is students who are hurtful to establish dominance and social status.[1] These students are often very popular with their peers. They have strengths that are easy to recognize. This includes social skills, athleticism, and attractiveness. They are frequently perceived by school staff as leaders.

> *Eve is in high school. She almost died when she was age 4, because she had Type I diabetes. She is slightly overweight. She has not been interested in engaging in sports. She focuses more on the arts. She has been bullied*

---

1 National Academies of Sciences, Engineering, and Medicine (2016). *Preventing Bullying through Science, Policy, and Practice*. The National Academies Press. https://doi.org/10.17226/23482.

throughout school. In high school, she applied to be in the leadership class, for several years. She was never selected for this activity. The mentor for these leadership activities was the assistant principal, who was also the athletic director. The students who were accepted into this class were the student athletes. These were the students who had bullied Eve throughout school.

The students who are treated badly and are also hurtful, discussed in Chapter 1, are more frequently boys. They engage in aggression that is reactive – reacting to negative situations they are experiencing. The dominance-motivated hurtful students engage in aggression that is proactive. They intentionally use hurtful strategies to obtain their desired goals. They do not have emotional outbursts. Their subtle and covert hurtful behavior is less obvious to a school staff observer. They often have a group of supporters who follow their lead in being hurtful.

High social status students may encourage "mobbing." Mobbing is when one hurtful student encourages everyone else to join in to also be hurtful. Their friends often join in because they are following their leader. They want to remain in the leader's group. This can result in many students attacking a student because one student started this.

Public Stereotype

The public stereotype about those who engage in bullying as maladjusted students is strong.[2] It is, unfortunately, not hard to find one source of this public stereotype. The US StopBullying.Gov website is one of the sources of this public stereotype.[3] Both in the past and currently on this website there has been an overemphasis on the idea that students who engage in bullying are doing so because they have challenges of their own.

The US National Academies of Sciences, Engineering, and Medicine (NAS), in a 2016 report entitled *Preventing Bullying Through Science, Policy, and Practice*, noted the significant concerns about this stereotype.[4] They stated as follows:

> There is evidence that supports a finding that individuals who bully others have contradictory attributes. Research suggests that there are children and adolescents who bully others because they have some form of maladjustment or … are motivated by establishing their status in a social network.

2 National Academies of Sciences, Engineering, and Medicine, *Preventing Bullying through Science, Policy, and Practice.*

3 https://www.stopbullying.gov/bullying/at-risk; https://www.StopBullying.Gov/bullying/why-some-youth-bully (accessed 1 August 2024).

4 National Academies of Sciences, Engineering, and Medicine, *Preventing Bullying through Science., Policy, and Practice.*

Consequently, the relation between bullying, being bullied, acceptance, and rejection is complex. This complexity is also linked to a stereotype held by the general public about individuals who bully. This stereotype casts children and youth who bully others as being high on psychopathology, low on social skills, and possessing few assets and competencies that the peer group values. Although some occurrence of this "stereotypical bully" or "classic bully" is supported by research, when researchers consider social status in relation to perpetration of bullying behavior, a different profile emerges. These studies suggest that most children and youth who bully others wield considerable power within their peer network and that high-status perpetrators tend to be perceived by peers as being popular, socially skilled, and leaders. High-status bullies have also been found to rank high on assets and competencies that the peer group values such as being attractive or being good athletes; they have also been found to rank low on psychopathology and to use aggression instrumentally to achieve and maintain hegemony. Considering these findings of contrasting characteristics of perpetrators of bullying behavior, it makes sense that the research on outcomes of perpetrating is mixed. Unfortunately, most research on the short- and long-term outcomes of perpetrating bullying behavior has not taken into account this heterogeneity when considering the impact to children and youth who have bullied their peers.[5]

Note specifically the concerns related to research and interventions because of the failure to recognize that these students being hurtful to obtain dominance are a primary source of bullying. The reason why so many strategies schools have been encouraged to use to address bullying have not been effective is because the underlying view about those who engage in bullying is so inaccurate. Efforts to reduce bullying by those students who are motivated to gain dominance and who are receiving significant rewards within their school community for engaging in such hurtful behavior will require an approach that is vastly different from the risk prevention practices schools consider appropriate for students who have greater challenges.

It is also important to recognize how this inaccurate public stereotype has impacted principals. If you report to your child's principal that a student who the principal knows to have behavior challenges is being hurtful to your child, the principal is likely to believe you. But if you report that a popular, socially skilled student who is compliant to school staff is being hurtful to your child, the principal is likely to think that your child is overreacting and that the accused student really has not done anything that wrong.

---

5 National Academies of Sciences, Engineering, and Medicine, *Preventing Bullying through Science., Policy, and Practice*, 133.

Insight on the motivations and behaviors of students who are hurtful to achieve dominance was well explained by researchers Robert Faris and Diane Felmlee:

> Clearly it is the strong who do the attacking: recent scholarship has debunked the traditional view of aggressive youth as socially marginal and psychologically troubled. Indeed, aggressors often possess strong social skills and harass their peers, not to reenact their own troubled home lives, but to gain status ...
>
> [A]ggression is highly related to dominance and territoriality. Most adolescents desire status, albeit to varying degrees, and this desire motivates much aggressive behavior: the more adolescents – or their friends – care about being popular, the more aggressive they become over time. Bullies appear to pursue status, as well as affection, as goals.
>
> Popularity is associated with increased physical and relational aggression, behavior used to maintain social dominance. As social status increases, aggressive behavior escalates, at least until youth approach the pinnacle of the school hierarchy, when such actions are no longer required and aggression again declines ...
>
> The adaptive bullying of pure bullies represents aggressive, dominance-seeking behaviors, therefore giving rise to the understanding of bullying as adaptive in the first place. In contrast, the bullying of bully-victims is characterized by the risky, impulsive, and hostile behavior typically described by the developmental psychopathological approach to bullying. This kind of behavior may be better explained by the social learning, maladaptive cognition, and impoverished environmental theories described previously. An important distinction between bullies and bully-victims lie in the associated outcomes as well. Bully-victims do not experience positive outcomes in terms of social dominance or intrasexual competition, indicating that the types of bullying employed by bully-victims are not adaptive strategies. In addition to failing to benefit from their bullying behavior, bully-victims also experience high levels of depression when compared to pure bullies, victims, and uninvolved individuals.[6]

Another researcher, Janna Juvonen, identified that students who were named by peers as the "coolest" were also often named the most hurtful and the ones

---

6 Faris, R. and Felmlee, D. (2014). Casualties of social combat: school networks of peer victimization and their consequences. *American Sociological Review* 79 (2): 228–257.

engaging in spreading of rumors.[7] This insight from Juvonen explains the ethological basis for this hurtful behavior:

> Ethological research suggests that aggression is a strategy to establish a dominant position within a group. Among a number of species (e.g., various non-human primates), physical aggression enables attainment of a dominant position, such that the most powerful fighter (typically male) acquires a top position within a group and therefore gains access to valued resources. Within human youth, aggression can be considered a strategic behavior that serves similar social dominance functions.[8]

Consider the social behavior of animals. What could be called "bullying" is apparent in most animal communities. Animal aggression varies based on the species. However, this aggression is primarily competition over mates, food, and territory.[9] I own mini donkeys, goats, chickens, and ducks. Anyone who owns livestock understands these ethological based dynamics. If a baby chick is sick, the other chickens will peck at it until it dies. If I were to put a new donkey or goat into a pasture, bullying in the form of kicking among the donkeys would occur; the goats would engage in head-butting.

Does any of this reflect on what you perceive is happening in your school'? Do students pick on your child because they are considered to be a "weak chick" or "not normal?" Is your child being treated badly based on their identity – as not appropriate to be considered members of the "herd" or "pack?" Is a student "head-butting" your child because they perceive your child to be a "rival?" Is your child being treated badly in the context of athletics or other activities such as getting a place on a team, playing time, a position on the field, a role in a play, or a seat in the orchestra? Is this associated with personal relationships – who someone is allowed to date or be seen with? Is the student who is being hurtful gaining rewards from their behavior in terms of attention, status, or other relationships?

7 Juvonen, J., Wang, Y., and Espinoza, G. (2013). Physical aggression, spreading of rumors, and social prominence in early adolescence: reciprocal effects supporting gender similarities? *Journal of Youth and Adolescence* 42: 1801–1810.
8 Juvonen, J. Wang, Y., and Espinoza, G. (1804). Physical aggression, spreading of rumors, and social prominence in early adolescence.
9 Wohlleben, P. (2016). The Hidden Life of Trees. Greystone Books.

Motivations for Bullying

Consider the motives of student who is being hurtful to your child.[10] It is exceptionally important to distinguish between reactive aggression and proactive aggression. Reactive aggression indicates that the student who is being hurtful is also experiencing profound challenges. The hurtful behavior of this student can not be expected to stop until the challenges they are facing are better addressed. When considering proactive aggression, it is important to understand their motivation.

An excellent article entitled "Why Do Bullies Bully? Motives for Bullying," provided a discussion on the identified motives of those who are hurtful.[11] It will be helpful for you and your child to look at this list of possible motives to identify what appear to be the motives of the student who is being hurtful to your child. Questions about this are in the Documentation Guide that is provided in this book and available online at the Rise Above Bullying website. The motives that have been identified include:

- **Dominance.** Social dominance and power within a group is a clearly recognized goal of students who are hurtful. Dominance-motivated students are hurtful in order to demonstrate control over others or over desired resources or opportunities.[12] Many of the other motives on this list can accurately be phrased "dominance and ..."
- **Status and popularity.** Status refers to a student's social standing and position within the school's "social ladder." Students may bully others to reduce the social status of those they are treating badly or to increase their own social standing.[13] Status is clearly associated with dominance. Status goals appear to be most active in the teen years.[14] Status goals are also strong when there is a school level transition. The transition from elementary to middle school, as well

---

10 Sanders, J.B.P., Malamut, S., and Cillessen, A.H.N. (2021). Why do bullies bully? Motives for bullying. In: The Wiley Blackwell Handbook of Bullying: A Comprehensive and International Review of Research and Intervention (ed. P.K. Smith and J. O'Higgins Norman), 158–176. Wiley Blackwell.

11 Sanders, Malamut, and Cillessen, Why do bullies bully?

12 Thornberg, R. and Knutsen, S. (2011). Teenagers' explanations of bullying. *Child & Youth Care Forum* 40: 177–192. https://doi.org/10.1007/s10566-010-9129-z. Thornberg, R., Rosenqvist, R., and Johansson, P. (2012). Older teenagers' explanations of bullying. *Child & Youth Care Forum* 41: 327–342. doi: 10.1007/s10566-012-9171-0.

13 Salmivalli, C. (2010). Bullying and the peer group: a review. *Aggression and Violent Behavior* 15 (2): 112–120. https://doi.org/10.1016/j.avb.2009.08.007.

14 LaFontana, K.M. and Cillessen, A.H.N. (2010). Developmental changes in the priority of perceived status in childhood and adolescence. *Social Development* 19: 130–147. https://doi.org/10.1111/j.1467-9507.2008.00522.x.

as into high school level is a time where their perceived place on the school's "social ladder" is important to many students.

- **Resources.** In modern society, aggression to achieve resources necessary for survival is no longer a predominant goal. However, the "resources" that secondary students might consider important could include a student-body position, a desired position on the field on an athletic team, or a leading role in a play or seat in the band.
- **Revenge or retaliation.** Those who bully often justify their actions as having resulted from being provoked and the need to retaliate against the wrongdoing of the one they were hurtful to.[15] More on this below.
- **Justice.** Some students may be hurtful out of a sense of their position to correct a student who has acted outside of the social or cultural peer norms of the school.[16] The objective is to demonstrate to the bullied student and the peer group which norms will not be tolerated. This motive may be involved in identity-based bullying when the hurtful student targets a student who is perceived to be "different."
- **Belonging.** Bullying can be used as a strategy to gain acceptance in a group or to acquire or maintain friends.[17] This is a frequent motive of supporters of a student who is the primary source of aggression.
- **Romance.** Especially during the teen years, dominance and status are often likely sought to achieve the end goal of obtaining romantic relationships.[18] Students may engage in bullying to show their sexual interest or deal with competitors.[19] They may also be hurtful to those who have spurned their attentions or after a relationship has ended.

---

15 Runions, K.C., Salmivalli, C., Shaw, T. et al. (2018). Beyond the reactive proactive dichotomy: rage, revenge, reward, and recreational aggression predict early high school bully and bully/victim status. *Aggressive Behavior* 44: 501–510. https://doi.org/10.1002/ab.21770. Fluck, J. (2014). Why do students bully? An analysis of motives behind violence in schools. *Youth & Society* 1–21: https://doi.org/10.1177/0044118X14547876.

16 Juvonen, J. and Galvan, A. (2009). Bullying as a means to foster compliance. In: *Bullying, Rejection, and Peer Victimization: A Social Cognitive Neuroscience Perspective* (ed. M.J. Harris), 299–318. Springer.

17 Thornberg, R. (2010). School children's social representations on bullying causes. *Psychology in the Schools* 47: 311–327. https://doi.org/10.1002/pits.20472.

18 Ellis, B.J., Volk, A., Gonzalez, J.M., and Embry, D.D. (2016). The meaningful roles intervention: an evolutionary approach to reducing bullying and increasing prosocial behavior. *Journal of Research on Adolescence* 26: 622–637. https://doi.org/10.1111/jora.12243.

19 Vaillancourt, T. (2013). Do human females use indirect aggression as an intrasexual competition strategy? *Philosophical Transactions of the Royal Society B: Biological Sciences* 368: https://doi.org/10.1098/rstb.2013.0080.

- **Identity.** Bullying may be used by a student as a way to boost their positive self-image.[20] This may be closely linked to revenge. Students may be hurtful in retaliation for the actions of another that attacked their identity.
- **Well-being.** This factor has not been extensively studied. However, in conversations with students who admitted to being hurtful, one of the reasons provided has been to create a distraction from their own negative feelings.[21]
- **Entertainment.** Bullying for entertainment or excitement, because one is "bored," is frequently mentioned as a motive by students.[22]

Successful Outcomes of Proactive Aggression

The proactive aggression of students who are hurtful to achieve dominance has many positive benefits, in the thinking of these hurtful students.[23] These students experience dating and first sexual intercourse at earlier ages. They report greater dating and sexual relations opportunities, are more likely to be in a dating relationship, and report a significantly greater number of sexual partners. Indeed, when one considers the sexual relationship objectives of some teens, bullying can be considered to be a highly effective "head-butting" strategy to achieve these objectives.

These students are also focused on other status goals, including the ability to dictate what is happening in social interactions, becoming leading players on athletic teams, obtaining admission to a high-ranking university, and obtaining a dynamite job where they can rise in status within a hierarchal corporation, and gain wealth.[24] Being willing and able to use power aggressively is supported by many in our society.

20 Salmivalli, C., Kaukiainen, A., Kaistaniemi, L., and Lagerspetz, K. (1999). Self-evaluated self-esteem, peer-evaluated self-esteem, and defensive egotism as predictors of adolescents' participation in bullying situations. *Personality and Social Psychology Bulletin* 25: 1268–1278. https://doi.org/10.1177/0146167299258008.
21 Fluck, Why do students bully?; Thornberg and Knutsen, Teenagers' explanations of bullying; Thornberg, Rosenqvist, and Johansson, Older teenagers' explanations of bullying.
22 Fluck, Why do students bully?; Thornberg and Knutsen, Teenagers' explanations of bullying; Thornberg, Rosenqvist, and Johansson, Older teenagers' explanations of bullying.
23 Connolly, J., Pepler, D., Craig, W., and Taradash, A. (2000). Dating experiences of bullies in early adolescence. *Child Maltreatment* 5 (4): 299–310. Faris and Femlee, Casualties of social combat.
24 Sijtsema, J.J., Veenstra, R., Lindenberg, S., and Salmivalli, C. (2009). Empirical test of bullies' status goals: assessing direct goals, aggression, and prestige. *Aggressive Behavior* 35: 57–67. Reijntjes, A., Vermande, M., Olthof, T. et al. (2013). Costs and benefits of bullying in the context of the peer group: a three wave longitudinal analysis. *Journal of Abnormal Child Psychology* 41: 1–13.

Now contrast this to what is happening with your students who are both being treated badly and are hurtful.[25] These hurtful students do not achieve such beneficial outcomes from their hurtful behavior. They generally experience high levels of depression. Other students do not want to be associated with them. Being considered "popular" is an outcome of proactive aggression. It is not an outcome of reactive aggression.[26]

Students who are hurtful to achieve dominance frequently appear to have a sense of entitlement grounded in privilege. They may feel they are entitled to determine who is to be considered a "misfit" – and thus deserve to be "put in their place." They may not recognize or be willing to admit their actions are hurtful. They are just reinforcing a natural social order which has them on top and those who are "different" far below on the school's social ladder. Throughout their schooling, they have likely experienced environments where their drive for dominance has been valued, such as in athletics or receiving token rewards for their compliance with school expectations. They are often well behaved in front of staff and are not considered "problem students."

These students very likely also have parents who are socially prominent in the community and in your child's school. This creates challenges in a disciplinary context. Having a disciplinary record of engaging in bullying would have a negative impact on their ability to gain admission to a top-level university. These students are headed to leadership positions in society.

Obviously, society would be greatly benefitted by helping these students change their approach to leadership.

Situation Dynamics

The dynamics of this must be more fully considered in situations where a socially skilled, compliant student has been hurtful to a student who has greater challenges. The hurtful actions of these students are likely to be sophisticatedly cruel, but largely invisible to any staff member. They engage in verbal and relational aggression that is subtle and covert – not physically aggressive hurtful acts.

Any student who has had challenges regulating their behavior in school has likely been disciplined. If a bullied student reports they are being bullied, the principal may view the situation based on what they think about the differences in the degree to which the student with challenges and the student who is accused

---

25 Faris and Felmlee, Casualties of social combat; Juvonen, Wang, and Espinoza, Physical aggression, spreading of rumors, and social prominence in early adolescence.
26 Stoltz, S., Cillessen, A.H., van den Berg, Y.H., and Gommans, R. (2016). Popularity differentially predicts reactive and proactive aggression in early adolescence. *Aggressive Behavior* 42 (1): 29–40. https://doi.org/10.1002/ab.21603.

of being hurtful are generally compliant to school staff. The principal may not think that the student who is compliant was really all that hurtful.

Sometimes students who are being persistently treated badly will trigger and have a more visible, emotionally aggressive outburst in response. This emotional outburst may be considered a violation of the disciplinary code. Even if this student strives to explain that their outburst was in response to being treated badly, these statements may be disregarded.

Rationalizations

People like to think of themselves as "being good." So when they engage in hurtful behavior, they often create what are called "rationalizations" for their behavior.[27] People use these rationalizations to convince themselves that certain ethical standards do not apply to them in particular situations. Rationalizations are excuses people tell themselves or others to justify that their behavior was appropriate – even when it clearly was not.

The four common rationalizations are:

- **Spin it.** A more neutral term is used to describe the action as not that bad. "I was just joking around." "It was a prank." "This is just locker room talk."
- **Deny personal responsibility.** This can occur when someone else can be blamed. "Someone else started it." "It wasn't my fault."
- **Deny the harm.** The harm that was caused is minimized. "What happened wasn't that bad." "They are just overreacting."
- **Blame the other.** Those who are targeted are blamed. "They deserved it." "They do not belong here." "If they would stop [describe behavior], this would not happen."

When you approach the school to raise concerns about the hurtful behavior of these students, you may hear rationalizations from the principal or school staff. For example:

- "You can view this as a learning opportunity for your child."
- "This is not bullying, so there is nothing we can do."
- "Your child is overreacting. It was not that bad."
- "If your child would stop [describe behavior], this would not happen."

---

27 Bandura, A. (1991). Social cognition theory of moral thought and action. In: *Handbook of Moral Behavior and Development*, vol. 1 (ed. W.M. Kurtines and J.L. Gewirtz), 45–96. Lawrence Erlbaum.

Bidirectional Aggression or Impulsive Retaliation

> *Liam is a freshman in high school. He is quick to trigger when he gets upset. He was carrying too many books at school and they all dropped. The other students laughed at him. That evening, Sam posted a photo of Liam and all of his books on the floor on Instagram with a nasty comment. Liam's father had always taught him to fight back if he was bullied. The next day at school, Sam walked past Liam with a group of boys. Sam asked Liam if he was going to clean the floor with his books again. The other boys laughed. Liam physically attacked Sam.*

Not all incidents of hurtful behavior are one-directional. Sometimes, both or many students are being hurtful to each other. Sometimes, these situations are indeed bidirectional "conflict" or "drama." Bidirectional aggression is situations where all parties have a relatively equivalent social status level and equivalent levels of hurtful behavior. The term "drama" is frequently used when students are engaging in back-and-forth hurtful acts, often with supporters on one or both sides. Impulsive retaliation occurs when one student has been treated badly and they retaliate against the student who treated them badly.[28]

In the survey I conducted of teens about bullying in 2015, impulsive retaliation appeared to have played a major factor in many of these hurtful incidents. Over two-thirds of students who reported they had been hurtful also reported someone had been hurtful to them. Students who indicated they had been hurtful to another student were asked what they were thinking at the time. The two key reasons students provided for when they were hurtful were:

- "I acted too fast when I was angry and really did not think."
- "This student had been hurtful to me or a friend of mine."

Obviously, retaliation against someone who has been hurtful – whether by a person, a group, a political leader, or a country – is something that happens quite frequently in our global society. Many in our society support this kind of retaliation. They say, "If someone is hurtful to you, hit them back ten times harder." Many times, young adults are sent to war – to risk their lives, kill others, be wounded, or be killed – because the leaders of one country are engaging in retaliation against the leaders of another country. Is this how you want to see our global society function?

---

28 Runions et al., Beyond the reactive proactive dichotomy; Mahady Wilton, M.M., Craig, W.M., and Pepler, D.J. (2000). Emotional regulation and display in classroom victims of bullying: characteristic expressions of affect, coping styles and relevant contextual factors. *Social Development* 9: 226–245. Tapper, K. and Boulton, M.J. (2005). Victims and peer group responses to different forms of aggression among primary school children. *Aggressive Behavior* 31 (3): 238–253. https://doi.org/10.1002/ab.20080.

Mahatma Gandhi tried to warn about this. "An eye for an eye only ends up making the whole world blind." Coretta Scott King said, "Revenge and retaliation always perpetuate the cycle of anger, fear, and violence."

Several key strategies grounded in Positively Powerful, which is discussed in Chapter 5, are helpful in reducing the likelihood that your child will engage in impulsive retaliation. These specific anti-retaliation strategies are discussed in Chapter 7.

Bullying by School Staff

Janice has dyslexia. She spent most of her time in a general education classroom in 3rd grade. But she struggles to get her work done. Her teacher says things to the whole class like, "Time for recess. Everyone has done a good job on their work and finished. Except for Janice that is." The other students also say hurtful things to Janice and she has no friends. Janice began experiencing profound nightmares. She experienced bullying by her peers throughout her time in school.

Staff bullying of students is an abuse of power and can cause significant harm. Staff bullying occurs when a school staff member degrades a student, often in front of other students.[29] This has a profoundly negative impact on the targeted student's emotional well-being. The manner in which school staff interact with students communicates to all of the other students how they should treat this student. The harms from such hurtful treatment have been described in this way:

Students who are bullied by teachers typically experience confusion, anger, fear, self-doubt, and profound concerns about their academic and social competencies. Not knowing why he or she has been targeted, or what one must do to end the bullying, may well be among the most personally distressing aspects of being singled out and treated unfairly. Over time, especially if no one in authority intervenes, the target may come to blame him or her self for the abuse and thus feel a pervasive sense of helplessness and worthlessness.[30]

Unfortunately, the issue of staff bullying of students has not received sufficient attention from researchers or policy makers.[31] The limited research that has been conducted provides the following insight:

• There appear to be two kinds of situations where such staff bullying occurs:

29 McEvoy, A. (2005). Teachers who bully students: Patterns and policy implications. Paper presented at the Hamilton Fish Institute's Persistently Safe Schools Conference, Philadelphia, PA, p. 3.
30 McEvoy, Teachers who bully students, 2–3.
31 McEvoy, Teachers who bully students;Twemlow, S.W., Fonagy, P., Sacco, F., and Brethour, J. (2006). Teachers who bully students: a hidden trauma. *The International Journal of Social Psychiatry* 52 (3): 187–198.

- Situations where staff intentionally humiliate students, frequently associated with some form of identity bias. This includes identity bias based on disabilities, sexual and gender minority, students with weight concerns, and students who are religious or racial minorities.
- Situations where staff appear to be overwhelmed by challenges in behavior management. This concern may be related to lack of training in effective classroom management, classes that are too large, and a lack of support from the administration.

• The issue of school staff who bully students is a known concern. But no clear way has been found to handle or assess the prevalence of this problem. Schools often do not have effective policies or processes in place to address these concerns. There are frequently no policies or procedures to follow when other staff members witness these hurtful acts. There are usually no negative consequences for staff who engage in such hurtful acts.

• Most public school teachers in the US are part of collective-bargaining groups that represent the teachers on labor issues. When the issue of teachers who engage in bullying becomes a labor conflict, an adversarial teacher–administrator dynamic is set up. The labor group often then acts to protect the bullying teacher, to the serious disadvantage of the bullied student.

• Students who are targeted often are vulnerable, have some devalued personal attribute, and are unable to stand up for themselves. Other students will not defend them. Frequently, there are references to how this student differs from other students who are more capable or valued. As a result, the student also becomes targeted by peers. Students perceived bullying by school staff as more distressing than bullying by a peer.[32]

• School staff most often will not recognize or acknowledge their behavior as bullying.[33] They often use rationalizations. Frequently, they will claim their actions are an appropriate disciplinary response or good classroom management.

On the youth survey that I conducted in 2015, students were asked how frequently in the last month they had been treated badly, were hurtful, or witnessed a student be hurtful to another student. They were also asked how frequently they had witnessed a school staff member be hurtful to a student. I analyzed the results in a way that allowed me to compare the findings. Those students who had witnessed staff be hurtful to a student were significantly more likely to report being treated badly, that they were hurtful, or they had witnessed a student be hurtful.

---

32 Whitted, K. and Dupper, D. (2008). Do teachers bully students? Findings from a survey of students in an alternative education setting. *Education and Urban Society* 40 (3): 329–341.
33 Sylvester, R. (2011). Teacher as bully: knowingly or unintentionally harming students. *Morality in Education. The Delta Kappa Gamma Bulletin* 77 (2): 42–45. http://www.deltakappagamma.org/NH/dkgbulletinwinter2011.PDF (accessed 1 August 2024).

Question: How frequently were students hurtful to you?

If they had "ever" witnessed staff be hurtful

If they had "never" witnessed staff be hurtful

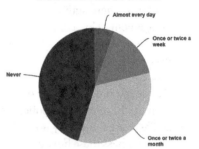

Question: How frequently were you hurtful?

If they had "ever" witnessed staff be hurtful

If they had "never" witnessed staff be hurtful

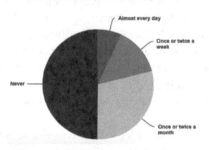
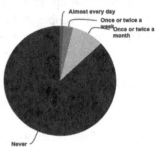

Question: How frequently did you witness students being hurtful?

If they had "ever" witnessed staff be hurtful

If they had "never" witnessed staff be hurtful

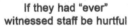
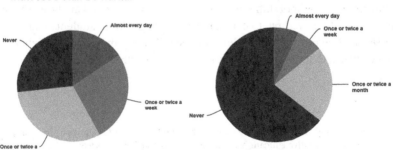

Based on these results, it appears that in schools where staff treat students in hurtful ways, this results in significantly higher levels of student hurtful behavior directed at peers. Dramatic declines could be achieved in reducing hurtful student behavior by reducing staff hurtful behavior directed at students.

There are also situations where students are hurtful to staff. The critical first question in these situations is whether these are situations of proactive aggression or reactive aggression. Is the hurtful student emotionally distressed, dysregulated, and lashing out? Or is this hurtful behavior intentional and planned, based on some level of bias against the teacher or other staff member?

If this is proactive aggression, the staff member may be a member of a minority identity group. If this is a reactive aggression situation, the critically important questions must be: What led this student to become emotionally distressed and dysregulated, resulting in an attack on the staff member? Was this student acting in an aggressive manner in reaction to how this student was treated by the staff member? It is always so very important to consider the differences between proactive and reactive aggression.

If your child has been accused of being hurtful to a teacher, it is very important to ask what happened that led to this. Your child absolutely must be held accountable and take steps to remedy the harm. However, if the staff member was hurtful to your child, that staff member must also be held accountable to take steps to remedy the harm to your child.

3

Lack of Effectiveness of Anti-bullying Efforts

Lack of Effectiveness

The way in which schools are addressing bullying is not achieving success in far too many situations. Your child's principal and all of the school staff want to have students in your school feel safe, welcome, and respected. Your child's principal is likely doing what they have been told to do. They are "following the book." The problem is the requirements and guidance in "the book." This chapter will outline why what schools are being directed to do to address bullying is not achieving success.

Survey Data on Bullying

In the United States, significant initiatives were launched by the Obama Administration in 2010.[1] It was hoped that these activities would result in a reduction in bullying. The CDC added a question related to bullying on the Youth Risk Behavior Survey (YRBS) in 2009.[2] The question they use is: "Bullying is when 1 or more students tease, threaten, spread rumors about, hit, shove, or hurt another student over and over again. It is not bullying when 2 students of about the same strength or power argue or fight or tease each other in a friendly way."[3] The question related to this statement asks about experiences in the last month.

---

1 Lee, J. (2011). President Obama & the First Lady at the White House Conference on Bullying Prevention. https://obamawhitehouse.archives.gov/blog/2011/03/10/president-obama-first-lady-white-house-conference-bullying-prevention (accessed 1 August 2024).
2 US Centers for Disease Control (CDC), Youth risk behavior survey (CDC YRBS). https://www.cdc.gov/healthyyouth/data/yrbs/index.htm (accessed 1 August 2024).
3 https://www.cdc.gov/healthyyouth/data/yrbs/questionnaires.htm (accessed 1 August 2024).

There are concerns about the wording of the YRBS statement. It uses terms that possibly could be implicated in more serious situations, but raises the potential that students may identify more typical youth relationship challenges as "bullying." This survey data also does not identify the percentage of students who were treated badly on a very frequent basis, felt emotionally distressed, and were unable to get this to stop. These are the students who are at greatest risk.

However, because the YRBS has been delivered to students every other year, it is possible to track trends. (However, the results on YRBS obtained during the pandemic are suspect.) Based on survey data in the United States, there has been no decline in the rate at which students report being bullied at school. This is the data from 2009 to 2019[4]:

The percentage of high school students who	2009	2011	2013	2015	2017	2019
Were bullied at school	19.9	20.1	19.6	20.2	19.0	19.5

Adapted from 4.

More effective survey language is used on the Program for International Student Assessment (PISA) survey, which is coordinated by the Organization for Economic Cooperation and Development (OECD). PISA is an international assessment that measures 15-year-old students' reading, mathematics, and science literacy. The survey is delivered every three years.[5] The PISA survey assessed students in over 80 countries. Starting in 2015, PISA has included questions about bullying.[6]

PISA 2018 asked about three distinct types of bullying, including physical, relational, and verbal. Students were asked how often they had experienced these types of bullying. The response options were: "never or almost never,"

4 CDC (2015). Youth risk behavior survey: data summary and trends report 2007–2019. https://www.cdc.gov/healthyyouth/data/yrbs/pdf/YRBSDataSummaryTrendsReport2019-508. pdf (accessed 1 August 2024). There was a reported reduction in the rate of bullying on the YRBS in 2021. This survey was conducted at a time when student experiences in schools were profoundly changed due to the pandemic. This is not a valid finding. My perspective is that we need to have more distance from the pandemic to determine what is happening in schools.

5 Organization for Economic Cooperation and Development (OECD) (2020). Bullying. In: PISA 2018 Results, vol. III: What School Life Means for Students' Lives. OECD Publishing https://doi. org/10.1787/cd52fb72-en. https:// www.oecd-ilibrary.org/docserver/cd52fb72-en.pdf?expires=1 721337739&id=id&accname=guest&checksum=97C6042F4C2E9D0DDF104A8E9834E7F5 (accessed 1 August 2024).

6 Schleicher, A. (2020). PISA 2018 results, vol III: what school life means for student lives. https://www.oecd-ilibrary.org/sites/cd52fb72-en/index.html?itemId=/content/component/ cd52fb72-en#fig10 (accessed 1 August 2024).

"a few times a year," "a few times a month," "once a week or more." This approach to asking about experiences of bullying will generate more helpful information about the extent to which students are experiencing persistent bullying than the YRBS.

On average across OECD countries, 23% of students reported being bullied at least a few times a month, with 8% classified as being frequently bullied. The PISA 2018 data for US students indicated that 26% of students reported being bullied at least a few times a month, with 10% reporting frequent bullying.

Note that the YRBS asks about experiencing bullying in the last month, but does not ask about frequency. If one evaluates the results of the YRBS based on the responses in PISA, it appears logical to assume that approximately 10% of US students are persistently bullied.

Bullying and Cyberbullying Data

Survey data related to what happened during the pandemic appears to demonstrate the interrelationship between bullying and cyberbullying. Given most students were in remote learning, it was reasonable to predict a decrease of in-person bullying and an increase in cyberbullying. But this is not what happened.

The researchers at the Cyberbullying Research Center have been regularly collecting data on bullying and cyberbullying in the United States since 2004.[7] They conducted studies in 2016, 2019, and 2021. These studies used the same method and survey. This allowed them to evaluate the trends in bullying and cyberbullying behaviors during the pandemic.[8]

Students overwhelmingly said that they had been bullied less at school since the start of the pandemic. This is logical because many times they were not in school or, if they were, their environments were severely restricted. When it came to cyberbullying, most said they had been bullied online less or about the same as before. These data provide support for the understanding that most cyberbullying is closely associated with in-person bullying.[9]

This insight is important for you to understand as a parent. If your child is experiencing cyberbullying, this is very likely related to in-person bullying at school. There must be an overall response that addresses the concerns both at school and online.

---

7 See generally, https://cyberbullying.org (accessed 1 August 2024).
8 Patchin, J.W. (2021). Bullying during the Covid-19 pandemic. https://cyberbullying.org/bullying-during-the-covid-19-pandemic (accessed 1 August 2024).
9 Gini, G., Card, N.A., and Pozzoli, T. (2018). A meta-analysis of the differential relations of traditional and cyber-victimization with internalizing problems. *Aggressive Behavior* 44 (2): 185–198.

Current Anti-bullying Approach

Effectiveness of Prevention Programs

The recent National Academy of Sciences, Engineering, and Medicine (NAS) report on bullying prevention, *Preventing Bullying through Science, Policy, and Practice*, noted that, despite a growing demand for bullying prevention programs, research had shown limited effectiveness of these programs, especially in the United States.[10] One huge concern was noted:

> Competing demands on student and teacher time, such as standardized testing, also limit U.S. teachers' perceived ability to focus on social-emotional and behavioral activities, as compared with traditional academic content. The challenges in designing and delivering effective bullying prevention programs in the U.S. may also include the greater social and economic complexities of U.S. school populations, including greater income disparities and racial/ethnic heterogeneity.[11]

The NAS report also noted the challenges of evaluating studies of approaches that are implemented at different school levels due to developmental issues. A recent analysis of the results of many studies demonstrated that programs implemented at the secondary level simply were not effective.[12] As mentioned previously, the NAS report noted the inaccurate stereotype of those who bully. If bullying prevention programs have been developed with the mistaken understanding that those who engage in bullying are at high risk, they will incorporate approaches that seek to address youth risk. Students who bully to achieve dominance and social status are not at high risk. An entirely different, peer-based, approach is necessary to reduce their hurtful behavior.

Student Perspectives of Staff Effectiveness

Research suggests that school staff overwhelmingly think that they have effective strategies and respond effectively to the bullying incidents they witness or are reported. The student perspective is that staff are not doing enough, ignore the

---

10 National Academies of Sciences, Engineering, and Medicine (2016). *Preventing Bullying through Science, Policy, and Practice*. https://doi.org/10.17226/23482.
11 National Academies of Sciences, Engineering, and Medicine, *Preventing Bullying through Science, Policy, and Practice*.
12 Yeager, D.S., Fong, C.J., Lee, H.Y., and Espelage, D. (2015). Declines in efficacy of anti-bullying programs among older adolescents: a developmental theory and a three-level meta-analysis. *Journal of Applied Developmental Psychology* 37: 36–51.

hurtful incidents they witness, and generally make things worse when they respond. The findings in studies from different countries are quite stark:

- **Different perspectives.** In one study of both staff and students, only 7% of school staff thought they made things worse when they intervened in bullying situations, whereas 61% of middle school students and 59% of high school students reported that staff who tried to stop bullying only made things worse.[13]
- **Ineffective staff.** A study found that students overwhelmingly believed that most teachers ignored or did not recognize such hurtful activities, were not prepared to intervene if asked, and were incapable of doing anything effective if they took actions.[14]
- **Where bullying occurs.** A study in middle schools found that the highest reported prevalence of bullying was in classrooms, hallways, and lunchrooms.[15] These are the places where presumably staff supervision should be the highest. The fact that these incidents were witnessed by staff and continued to occur increased the distress of the students.

Effectiveness of "Tell an Adult"

The primary approach schools are directed to take to address bullying is to tell students to "tell an adult." As reported in a book entitled *Youth Voice Project*, the researchers conducted a survey of students that asked whether they reported bullying and the effectiveness of the response by the school.[16] Only about a third of students who reported they had been bullied and were feeling distressed also indicated that they had reported this to the school. For those who did report, things got better only about a third of the time. Things stayed the same a third of the time and got worse a third of the time.

---

13 Bradshaw, C.P., Sawyer, A.L., and O'Brennan, L.M. (2007). Bullying and peer victimization at school: perceptual differences between students and school staff. *School Psychology Review* 36 (3): 361–382.
14 Thomson, P. and Gunter, H. (2008). Researching bullying with students: a lens on everyday life in an "innovative school." *International Journal of Inclusive Education* 12: 185–200.
15 Perkins, H.W., Perkins, J.M., and Craig, D.W. (2014). No safe haven: locations of harassment and bullying victimization in middle youth organizations. *The Journal of School Health* 84: 810–818.
16 Davis, S. and Nixon, C. (2013). *Youth Voice Project: Student Insights into Bullying and Peer Mistreatment*. Research Press. Davis, S., and Nixon, C. (2011). Youth Voice Project: national data set. Youth Voice Project. https://www.researchpress.com/product/youth-voice-project/ (accessed 1 August 2024).

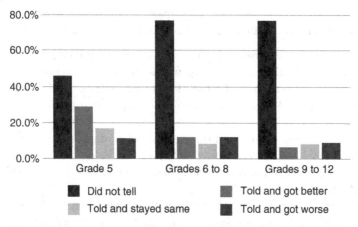

Adapted from data presented in 16.

The survey I conducted in 2015 used similar questions and got almost identical results, even though we conducted our surveys in different ways.[17] The GLSEN 2019 School Climate Report indicated that 76% of sexual minority students experienced in-person verbal harassment and 31% were physically harassed.[18] Only 35% of these students reported the harassment to the school and, of those who reported, 60% said staff did nothing in response.

This consistent data translates to roughly a 10% level of success in the "tell an adult" approach to addressing bullying. Of concern is that when students either do not report or do not report again if things became worse after the first report, school leaders may mistakenly believe that bullying is not a significant concern in their school, despite survey data indicating otherwise.

Students appear to think that there are many barriers that prevent them from obtaining help from adults at school. They will determine whether the risks outweighed the benefits. Most students believe that school staff will make the situation worse if they intervene.[19] There is a perception among the students that the school tolerated bullying because nothing is ever done if they do report. Therefore, it is a waste of time to report.[20]

17 Willard, N.E. (2015) Embrace Civility Student Survey. Embrace Civility in the Digital Age. https://www.embracecivility.org/wp-content/uploadsnew/ECSSFullReportfull.pdf (accessed 1 August 2024).
18 Kosciw, J.G., Clark, C.M., Truong, N.L., and Zongrone, A.D. (2020). The 2019 National School Climate Survey: The Experiences of Lesbian, Gay, Bisexual, Transgender, and Queer Youth in Our Nation's Schools. GLSEN. https://www.glsen.org/sites/default/files/2021-04/NSCS19-FullReport-032421-Web_0.pdf (accessed 1 August 2024).
19 Bradshaw, C.P., Sawyer, A.L., and O'Brennan, L.M. (2007). Bullying and peer victimization at school: perceptual differences between students and school staff. *School Psychology Review* 36: 361–382. https://doi.org/10.1080/14680777.2015.1137959.
20 MacDonald, H. and Swart, E. (2004). The culture of bullying at a primary school. *Education as Change* 8: 33–55.

Educators often appear to think that they are effectively responding to the hurtful incidents that are reported to them.[21] Many students believe that school staff will respond in a way that will make their situation worse. The results of many studies document that students' perspectives of the lack of effectiveness are accurate.[22]

Students may not report for fear of being viewed as a "tattling," which will result in retaliation and harm to their reputation. Do a search on the term "bullying" and then look at "images." Look specifically at the images of those being bullied. Do the terms "wimp" or "helpless" come to mind. To report that you are being bullied may be perceived by other students as a confession that they are a "help-less wimp." Teens expect that they are becoming independently effective, including in managing their own personal relationships. To report that they are being bullied and cannot get this to stop is, essentially, reporting that they are failing in the task of managing their life.

It appears that many students think that "official channels" for reporting may be risky because this could lead to public disclosure that they had reported. They may not trust the digital reporting systems because they do not know who might receive the report or how this will be handled. They also do not trust school staff to keep secrets told to them in confidence.[23]

Statutes and Directives

This following section is based solely on US laws. Hopefully, the insight will also benefit those who live in other countries.

In the United States, there are no federal statutes that address "bullying." There are federal civil rights laws that address discriminatory harassment of "protected class" students that provide a significantly better approach to use to intervene in bullying situations.[24] These laws are discussed in Chapter 11. The federal civil rights laws require that public schools respond to situations that have created a

---

21 Bradshaw, Sawyer, and O'Brennan, Bullying and peer victimization at school.

22 Davis and Nixon, Youth Voice Project: national data set;Fekkes, M., Pijpers, F.I.M., and Verloove-Vanhorick, S.P. (2005). Bullying: who does what, when and where? Involvement of children, teachers and parents in bullying behavior. *Health Education Research: Theory and Practice.*Rigby, K., and Johnson, K. (2016). The prevalence and effectiveness of anti-bullying strategies employed in Australian schools. University of South Australia. www.unisa.edu.au/siteassets/episerver-6-files/global/eass/eds/184856-anti-bullying-report-final-3large.pdf (accessed 1 August 2024).

23 Garpelin, A. (2004). Accepted or rejected in school. *European Educational Research Journal* 3: 729–742.

24 In the United States, Title IX of the Education Amendments of 1972. 20 USC. §§ 1681–1688. Title VI of the Civil Rights Act of 1964. 42 USC. §§ 2000d-2000d-7. Section 504 of the Rehabilitation Act of 1973. 29 USC § 794. The Americans with Disabilities Act of 1990. 42 USC. §§ 12131–12134.

"hostile environment" for a student based on race, color, native origin, religion (if grounded native origin), gender identity or sexual orientation, sex, or disabilities. A "hostile environment" exists when serious, persistent, or pervasive hurtful behavior has caused an interference in the ability of a protected-class student to learn and participate in school activities. "Persistent" means frequent hurtful acts that, individually, may be more minor. The cumulative impact is harmful. "Pervasive" means widespread hurtful acts directed at a group of students within a similar identity group.

If a hostile environment is found to exist, the school is required to take steps that are reasonably calculated to stop the harassment (more than punishment), remedy the harm to the targeted student, correct any aspects of the school environment that are supporting the hurtful behavior, and monitor to ensure effectiveness. If an involved student has disabilities and is receiving services on an Individual Education Plan (IEP) or Section 504 plan, the comprehensive plan to address this situation must be developed by that student's IEP or 504 team and included in their IEP or 504 plan.

The guidance set forth in Chapter 12 on how to insist upon in an intervention by your child's school is in line with federal civil rights laws, even if your child does not currently qualify as being in a protected class. Chapter 12 outlines a way to have your child considered to be in a protected class under Section 504 if they are now experiencing a mental health concern and interference with their learning.

State Statutes and District Policies

School districts in the United States are required by the statutes in each state to have anti-bullying policies. These policies are part of the district's disciplinary code. Thus, an accusation of bullying is considered an accusation that the hurtful student has violated the disciplinary code. These statutes and the policies adopted under them are a significant reason why the manner in which schools are seeking to address bullying is not working at all effectively.

In December 2010, USDOE released a document entitled "*Key Components for State Anti-Bullying Laws.*"[25] This guidance encouraged states to enact more comprehensive bullying prevention statutes and for districts to address bullying

---

25 Duncan, A. (2010). Key policy letters from the Education Secretary and Deputy Secretary. US Department of Education, December 16. https://www2.ed.gov/policy/gen/guid/secletter/101215.html (accessed 1 August 2024). See also Federal Partners in Bullying Prevention, Key components in state anti-bullying laws. http://www.StopBullying.Gov/laws/key-components/index.html (accessed 1 August 2024).

as a disciplinary code violation. The following were their recommendations for state statutes:

- **Purpose statement.** The purpose statement outlines the harms of bullying and declares this behavior to be unacceptable.
- **Definition.** The definition of "bullying" often includes other terms, such as "harassment" or "intimidation." This includes reference to intentional hurtful behavior that causes harm to other students. The definition may include a list of specific behaviors that are considered bullying. The definition generally includes conduct that occurs on school grounds, at school-sponsored activities, on school-provided transportation, or through school-owned technology, or that otherwise creates a significant disruption to the school environment. USDOE made a recommendation that the definition include an "enumeration of specific characteristics" that describes students who are within protected classes under civil rights statutes, but to make it clear that bullying does not have to be based on any particular characteristic.
- **District policy requirement.** State statutes require that school districts adopt an anti-bullying policy that contains the following provisions:
  - **Reporting and investigations.** District policies include a procedure for students, students' families, staff, and others to report incidents of bullying. The procedure identifies the appropriate school personnel responsible for receiving the report and investigating the incident. This is usually the assistant principal or principal. Policies often require that school personnel report incidents of bullying they witness or are reported to them.
  - **Investigation and notification.** Policies include a procedure for the designated school personnel to promptly investigate and respond to any report of an incident of bullying. The policy also generally includes requirements of notification to parents and others.
  - **Consequences.** The overall disciplinary code includes graduated range of consequences and sanctions for any violation of the code.
- **Other components.** Other components of state statutes may include that the school will also implement a prevention program, how the policy will be communicated, supports that may be provided to students, preventive education, staff training, and parent involvement.

The Problems

Note that the entire focus of this recommended statutory approach is based on the perception that students will readily report to the school if they are being bullied and that school-imposed punishment will be effective in stopping the hurtful behavior. There are critically important reasons why this approach is not effective.

Shift of Focus Away from the Harmed Student

The disciplinary code approach turns the situation from a harmful offense that should require remedy to the student who was harmed into an investigation of an alleged violation of a school rule by the accused. Instead of responding in a way that best supports the harmed student, the attention of the principal most often shifts away from the harmed student and focuses solely on a determination of whether the accused student has violated the disciplinary code. A disciplinary consequence response generally ignores the concerns of the bullied student. Because of privacy restrictions, the consequence imposed on the hurtful student cannot even be disclosed to the student who reported they were bullied.[26]

Lack of Effectiveness of Punishments

Punishing students is an ineffective strategy to influence a change in their behavior.[27] Punishment often causes problem behaviors to increase, not decrease.[28]

Enumeration of Specific Characteristics

State statutes and district policies often include what is called "enumeration of specific characteristics" that reference protected-class students. This has caused significant confusion among school leaders. Many school leaders appear to think that their district's anti-bullying policy sets forth the *only* requirements for their response to a complaint.

Take a moment right now to look at what is set forth on the http://StopBullying.Gov website. Look under the Resources tab, for Laws & Policies. This will take you to a page that discusses the "Common Components" set out above. Look below the map of the state statutes for the heading "Federal Law." Click on the link and you will see guidance that will be discussed in Chapter 11.

Now, go to the map and select your state. Look at the question that reads: "Do [name of state] anti-bullying laws and regulations include protections for specific groups?" Note the reference to protected classes and then the language: "[Name

---

26 The Family Educational Rights and Privacy Act (FERPA) contains provisions restricting release of information pertaining to disciplinary actions taken against students. (20 USC. § 1232g; 34 CFR Part 99).

27 Alvarez, B. (2021). School Suspensions Do More Harm Than Good. NEA Today, September 10. https://www.nea.org/nea-today/all-news-articles/school-suspensions-do-more-harm-good#:~:text=New%20study%20finds%20more%20severe,behavior%3B%20educators%20have%20better%20solutions (accessed 1 August 2024).

28 Swearer, S.M., Espelage, D.L., Love, K.B., and Kingsbury, W. (2008). School-wide approaches to intervention for school aggression and bullying. In: *Transforming School Mental Health Services* (ed. B. Doll and J.A. Cummings), 187–212. Corwin Press.

of state] schools that receive federal funding are required by federal law to address discrimination based on certain personal characteristics. Find out when bullying may be a civil rights violation." This link will take you to the same page as the Federal Laws link above.

When you approach the school with your complaint, the first response of the principal will likely be that they will address this situation under the district's disciplinary code. This needs to be corrected. "We are filing this complaint under federal civil rights laws, not the district disciplinary code." You can show them the path on the StopBullying.gov website to see the differences.

Substantial Disruption Standard

Under your district's disciplinary code, the misbehavior of a student generally must meet the standard of causing a "substantial disruption" to result in any disciplinary consequence. This is grounded in a free speech case, *Tinker v. Des Moines,* which is discussed in Chapter 11.[29] The actual decision set forth the standard that schools can restrict student speech if it has caused or foreseeably could cause a substantial disruption or significant interference with the rights of other students. However, many principals think only in terms of substantial disruption.

A serious bullying situation, especially one involving violence, would likely meet this standard. However, most bullying is more in the form of persistent verbal aggression or exclusion that are subtle and covert, that, when viewed as individual incidents, are not generally disruptive. The persistent nature of the hurtful behavior is what is causing the profound harm.

In many state statutes, this persistent hurtful behavior will not even fit the statutory definition of "bullying." The statutes and resulting policies often focus on "an act" of hurtful behavior. Often, students experiencing such persistent harm will not even report, because they do not think the principal will do anything about such minor incidents. Or, if they do report, the principal tells them "this is not bullying, so there is nothing I can do." This is the other reason it is important to pursue an intervention under federal civil rights laws, as discussed in Chapters 11 and 12.

Reduce Exclusionary Discipline

At the same time as states and school districts were being encouraged to better address bullying through state statutes and district policies that focus on the use of disciplinary consequences, schools were also directed to reduce the imposition of disciplinary consequences. In early 2014, the US Department of Justice

---

29 Tinker v. Des Moines, 393 US 503 (1969).

(USDOJ) and US Department of Education (USDOE) jointly released guidance that directed schools to identify, avoid, and remedy discriminatory discipline.[30] In 2015, the Every Student Succeeds Act (ESSA) was signed into law.[31] ESSA requires that school districts reduce the overuse of exclusionary discipline policies.

These efforts were for the purpose of addressing very serious concerns. The data are clear that students of color and those with disabilities are far more frequently suspended for engaging in the same kinds of misbehavior as dominant-culture students.[32] These are the students who are more likely to experience being bullied.

However, this has created a situation of confusion for school leaders. State legislatures and school leaders were told: "Impose disciplinary consequences to stop bullying." Then, they were told: "Do not impose disciplinary consequences."

Required Public Bullying Reports

In the 2010 Key Components guidance, USDOE also advised states to increase what they called "Transparency and Monitoring" by requiring schools to make annual public reports on the number of bullying incidents. This section of guidance is not present on the StopBullying.Gov page on the components. If you go to a report entitled "Analysis of State Laws and Policies," you can see the original guidance, which reads:

- Includes a provision for LEAs to report annually to the state on the number of reported bullying incidents, and any responsive actions taken.
- Includes a provision for LEAs to make data regarding bullying incidence publicly available in aggregate with appropriate privacy protections to ensure students are protected.[33]

In states that have made this a statutory requirement, the rates of bullying reported by the schools have plummeted, while the rate at which students report

---

30 USDOJ and USDOE (2015). Dear colleague letter. https://www2.ed.gov/about/offices/list/ocr/letters/colleague-201401-title-vi.html (accessed 1 August 2024); USDOE (2015). Rethink school discipline: school district leader summit on improving school climate and discipline, Resource Guide for Superintendent Action, Washington, DC. http://www.ed.gov/school-discipline (accessed 1 August 2024).

31 Pub.L. 114–95; https://www.ed.gov/essa?src=rn (accessed 1 August 2024).

32 Pub.L. 114–95; https://www.ed.gov/essa?src=rn (accessed 1 August 2024); see also American Psychological Association (APA) Zero Tolerance Task Force (2008). Are zero tolerance policies effective in the schools? An evidentiary review and recommendations. American Psychologist 63 (9): 852–862. https://doi.org/10.1037/0003-066X.63.9.852. https://www.apa.org/pubs/reports/zero-tolerance.pdf (accessed 1 August 2024).

33 https://www2.ed.gov/rschstat/eval/bullying/state-bullying-laws/state-bullying-laws.pdf, 93–94 (accessed 1 August 2024).

being bullied on the YRBS has remained constant. You will need to look at your state statute to determine whether this is a requirement in your state. Look again at the page on StopBullying.Gov for your state's statute. Then, look at the end of the analysis under the question that reads: "What are the policy requirements for schools to prevent and respond to bullying behavior?" This will tell you whether your state has this requirement.

An analysis of what has happened in the state of New York after the 2011 passage of the Dignity Act for All Students (DASA) statute is helpful. DASA requires that all schools make an annual report of bullying incidents.[34] In 2017 the New York state comptroller analyzed the data from the 2013 to 2014 school year. This analysis found that 71% of New York City schools had reported zero incidents of harassment, bullying, or discrimination of students for that entire year.[35] Similar concerns about reporting were evident throughout the state. By comparison, the rate at which students report being bullied on the New York YRBS has steadily increased since 2011 from 17.7% in 2011 to 20% in 2019.[36] Similar reports of low levels of bullying incidents by schools are evident in other states with this annual state statute reporting requirement.[37]

So what likely is happening? Schools want to avoid "black mark" reports. Principals who admit to problems with bullying in their schools may be seen as ineffective leaders. This very likely influences them to provide a socially desirable response that "there is no or little bullying occurring in my school." Principals have total control over the determination of whether a reported incident meets the policy definition of "bullying." This gives them the ability to control the number of reports. If the principal determines that the reported incident does not constitute "bullying" they do not have to include this incident in their report.

---

34 http://www.p12.nysed.gov/dignityact (accessed 1 August 2024).

35 https://ag.ny.gov/press-release/2016/ag-schneiderman-and-state-education-commissioner-elia-release-guidance-and-model (accessed 1 August 2024). Chapman, B. (2018) NYC Public Schools Have Been Underreporting Bullying, Report Suggests. *NY Daily News*. https://www.nydailynews.com/2016/08/31/nyc-public-schools-have-been-underreporting-bullying-report-suggests/ (accessed 1 August 2024).

36 Youth risk behavior data for New York state. https://nccd.cdc.gov/youthonline/app/Results.aspx?LID=NY (accessed 1 August 2024).

37 Duffort, L. (2018). Data Indicates Schools Are Likely Underreporting Bullying. Vtdigger, May 6. https://vtdigger.org/2018/05/06/data-indicates-schools-may-underreporting-bullying (accessed 1 August 2024);Kenney, K. (2017). Despite Law, Indiana Schools Are Misreporting Their Bullying Data, Call6 Investigation Finds. Theindychannel, October 30. https://www.theindychannel.com/longform/despite-law-indiana-schools-are-misreporting-their-bullying-data-call-6-investigation-finds (accessed 1 August 2024).

To make matters worse, this annual reporting-of-incidents requirement was incorporated into the ESSA.[38] However, at the federal level, the reporting requirement is only of allegations of harassment based on protected class under the federal civil rights statutes. The bullying and harassment data from each school and district are reported directly to the USDOE Office for Civil Rights (OCR). Data for individual districts and schools can be viewed on this website: https://civilrightsdata.ed.gov.

You are encouraged to make a public record request for your district and school's annual report, if your state requires these, and look at your district and school reports on the OCR website. Every school or district report I have reviewed defies logic.

Characteristics of Hurtful Students

In addition to all of the above reasons for why the disciplinary code approach is ineffective is a critically important understanding about the nature of bullying behavior. If the student being hurtful to your child also has other challenges in their behavior, it is probable that you could convince a principal to suspend that student. The problem with this approach is that this suspension will do nothing to address the underlying conditions that are resulting in this student being hurtful.

A more significant challenge is related to the insight set forth in Chapter 2 that students with challenges are not the most common source of bullying. The most common source of bullying are those students who are hurtful to achieve dominance and social status. These students are compliant to school staff and often considered to be leaders. They engage in persistent, but more minor, hurtful acts that certainly will not be considered to have created a substantial disruption. They also very likely have parents who are in prominent positions in the community who would immediately protest to school board members if a principal suspended their child.

This challenge is grounded in privilege. In far too many schools, the students who are hurtful to achieve dominance and social status have the privilege of being able to be hurtful to "misfits" without fear of any negative consequences.

Failure to Consider the Data

While USDOE tried to find a way to ensure greater accountability through its recommended requirement of annual bullying reports, this is absolutely not an effective approach. A better way to ensure accountability is to insist that schools and districts

---

38 ESEA section 1111(h)(1) and (h)(2).

engage in effective analysis of their school climate data, engage in the necessary planning to address identified concerns, and use subsequent data to evaluate their effectiveness. Further, schools and districts should provide this analyzed data, their plans, and their evaluation of effectiveness to their school and district communities.

An example of how badly schools and districts are ignoring their own data is evident in some data from Oregon, which is the state I live in. For years, Oregon used a survey called the Oregon Healthy Teens Survey. This survey is equivalent to the YRBS. The name has changed to Student Health Survey. However, many of the questions are the same.

My focus is on two questions. One question asks students to respond to statements on a four-point scale. One statement is: "There is a teacher or other school staff member who really cares about me." In 2013, 7.9% of 8th grade students and 5.9% of 11th grade students said this was "Not at all true." In 2022, 7.1% of 8th grade students and 7.0% of 11th grade students said this was "Not at all true." The survey solicits demographic data on the students, as well as outcomes data like student mental health. No analysis was ever provided to allow Oregon educators to know what groups of students might feel that school staff do not care about them. Positive school staff–student relationships are foundational for student happiness and success. If this percentage of students are not feeling like anyone at school really cares about them, this is a situation that should have been identified for improvement.

The second question changed a bit between 2013 and 2022. However, on both surveys there was a question that asked if students had experienced harassment or bullying in the last 30 days at school. The most consistent wording of the possible responses focused on not being harassed or bullied. In 2013, 65.4% of 8th grade students and 77% of 11th grade students said "I have not been harassed." In 2022, 64.7% of 8th grade students and 75.3% of 11th grade students said "I have not been bullied at school." There was an attempt to determine the demographic basis upon which students had been bullied. However, there was no analysis of the data to determine what percentage of students who experienced bullying also reported mental health concerns.

If there is a desire to address concerns of how safe, welcome, and respected students feel in school it is essential to hold schools and districts accountable by analyzing the data more effectively, evaluating progress in addressing critically important concerns based on such data, and making the data and the plans to address the concerns available to the school and district communities. I call this a continuous improvement approach. More insight on what I think schools need to be required to do is set forth in Chapter 12.

Institutional Betrayal

When schools do not respond effectively to bullying by students, their failure to effectively respond can cause profound harm. The concept of "institutional betrayal" is used when an institution fails to respond in an effective manner when it knows or should know of the harmful treatment being experienced by a member of the institution's community.

The concept of institutional betrayal has not yet been integrated into the bullying prevention field of research.[39] This concept has been developed in the context of an analysis of university responses to sexual harassment and assault among university students.

Institutional betrayal is grounded in betrayal trauma. Betrayal trauma theory holds that abuse that occurs within close relationships is more harmful than abuse by strangers. This is because in addition to the abuse, there has been a violation of trust and the situation involves a continuation of the relationship.

Institutional betrayal occurs when the person who has engaged in the abuse and the one who is being victimized are within the same institution and the victimized person must reach out for help from the institution to get the abuse to stop. When those who are victimized reach out for help, they must place a great deal of trust in the institution from which they are seeking that help. When the institution does not respond in an effective manner to such reports of abuse, this results in a significant increase of additional trauma for the one who has already been victimized.

Institutional betrayal is clearly associated with the profound challenges experienced by those who are sexually assaulted within an institutional setting. This includes sexual assault within universities, religious institutions, athletic teams, other youth organizations, and secondary schools.

Researchers Smith and Freyd created an Institutional Betrayal Questionnaire for use in studies of students who had experienced sexual harassment or assault at the university level.[40] The questionnaire asks:

In thinking about the events described in the previous section [an instance of a sexual assault], did an institution play a role by (check all that apply):

- Not taking proactive steps to prevent this type of experience?
- Creating an environment in which this type of experience seemed common or normal?

---

39 Smith, C.P. and Freyd, J.J. (2014). Institutional betrayal. *American Psychologist* 69, 575–587.
40 Smith, C.P. and Freyd, J.J. (2017). Insult, then injury: interpersonal and institutional betrayal linked to health and dissociation. *Journal of Aggression, Maltreatment & Trauma.* https://dynamic.uoregon.edu/jjf/institutionalbetrayal/ibq.html (accessed 1 August 2024).

- Creating an environment in which this experience seemed more likely to occur?
- Making it difficult to report the experience?
- Responding inadequately to the experience, if reported?
- Mishandling your case, if disciplinary action was requested?
- Covering up the experience?
- Denying your experience in some way?
- Punishing you in some way for reporting the experience (e.g. loss of privileges or status)?
- Suggesting your experience might affect the reputation of the institution?
- Creating an environment where you no longer felt like a valued member of the institution?
- Creating an environment where continued membership was difficult for you?

These questions clearly also relate to the characteristics of a school that is not responding effectively to address bullying, including when reported. The term DARVO was coined by Smith and Freed. This refers to a reaction those engaged in wrongdoing may display in response to being accused of such behavior. It is described as follows:

> DARVO refers to a reaction perpetrators of wrong doing, particularly sexual offenders, may display in response to being held accountable for their behavior. DARVO stands for "Deny, Attack, and Reverse Victim and Offender." The perpetrator or offender may Deny the behavior, Attack the individual doing the confronting, and Reverse the roles of Victim and Offender such that the perpetrator assumes the victim role and turns the true victim – or the whistle blower – into an alleged offender. This occurs, for instance, when an actually guilty perpetrator assumes the role of "falsely accused" and attacks the accuser's credibility and blames the accuser of being the perpetrator of a false accusation.[41]

Has this happened to you and your child when seeking assistance from your child's school to get the bullying of your child to stop?

To remedy these concerns requires "institutional courage." Having institutional courage requires that your child's school: maintains a commitment to responding effectively and sensitively to reports of bullying; accepts responsibility for taking steps to remedy the harm; encourages witnesses to report; engages in self-study through focus groups and by conducting surveys; ensures that leadership and

---

41 https://dynamic.uoregon.edu/jjf/defineDARVO.html (accessed 1 August 2024).

staff have received effective professional development, are transparent about data and policy, and use the power of the school community to address the larger societal issues; and commits resources to these actions.

What Schools Should Be Doing

Having studied these issues for a very long time, it is my perspective that the three key things schools need to do are:

- **Continuous improvement.** Implement a continuous improvement planning approach. The positive school climate task forces at the school level and at the district level should include both parent and student participation as representatives of their community. This task force must engage in an effective analysis of data from an annual school climate survey to identify concerns, looking at demographics, relationships, and outcomes. Based on this analysis, the task forces should develop objectives for improvement that are grounded in the data. The task force should develop strategies to address identified concerns and plan for their implementation. An evaluation of progress or lack thereof should be based on the subsequent surveys. This evaluation should be followed by a reassessment of objectives and strategies.
- **Student leadership.** Empower a team of kind, respectful, and inclusive students to provide leadership within the school. These students should be trained and empowered to provide peer support and engage in conflict resolution and restorative practices. They should also be empowered in a teen court-like manner to engage in a process with hurtful students and their supporters, to support these students in entering into accountability agreements to acknowledge personal responsibility for wrongdoing, remedy the harm to the person they harmed and to the school community, and commit to avoid all further harmful acts. The kinds of activities students could be engaged in are set forth in Chapter 10.
- **Effective interventions.** Interventions in both minor and more serious situations involving hurtful behavior should be implemented in an instructional manner to support all involved students in gaining the insight and skills to maintain positive relationships. All staff must have expertise in supporting students in resolving more minor incidents. Interventions in serious or persistent situations must be handled in accordance with the civil rights guidance set forth in Chapter 11. This should involve a resolution plan, developed by a team, that is reasonable, calculated to stop the harassment, remedy the harm to the targeted student, and correct any aspects of the environment that are supporting such hurtful acts.

4

Youth Development, Trauma, and Post-traumatic Growth

This chapter will address youth development. This includes learning about key parts of your child's brain and how their brain develops as they grow. The chapter also focuses more closely on teen development, because the teen years are when more bullying occurs. The teen development issues include identity development and moral development, as well as the greatest risks in decision making during the teen years. The chapter will also address trauma, intergenerational trauma, and post-traumatic growth.

It will be helpful for your child to understand the insight that is presented in this chapter. There are short videos and other resources on the Rise Above Bullying website for young people.

Key Areas of the Brain

Let us first learn about the areas of the brain that are most involved with guiding the decisions and actions your child might make.[1] You should know that this section is highly simplified – overly so. Your child's brain (and your brain) is composed of different centers that work together with the rest of the brain to make decisions and guide behavior. The brain is highly interconnected and no one area completely controls any specific behavior. However, it is my perspective that thinking about these four areas and the activities they are engaged in is helpful.

---

1 Siegel, D.J. and Payne-Bryson, T. (2002). *The Whole-brain Child: 12 Revolutionary Strategies to Nurture Your Child's Developing Mind.* Random House. Steinberg, L. (2015). *Age Of Opportunity: Lessons from the New Science of Adolescence.* Harper Paperbacks. Armstrong, T. (2016). *The Power of the Adolescent Brain: Strategies for Teaching Middle and High School Students.* ASCD. Jensen, F.E. and Nutt, A.E. (2015). *The Teenage Brain: A Neuroscientist's Survival Guide to Raising Adolescents and Young Adults.* Harper.

Rise Above Bullying: Empower and Advocate for Your Child, First Edition. Nancy E. Willard.
© 2025 John Wiley & Sons, Inc. Published 2025 by John Wiley & Sons, Inc.

Prefrontal Cortex – Thinking Center

The prefrontal cortex or "thinking center" of the brain is located near the top of our head, behind the forehead. The prefrontal cortex is involved with a wide range of functions, known as "executive functions." What does an "executive" do? An executive is the "boss" who is in charge. The executive functions of the prefrontal cortex include assessing situations, solving problems, planning, impulse control, and focusing attention.

The prefrontal cortex is the last part of a young person's brain to develop, and is not fully developed until a person is around the age of 25. When the prefrontal cortex is well developed and fully functioning a person is able to think clearly, be aware of oneself and others, evaluate situations, engage in effective problem solving, and make good decisions.

Anterior Cingulate Cortex – Emotional Regulation Center

The anterior cingulate cortex or "emotional regulation center" of the brain is located next to the prefrontal cortex. It is deeper inside our brain. This area is responsible for regulating and controlling emotions. Ideally, the anterior cingulate cortex works closely with the prefrontal cortex. When this connection is working well, a person is able to manage difficult emotions while they are evaluating situations and making decisions on how they will respond without being totally overwhelmed. This is also one of the later parts of the brain to fully mature.

Hippocampus – Memory Center

The hippocampus or "memory center" is located much deeper inside the brain. The hippocampus is where our memories are first processed. These memories are then sent out to long-term storage in other parts of the brain. Because our brains store these memories, this helps us to learn from our experiences. When we have an experience, the memory of this experience is processed by our hippocampus and then stored. Then, the next time we have a similar experience, we already have insight into a response which is based on our prior experiences. This part of the brain is functional very early.

One reason the hippocampus is so important is for personal safety. If your child is crossing the street and all of a sudden they note a car moving fast toward them, their hippocampus will facilitate access to the memories it has stored to make sure they move really quickly to get out of the way. Their brain does not take the time to problem solve.

Most often the hippocampus and our stored memories work subconsciously. This means that we react quickly to situations based on our past experiences. We are not consciously remembering past experiences in our immediate response. A challenge with this is if we have experienced too many sad or hurtful happenings in our life. The memories of these sad or hurtful past happenings are stored in the hippocampus. These stored memories can subconsciously guide how we respond to new situations.

The Amygdala – Threat Response Center

The amygdala is located way deep inside of the brain. This is the "threat response center." This is in an older part of the brain that first evolved in prehistoric times. Our amygdala is focused on what is necessary to ensure our physical survival. The most important job of the amygdala is to receive all incoming information – that is everything we see, hear, touch, smell, and taste – and answer one question: "Is there a threat to my safety?"

When our amygdala detects that a threat may be present, our whole body goes into a fight, flight, or freeze mode. When this happens, two stress hormones, adrenalin and cortisol, rush through our bodies. Our heart rate, respiration, and blood flow all also increase. This response allows our bodies to respond effectively to the threat – by running away, fighting, or freezing in place.

The amygdala often works closely with the hippocampus in assessing threats. The hippocampus has stored memories from past threats. If something happens that the hippocampus perceives to be a threat, based on past stored memories, this can immediately trigger the amygdala to believe that there is a present threat.

When the amygdala's threat response has been activated, what also happens is that our prefrontal cortex shuts down and becomes disconnected from our anterior cingulate cortex. This response to a threatening situation is just what we want our brains and bodies to do when a physical threat like a dangerous wild animal is present. "Do not think. Just get out of here."

However, these days the threats young people face do not generally involve dangerous wild animals. Many of the challenges they face require the ability to engage in effective problem solving. It is much harder to engage in effective problem solving if they are feeling threatened. This is because their amygdala has been activated and their prefrontal cortex has shut down.

Also, many of the concerns young people face are more constant – for example, constant pressure for grades or persistent bullying. Their amygdala can get stuck in "threat mode." If this is happening to your child, this means that the stress hormones adrenalin and cortisol are always at a higher level in their bodies. As a result, they are hypervigilant. They have difficulty thinking clearly. They are constantly assessing potential threats around them. If they continue in this state, they could experience significant physical and mental health concerns that could last a lifetime.

Neurons and Neural Pathways

The working parts of the brain are the neurons. Neurons are cells in the brain and nervous system that communicate with each other to send messages throughout the body – telling the body what to do. Neurons form connections, called synapses, with other neurons. The connections of synapses form neural pathways. It is said they are "wired together." Neurons send messages through these neural pathways that guide what people normally think about and how they normally respond.

As a young person's brain is developing, especially during the teen years, two basic processes are taking place. These are synaptic pruning and the strengthening of the neural pathways. When someone prunes an apple tree, the weak and unwanted branches are removed. This allows the stronger branches to grow even more strong. This results in a healthier tree, with strong branches to bear fruit. Synaptic pruning in a teen's brain is basically the same thing. Pruning reduces weak and unnecessary neural pathways. This allows the more frequently used neural pathways to become stronger.

This synaptic pruning occurs throughout the teen years and into early adulthood. The pruning is being facilitated by what young people are learning, based on their experiences. Their ability to think and solve problems improves with age, because the neural pathways that support this are being strengthened. The pruning process helps to build connections. This pruning will not ensure that your child will make wise decisions. Making wise decisions depends more on what the person has learned so far and will continue to learn during their development.

The things young people experience as they are growing guide how their neural pathways are established. If they generally experience happiness and success, their neural pathways will be established in a way that will keep them focused on a happy and successful path.

Unfortunately, if a young person is having more consistent negative experiences, their neural pathways will be established in a way that will tend to keep them focused on the negative experiences they have had. This will undermine their happiness and success.

The good news is that it is possible to rewire neural pathways. The Positively Powerful strategies set forth in Chapter 5 are designed to help your child to develop positive neural pathways that will support their happiness and success.

Feel Good Hormones – DOSE

The two stress hormones are adrenalin and cortisol. We absolutely need these hormones to allow us to respond effectively under challenging situations. However, these two stress hormones do not support happiness and success. There are four other hormones that are considered the "feel-good" hormones. These feel-good hormones are dopamine, oxytocin, serotonin, and endorphins – or DOSE.

- **Dopamine.** Dopamine is associated with feeling happy. It is also involved with motivation, learning, and memory. When you meditate, this will increase your dopamine.
- **Oxytocin.** Oxytocin is often called the "love hormone." Oxytocin is responsible for our social connections. Oxytocin helps promote trust, empathy, and bonding in relationships. Oxytocin increases when you get or give a hug, play with your pet, spend time in nature, or hug a tree.
- **Serotonin.** Serotonin helps regulate our mood. Serotonin also regulates sleep patterns, appetite, digestion, learning ability, and memory. The best way to increase serotonin is through physical activity and getting out into the sun.
- **Endorphins.** Endorphins are our body's natural pain reliever. Our body produces endorphins in response to stress or discomfort. You can increase endorphins when you engage in activities such as physical activity, meditation, playing music, and having a good laugh.

The Positively Powerful strategies set forth in Chapter 5 are all designed to increase your child's feel-good DOSE hormones.

The Brain Development Process

A young person's brain develops in a manner that emulates the evolution of the human brain through prehistoric times. The neural pathways in the older portion of their brain, including the amygdala and hippocampus, develop earlier. These parts of the brain were most important to keep humans safe – especially from those dangerous wild animals. The neural pathways of the prefrontal cortex are the last part of the brain to mature. The pruning and strengthening of the neural pathways in the prefrontal cortex continues until around age 25. Even after this age, the brain will continue to change and to develop new and stronger neural pathways.

As the brain matures, the prefrontal cortex takes over greater control, resulting in a much greater ability to analyze situations and engage in problem solving before taking action. Before the prefrontal cortex fully matures, the amygdala and hippocampus are often more in charge. This means young people may be more likely to act in a way that is an emotional reaction, rather than engaging in problem solving.

As the brain continues to develop and young people gain more experience, they will gain greater awareness, insight, and judgment. Every time they are involved in a new situation, they will learn from that experience, new memories will be processed by the hippocampus, and new neural pathways will be established. Each experience helps to guide how they will respond to additional new similar situations.

They will also become better at reasoning and exploring logical solutions. They will be better able to predict the future consequences of certain actions. This supports their ability to think and plan ahead. In addition to being better able to reflect on their own thinking, they will get better at detecting how others are motivated and how others are thinking and feeling.

It is possible for young people to engage in intentional activities that will create neural pathways that can increase their resilience, empowerment, and happiness, as well as to enable them to more effectively self-regulate and engage in problem solving and action planning. These are the Positively Powerful strategies that are set forth in Chapter 5.

Stages of Brain Development

The human brain is the only organ that is not fully developed at birth. The average baby's brain is about a quarter of the size of the average adult brain. The brain doubles in size in the first year. It keeps growing to about 80% of adult size by age 3 and to 90% by age 5. A baby's brain has all of the neurons they will have for the rest of their life. What we refer to as "brain development" is the development of the neural pathways. These neural pathways are what allow the human brain to function – to move, think, communicate, solve problems. During the early years of a child's life at least one million new neural synapses are formed every second. This is far more than at any other time in life. *The Whole-Brain Child: 12 Revolutionary Strategies to Nurture Your Child's Developing Mind* by Daniel Siegel and Tina Payne Bryson is an excellent resource if you want to learn more about how you can support your child's brain development.[2]

Jean Piaget's research on cognitive development provides a foundation for understanding your child's brain development.[3] Piaget identified four stages of cognitive development. These stages are associated with different ages. Each stage builds on the earlier stages. These stages are sensorimotor, preoperational, concrete operational, and formal operational.

---

2 Siegel and Payne-Bryson, The Whole-brain Child.
3 Piaget, J. and Cook, M.T. (1952). *The Origins of Intelligence in Children*. International University Press. Mcleod, S. (2024). Piaget's theory and stages of cognitive development. Simply Psychology, January 24. https://www.simplypsychology.org/piaget.html (accessed 1 August 2024).

Sensorimotor Stage

The sensorimotor stage lasts from birth until a child is about two years old. As the name suggests, during this stage, children learn about their senses and gain motor skills. The main goal of the sensorimotor stage is to develop an understanding that objects are permanent. Young children's delight in playing the game of "peek-a-boo" is based on the fact that they are learning that objects, including your smiling face, continue to exist – even if your face is hidden behind your hands.

At this stage children learn things about themselves and their environment by seeing, touching, sucking, and feeling. They gain an understanding of cause and effect. They come to realize that they are separate from the people and objects around them.

Preoperational Stage

The second stage is the preoperational stage, which lasts from ages two to seven. During the preoperational stage, children develop language and the ability to communicate. The end of this stage can be kind of sad. This is when children realize that mystical creatures, such as unicorns, are not real.

During this stage, children cannot effectively see situations from another person's perspective. Toward the end of this stage, children begin to understand the concept that a quantity stays the same even if the size, shape, or container it is in changes.

At the beginning of this stage, children engage in what is called parallel play. This means they are playing beside other children, but they do not significantly interact with them. During this stage, they begin to play with other children. Children at this age love to engage in pretend play. Playing and collaborating with other children is a key way that they learn about the world around them and begin to gain insight into other people's feelings. However, their ability to understand the feelings of others is just forming.

Concrete Operational Stage

The concrete operational stage lasts from ages 7 to 11. During this stage, children begin to think logically and rationally about physical objects. They learn to identify how things fit into categories and how those categories relate to each other. They can follow instructions with multiple steps. They are able to arrange a group of items into a sequence, such as organizing items from thinnest to widest. They understand that some things can be changed and then returned to their original state – for example, water can become ice and then can be melted.

Children also gain the skills for what is called "inductive reasoning."[4] This is also referred to as bottom-up reasoning. They make observations, then search for

---

4 Bhandari, P. (2022). Inductive reasoning: types, examples, explanation. Scribbr, January 12, rev. June 22, 2023. https://www.scribbr.com/methodology/inductive-reasoning/#:~:text=is%20 inductive%20reasoning%3F-,Inductive%20reasoning%20is%20a%20method%20of%20drawing%20 conclusions%20by%20going,logic%20or%20bottom%2Dup%20reasoning (accessed 1 August 2024).

patterns, and finally, make general conclusions. "That black cat is purring. Every cat I have seen purrs. All cats purr."

During this stage, children tend to be self-centered and have challenges seeing things from the perspective of others. They are gaining an understanding that other people have their own thoughts and perspectives, which may be different than their own.

Young people's development of empathy is exceptionally important. The development of empathy begins with recognizing one's own feelings. A helpful way to support young people's development of empathy is to help them to "Tell My Story." First, they should label their emotions – "I feel sad." The next step is to identify the reasons for those emotions – "I feel sad because I do not want to stop playing and go to bed." As they develop the ability to "Tell My Story," they should be challenged to learn how to identify the emotions of others and consider the reasons for those emotions – to seek to "Learn the Story" of others when interacting with them.

Young people need to learn the common emotions, what they look and feel like, and how others might appear when feeling these emotions. Common emotions include: happy; sad; afraid; guilty; excited; sorry; jealous; proud; tired; angry; bored; loved; embarrassed; irritated; frustrated; surprised; hopeful; and shy. The best way to learn about these emotions in through face-to-face interactions with others, combined with discussions of both their emotions and the emotions of those others.

As young people grow older, this activity becomes more complex. They learn how attitudes, expectations, and beliefs can shape how they think and feel about how others are feeling. They become even better at analyzing the verbal and non-verbal cues about how others are feeling. Embracing the concepts of telling the story of their own emotions and the reasons for these emotions and identifying the stories of others can be very helpful for them to maintain positive relationships with others.

Formal Operational Stage

The final stage of is the formal operational stage, which starts at age 12 and lasts until adulthood. During this stage, young people begin to think abstractly and use what is called "deductive reasoning," or top-down reasoning.[5] Deductive reasoning starts with one assumption and then another assumption is noted. Through logical analysis, those assumptions are then linked. "All insects have six legs. Spiders have eight legs. Therefore, spiders are not insects."

---

5 Bhandari, P. (2022) What is deductive reasoning? Explanation & examples. Scribbr, January 20, rev. June 22, 2023. https://www.scribbr.com/methodology/deductive-reasoning (accessed 1 August 2024).

During this stage, young people learn to develop solutions to problems by using logic and systematic analysis. They can consider possible outcomes and logically analyze the situation to solve problems. They can think about hypotheticals and formulate various solutions to solve them. They are able to use symbols related to abstract concepts, which enables them to learn things like algebra. They begin to think more about moral, philosophical, ethical, social, and political issues. This allows them to systematically plan for their future.

Teen Development

It is important to discuss teen development in more detail. This period of time is when bullying can significantly increase. The reasons for this are related to many different developmental issues that arise during the teen years.[6]

During your child's teen years, their brain is still "under development." Because of how their brain is developing, some challenges could arise in their decision making – even if they are intent on making good decisions. Your child's brain is developing in the way it should to prepare them for adulthood. This is how Daniel Romer describes teen development:

> Risky behavior is a normal part of development and reflects a biologically driven need for exploration – a process aimed at acquiring experience and preparing teens for the complex decisions they will need to make as adults.[7]

Teens are also exploring questions about themselves. These explorations include who they are, what skills they have, what directions they want to go in their life, and who among their peers is worth having continued close relations with.

As a result of how your child's brain is developing, they may be more likely to engage in behaviors that some might consider to be "risky." Taking risks is actually a normal part of teen development. Another term for taking risks is "exploration." As a teen, they have an intense need to explore. As they explore, they will learn new things. This helps them to make decisions in different kinds of situations. As they gain more experience, they will become better prepared to make the complex decisions they will need to make as an adult.

---

6 Romer, D., Reyna, V.F., and Satterthwaite, T.D. (2017). Beyond stereotypes of adolescent risk taking: placing the adolescent brain in developmental context. *Developmental Cognitive Neuroscience* 27: 19–34.

7 Romer, D. (2017). Why it's time to lay the stereotype of the "teen brain" to rest. The Conversation, October 30. https://theconversation.com/why-its-time-to-lay-the-stereotype-of-the-teen-brain-to-rest-85888 (accessed 1 August 2024).

Exploring and taking risks is very important for your child's development. What is important, obviously, is that they do not take risks that could potentially cause harm to their safety and well-being – or the safety and well-being of others.

Key Developments During the Teen Years

Identity Development

During your child's teen years they are engaged in in a process known as "identity development."[8] Identity development is answering the question: "Who am I?" It is a process that will hopefully lead to the development of a strong and stable sense of self.

Identity development is an ongoing process. Their identity includes two components:

- **Self identity.** Self identity is how they identify themself.
- **Social identity.** Social identity is how they view themself in relation to others. They may identify with different social identities. This could include identities based on their gender, race, nationality, sexual identity or gender orientation, disabilities, neurodiversities, political party, passionate interests, or more. People can have many different identities. This is often called intersectionality.

All young people engage in this process of identity development. However, if your child is a member of a identity group that is a minority within a dominant culture, their identity development process is more complicated.[9] Not only do they have to figure out who they are, they have to figure out who they are within a dominant culture that may, unfortunately, consider them to be "different" and "less worthy."

If you and other family members are also part of this minority identity group, then your child will have a family and extended family basis for understanding and developing their identity. However, if your child has a minority sexual identity or gender orientation or has disabilities or is neurodiverse, your child will have to develop an identity that is likely also a minority in your own family and extended family.

---

8 Pfeifer, J.H. and Berkman, E.T. (2018). The development of self and identity in adolescence: neural evidence and implications for a value-based choice perspective on motivated behavior. *Child Development Perspectives* 12 (3): 158–164. http://dx.doi.org/10.1111/cdep.12279.
9 Yakushko, O., Mack, T., and Iwamoto, D. (2010). Minority identity development model. In: *Encyclopedia of Cross-Cultural School Psychology* (ed. C.S. Clauss-Ehlers). Springer. https://doi.org/10.1007/978-0-387-71799-9_257. Rivas-Drake, D., Seaton, E.K., Markstrom, C. et al. (2014). Ethnic and racial identity in the twenty-first century study group: ethnic and racial identity in adolescence: implications for psychosocial, academic, and health outcomes. *Child Development* 85 (1): 40–57. http://dx.doi.org/10.1111/cdev.12200.

Most of the research that has investigated identity development of those who are a minority within a dominant culture has focused on racial and ethnic minorities. However, much of this insight can be applied to other minorities, such as religious affiliation, sexual identity or gender orientation, and disability or neurodiversity. It appears that there are four stages in identity development of those who are a minority within a dominant culture:

- **Pre-encounter.** They may not be consciously aware of differences between them and others.
- **Encounter.** They have a positive or negative experience that causes them to realize that they are "different" from others. Unfortunately, for most minorities, this experience is a communication by a member of the dominant culture that, by being a member of a minority group, they are considered to be less worthy.
- **Immersion.** Generally during their teen years, they immerse themself in an exploration of how they are going to identify themself as a minority within a dominant culture. Much of this exploration will occur with others within their same identity group. This is why students who are within minority groups so often sit together in the lunchroom at school.[10]
- **Internalization and commitment.** At this point, they have hopefully developed a secure sense of their positive identity and are comfortable socializing both within and outside of their group.

Unfortunately, our society today shows lots of evidence of what is called "identity politics." This has generated a lot of hurtful communications and situations. Given the discriminatory treatment of too many members of minority identity groups in our current society, this can interfere with the development of a secure sense of positive identity.

We are all humans, sharing life with other living beings on this planet. Both welcoming and embracing diversity, as well as achieving unity and inclusion, are of great importance. Teens today appear to be farther on this path than many adults.

Moral Development
The changes that are taking place in your child's brain also involve what is called "moral development."[11] Moral development is the development of personal values regarding how they will behave and interact with others. When your child is younger, their moral reasoning is more focused on obeying rules to avoid punishment or to receive a reward from an adult.

---

10 Tatum, B.D. (2017). *Why Are All the Black Kids Sitting Together in the Cafeteria?* Basic Books.
11 Kohlberg, L. (1981). *Essays on Moral Development, I: The Philosophy of Moral Development: Moral Stages and the Idea of Justice.* Harper & Row. Gilligan, C. (1982). *In a Different Voice: Psychological Theory and Women's Development.* Harvard University Press.

When your child enters the teen years, they are learning to make important decisions based on their own personal values. They are deciding what their personal values are, what they consider to be "right" and "wrong," and how they want to present themself in society. They are also evaluating the behaviors of their friends, other peers, and adults to decide if they are comfortable with the values and behaviors these others hold. As they explore their personal interests and values, their friendships may change. This is to be expected.

Peer Relationships

During your child's teen years, they have an increased interest in peer relationships.[12] When they are younger, they are more focused on how they are perceived by important adults. This includes you and other important adults in their life.

During their teen years, their focus is much more on how they are perceived by their peers. They can be very susceptible to peer influence at this time. The last thing they want is to be excluded by their friends, be disparaged by peers, or engage in public actions that impact how peers think about them. Because they really do not want to be excluded, they may be more likely to engage in risky or inappropriate actions if their friends are also engaging in those actions. If they go to a party where everyone is drinking, they will feel compelled to drink also – even if this is not what they think they should do.

This is one reason why it is very important for them to be careful when choosing which peers they want to maintain close relationships with. Are these peers making the kinds of choices that are in accord with their and your family's personal values? Are these peers effectively thinking before acting or are they acting without thinking?

Greatest Risks During the Teen Years

The following are the greatest risks your teen faces during these years.[13] Remember, your teen is developing as they should to gain the insight and skills to be effective and functional adults. However, there are some challenges associated with this exploration.

Acting Without Thinking, Especially When Upset

Because of how your child's brain is developing, they are at greater risk of engaging in actions that are not wise – simply because they act without thinking. Acting without thinking occurs because the development in their prefrontal cortex is still

---

12 Romer, Reyna, and Satterthwaite, Beyond stereotypes of adolescent risk taking.
13 Romer, Reyna, and Satterthwaite, Beyond stereotypes of adolescent risk taking.

a "work in progress." They are at greater risk of engaging in impulsive, inappropriate actions without thinking if they act when they are upset. Remember, when their amygdala goes into action, their prefrontal cortex goes offline.

To protect themself, establish a good reputation, maintain positive relationships, and keep themselves out of trouble, it is exceptionally important that they learn to recognize when they are about to act without thinking and stop themselves. They need to have the skills to wait until they have calmed down and can engage in effective problem solving before they respond in any situation that has made them upset.

Consider these questions: What kinds of situations tend to make your child upset? What steps they can take to avoid those situations or recognize when they are in such situation? What plans can they make in advance on how they intend to remain in control and think before they act?

Failing to Predict the Consequences of Their Actions on Others

During your child's teen years, their brain is in the process of learning to better understand how others think and feel and the possible consequences of their own actions. They may truly believe that they know what someone else is thinking or how they are feeling – only to find out later that they were really wrong. When they pay close attention to the reactions of others, they are able to gain greater abilities in predicting and recognizing what others are thinking and how they are feeling – as well as the consequences of their actions on others.

Knowing how someone else is thinking and feeling can be especially challenging when teens use social media. When they send or post something online, they cannot see how others respond. This makes it more difficult to accurately recognize the consequences of their actions on others.

To be able to effectively predict or recognize the consequences of their actions on others requires that they have empathy for the feelings of others. Your child must learn to recognize emotions of others and to then guide their actions in accord with how they may impact others. This is why it is important for your child to learn to "Tell Their Story" and then to "Learn the Stories" of others.

Some good questions to propose to your child so they can learn to avoid harmful consequences of their actions on others are: "How do you think your actions will make someone else feel?" "How would you feel if someone treated you like this?" "What would I think about your actions?" "How would you feel if everyone in your school or community saw you act in this way?" "Would you say or do what you are about to post online if others you care about were with you in person?"

Playing "Follow the Leader"

Think of this situation: A popular student just posted something that is exceptionally hurtful about another student on social media. Will your child play "follow the leader" and "like" this post or add a hurtful comment? How will your child respond if several other teens "like" the post or add hurtful comments? Will your child follow a hurtful leader? Or will they think for themselves and act in accord with their personal values?

Your child's teen years are the time when they are exploring essential questions about themselves – their identity and personal values. This includes deciding what qualities, values, and actions of others they are inclined to follow. Because teens are highly motivated to gain peer acceptance and not be excluded this may lead them to think that it is necessary to go along with what someone who appears to be a leader does – even if this is against their personal values. They may feel even more pressure to do this if other teens start to follow this person's lead.

In discussions with your child, ask them: "What will you do if someone you think of as a friend encourages you to do something that you do not think is appropriate?" "How will you respond if a friend of yours is hurtful to another?"

Judging Their Value Based on Attention from Others

Some teens appear to think that their value as a person is determined by how many friends they have and how much attention they get. This is especially evident on social media. Too many teens post outrageous material just to get attention. Many teens appear to be obsessed with how many "friends" they have or how many "likes" each of their posts receives.

During these years, many teens have concerns about their bodies. How teens view their appearance is strongly tied to their sense of self-worth. Teens appear to be more concerned about how they appear than about their academic and athletic ability.[14]

This appears to be of significant concern for girls. Females have always been judged by their appearance. The media young people see very often sets forth images for appearance and beauty standards that are basically unattainable.[15] However, boys also have concerns about their bodies based on appearance of masculinity.[16]

Teen use of social media often has a strong focus on self-images. Many teens post images of themselves online with the aim of receiving likes, comments,

---

14 Harter, S. (2012). *The Construction of the Self: Developmental and Sociocultural Foundations*, 2e. The Guilford Press.

15 Fredrickson, B.L. and Roberts, T.A. (1997). Objectification theory: toward understanding women's lived experiences and mental health risks. *Psychology of Women* 21 (2): 173–206.

16 Lawler, M. and Nixon, E. (2011). Body dissatisfaction among adolescent boys and girls: the effects of body mass, peer appearance culture and internalization of appearance ideals. *Journal of Youth and Adolescence* 40: 59–71. http://doi.org/10.1007/s10964-009-9500-2. Berne, S., Frisén, A., and Kling, J. (2014). Appearance-related cyberbullying: a qualitative investigation of characteristics, content, reasons, and effects. *Body Image* 11 (4): 527–533. http://doi.org/10.1016/j.bodyim.2014.08.006.

views, and shares. Teens may also strive to post carefully edited or upgraded images of themselves to attract better attention.

When peers respond by providing positive feedback, this can increase the poster's self-esteem. Liking each others' posts is a way they show support and friendship. However, failing to receive such positive feedback or receiving negative feedback can have a damaging emotional impact.

Some questions to ask your child: "What standards will you use to judge your own personal value?" "What is more important, the number of friends or the quality of your friendships?" "How do you want to measure your self-worth?" "Are you acting in ways either at school or on social media for the purpose of gaining attention of others?"

Experiencing Trauma and Distress

A traumatic event is an event that threatens a person's life, safety, or well-being – or the lives, safety, or well-being of people around them. The National Child Traumatic Stress Network provides a wealth of insight into trauma and protective factors.[17] The California Surgeon General has also placed a strong focus on concerns about trauma and provides excellent resources.[18]

A serious traumatic event is a very stressful incident that has a significant, immediate impact on a person's emotional state. Your child might experience such an event or witness someone else experiencing a traumatic event. An ongoing traumatic situation is more chronic – ongoing distressing challenges. Both a traumatic event and chronic stress are considered forms of trauma.

These are some common forms of traumatic events or chronic stress experienced by young people:

- Emotional abuse by a loved or trusted one.
- Interpersonal violence, such as physical or sexual assault or witnessing violence.
- A serious bullying or harassment incident or persistent, chronic bullying by peers, siblings, school staff, a coach, or others.
- Community violence, including community or school shootings, as well as school shooter drills.

---

17 https://www.nctsn.org (accessed 1 August 2024).
18 Bhushan, D., Kotz, K., McCall, J. et al. (2020). *Roadmap for resilience: The California Surgeon General's Report on Adverse Childhood Experiences, Toxic Stress, and Health.* Office of the California Surgeon General. https://osg.ca.gov/wp-content/uploads/sites/266/2020/12/ Roadmap-For-Resilience_CA-Surgeon-Generals-Report-on-ACEs-Toxic-Stress-and-Health_12092020.pdf (accessed 1 August 2024).

- Natural disasters or terrorism.
- Traumatic loss and grief after the death of a loved one.
- Medical trauma including severe injury, diagnosis, and treatment of a life-threatening illness, or other serious medical procedure.
- Multiple, chronic adversities beginning in early childhood, including neglect, maltreatment, and witness to domestic violence.

Our society has recently experienced distressing challenges related to the global pandemic. Some in our society experienced more intense trauma from this. This pandemic forced most students to have to learn from home. The pandemic may have created distressing challenges for your family. This may have included your employment, your family's income, or may have resulted in the tragic loss of a loved one.

Focus on the Negative and Possible Threats

Human brains developed with a natural tendency to focus on the negative – to focus on potential danger and risk. Why? Because this was necessary for survival. Failure to note that a dangerous wild animal is close by could result in you becoming lunch.

As was discussed earlier, when a person's brain detects that a threat may be present, their amygdala takes over. Their body goes into a fight, flight, or freeze mode. When this happens, adrenalin and cortisol rush through their body and their prefrontal cortex shuts down. This response to a threatening situation is just what we want our brains to do when a threat is present. This allows our physical bodies to respond effectively to that threat.

Because the human brain developed in a way that was necessary to ensure survival, our brains are really focused on the bad things that might happen. Our brain also does a really good job of storing memories of those bad things so we can avoid risk in the future. Memories of bad things will "stick like on Velcro" while memories of good things will "slip away like on Teflon."

These days, the odds of encountering a dangerous wild animal on everyday walks are low. Unfortunately, many young people encounter other kinds of very stressful situations, like having to walk past a group of students who always denigrate them. If they are experiencing ongoing distressing challenges, their amygdala is always on alert and their body always has higher levels of adrenalin and cortisol.

What is also happening in their brain is that those neurons that keep "firing together," to deal with the ongoing stressful situation, end up getting "wired together." This results in the creation of neural pathways that cause them to be even more focused on potential threats and bad things. Instead of developing neural pathways that will support their success and happiness, their neural pathways are being formed in a way that seeks to ensure their survival in a dangerous environment. These threat-focused neural pathways will cause them to be overreactive in any new challenging situations. They are more likely to trigger, get upset, and become disruptive.

If your child's amygdala is over-activated and more frequently pumping adrenalin and cortisol through their body, they will experience chronic stress, fear, anxiety, and irritation. They will have a harder time feeling safe, calming down, sleeping, or learning. Because their prefrontal cortex is not effectively engaged, this also makes it more likely they will trigger, overreact, and act badly without thinking if they perceive a threat. They will also have significant challenges in learning.

Recall that the hippocampus regulates the storage and retrieval of memories. The increased stress hormones make it more challenging for the hippocampus to function well. When your child's hippocampus is not functioning well, this causes them to have more challenges in telling the difference between past and present experiences. Situations that might resemble prior distressing incidents can cause more intense panic and fear – even though the current situation does not present a threat or that much of a threat.

Painful memories can become reactivated by different "cues" from the outside world. This might be how someone simply looks at them or even being in a place where someone was hurtful in the past. They are always alert to when someone might be hurtful. They pay closer attention to those who are around so that they are prepared to respond.

At these times, it is harder for their brain to figure out what is actually happening. Their brain has a harder time telling whether a current situation is actually threatening or determining how threatening the situation actually is. This can, at times, lead them to draw mistaken conclusions. They may translate a minor hurtful incident as being a more significant incident. They can be more easily triggered by a situation that they perceive to present a threat – even when no threat is actually present at this point in time.

When they perceive that they might be in danger, they are more likely to trigger. They may respond in a way that is an overreaction – an outburst. They are reacting, not thinking. This is because their amygdala and stress hormones are preparing them to fight or run from that wild dangerous animal and their prefrontal cortex is not functioning. Because their anterior cingulate cortex has also been affected, even when they want to calm down and feel better, they just cannot. Because of this, they likely will have a harder time concentrating, learning, and remembering what they have learned. This is why being bullied has such a damaging impact on the ability of a child to learn.

A good example of how this happens is what happens when a veteran with post-traumatic stress disorder (PTSD) hears a loud noise. The bad memories stored in their hippocampus tell them that they are in danger. Their amygdala immediately goes into action to protect themselves. This will happen within seconds.

Now think of how this process might be impacting your child if they have experienced serious or persistent bullying. When they have to walk past a student or staff member who has been hurtful to them in the past, their hippocampus will immediately communicate, "Watch out, danger." If this student or staff member says or does something that is not really intended to be hurtful, your child could overreact because they perceived a threat. Your child's principal may say to your child, "Why did you get so upset? They really did not do anything wrong." The problem is that they, or someone else, has been hurtful to your child in the past in similar circumstances. These memories are stored in your child's hippocampus. When this similar act occurred, your child's overreaction was grounded in their stored memories.

If your child's brain is primed to look for the potential threats, they may also not see the good things that are actually happening to them. If they are always worried about someone saying something hurtful to them, they may very well miss the fact that someone just smiled at them.

Intergenerational Trauma

Children of parents who have experienced trauma often show signs that they have experienced trauma, even if they have not experienced trauma in their lives.[19] This is called intergenerational trauma. The experiences of intergenerational trauma are higher for those in identity groups that are marginalized within our society.

Intergenerational trauma can be passed from parents and families to their children in three ways:

- **Pregnancy.** The health and emotional well-being of the mother through pregnancy can have an impact. If the mother is experiencing times of distress during pregnancy those stress hormones can affect their unborn child.
- **Genetic expression.** Epigenetics is the study of how our environment influences our genes. Genes themselves do not change, but the manner in which genes are expressed can be influenced by trauma experienced by the parents. This process was first identified in children who were offspring of survivors of the Holocaust.
- **Messages.** Messages received from family members related to the dangers they will encounter in the world, especially when children are younger, can become stored in their hippocampus. These unconscious messages can have a profound impact on the way they see themselves and others.

---

19 Bhushan et al., *Roadmap for Resilience.*

All of these processes can impact how a child experiences the world. These processes can lead a child to have deep feelings that they are not safe. The perception they are not safe then shapes how they translate their experiences. This, in turn, can impact how they respond when treated badly and whether they will feel comfortable telling anyone that this is happening in order to gain assistance.

Two of these processes are not possible to go back and fix. Parents cannot redo their pregnancy and cannot fix the gene expression from their past trauma or their parent's past trauma. Parents and families can address issues of messages. Please think about the kind of messages you are transmitting to your child about their safety and acceptance in the world.

If you have experienced trauma in your own life – especially including if you experienced bullying as a child – you will need to be totally mindful of the possibility that you may communicate messages to your child that reflect the anguish you personally felt as you were experiencing these situations. These messages are, unfortunately, not likely to be helpful for your child or in resolving the current challenges.

What can you do to handle this situation? The first step is to love yourself. You are not at fault for the bad things that have happened to you. A second step is to look for how those past bad experiences have provided you with insight and strengths that you are currently using in ways that benefit your life. A third step is to forgive yourself for comments you may have made to your child before you realized this is a concern.

Realize that the Positively Powerful strategies set forth in Chapter 5 are designed to work for everyone – not just children or teens. By actively engaging in the use of these strategies along with your child, you will be able to achieve resilience and empowerment that will help you to move past the trauma based on what you experienced as a child or teen.

Asking for Help

Young people respond to trauma and chronic stress in different ways. This depends on the individual, as well as their past experiences, their levels of support, and the nature of the event.

Experiencing a traumatic situation or chronic stress might leave them with many questions about safety and control over their life. If they have experienced trauma or other challenges and they have become emotionally distressed, it is important that they talk with a trusted adult.

Hopefully, one trusted adult is you. However, recognize that sometimes teens do not want to tell a parent about a concern for fear that they will disappoint their parent. They may also have engaged in behavior that was not appropriate that they do not want you to find out about. It is important that your child has connections with several trusted adults who are outside of your family.

The following is a list of the symptoms of trauma or chronic stress. These could also be considered signs of mental health concerns. It is really important that we remove the stigma from the term "mental health concerns." If you think that your child is experiencing any of these symptoms, even just some of the time, please support your child in connecting with a counselor or other support provider.

- **Profound sadness.** Feeling hopeless and empty and that, no matter how hard they try, they just cannot control their negative thoughts.
- **Hypervigilance.** Always feeling on alert to the potential that something bad may happen.
- **Guilt.** Feeling that they are worthless and helpless.
- **Irritability.** Feeling angry, anxious, or restless.
- **Trouble thinking clearly.** Difficulties concentrating, making decisions, or remembering details.
- **Physical symptoms.** Aches and pains, headaches, or digestive problems that do not seem to have any other medical cause.
- **Fatigue.** Feeling tired all the time and having no energy.
- **Loss of interest.** Not interested in fun activities, like hobbies or getting together with friends.
- **Sleep changes.** Waking up too early in the morning, not being able to fall asleep, not sleeping enough, or sleeping too much.
- **Appetite changes.** Changes in eating habits, like eating too much or too little.
- **Self-harm or risky behavior.** Self-cutting, burning, and other forms of self-harm. Exceptionally risky behavior that could result in harm to them or others.
- **Violence and fighting.** Getting into fights with others. Taking a weapon to school because they think they need to protect themself.
- **Suicidal thoughts.** Having thoughts of harming or killing themself. If your child is thinking about suicide, you need to get help immediately. The National Suicide Lifeline phone number is 1-800-273-8255. They are available 24/7 with someone you can talk to get support for your child.

Your Child's Brain Can Change

The degree to which young people are impacted by trauma or chronic stress can vary. If a young person has feelings of self-confidence and positive connections with supportive others, it is less likely that the traumatic event or chronic stress will cause long-term damage.

Even if they have experienced a traumatic event or are experiencing chronic stress, it is possible for them to change their brain so that the harm that has been created can be overcome.[20] Remember that neural pathways can be rewired. Young people can rewire their brain to achieve greater resilience and empowerment. They can overcome the damage that past challenging experiences have caused in the way their brain functions.

"Neuroplasticity" is the term that describes the brain's ability to change.[21] The brain's neural pathways can reorganize by forming new connections. Neuroplasticity is possible because of the capacity of the brain's neural pathways to change their synaptic connections in response to new information. Even if your child's neural pathways have formed in a way that has kept their brain functioning in a hypervigilant manner, with a focus on possible threats and a tendency to trigger, their brain does not have to remain in this way. Their brain can create new neural pathways that support greater calmness and happiness.

By helping your child to focus on the positive things that are happening in their life, you can help them to rewire their brain. The Positively Powerful strategies that are provided in Chapter 5 are strategies identified by researchers that allow people who have experienced trauma or chronic stress to change the neural pathways in their brains so they can achieve greater resilience, self-control, empowerment, happiness, and success.

While this book is written for parents who are seeking to support their child's resilience and well-being, realize that the insight that has been provided in this chapter about how the human brain functions and the impact of trauma also applies to your brain. You may also have experienced trauma. Your brain can also change. The Positively Powerful strategies are very effective strategies that you can also use to rewire *your* brain to become more resilient and happier.

The key important insight into changing your child's brain (and your brain) relates to how the brain naturally focuses more attention on negative, rather than positive, experiences. To rewire your child's brain (and your brain), it is necessary to maintain focused attention on the positive. This rewiring is not going to happen rapidly. This will require intentional focused effort for a period of time.

Post-traumatic Growth

Post-traumatic growth is positive change that results from having experienced more significant challenges and responding to those challenges in an effective

---

20 Doidge, N. (2007). *The Brain That Changes Itself: Stories of Personal Triumph from the Frontiers of Brain Science*. Viking.
21 Cherry, K. (2022). What Is Neuroplasticity? Verywellmind. https://www.verywellmind.com/what-is-brain-plasticity-2794886 (accessed 1 August 2024).

manner.[22] Many of the strong and positive leaders in our society have grown through – and as a result of – the traumatic challenges they faced and overcame when younger. This can be your child (and you).

Post-traumatic growth can result in many positive benefits.

- New opportunities, opening up possibilities that were not present before.
- Closer relationships with people. An increased sense of connection with others, especially those who are also suffering.
- An increased sense of one's own personal strengths.
- A greater appreciation for life in general.
- A deepening of spiritual life and commitment to spiritual values.
- Increased engagement in actions that support social justice and that support a more kind, compassionate, and just society.

The new word that essentially describes someone who is demonstrating post-traumatic growth is "Thriver." As you may recall from the introduction, a Thriver is a person who experienced challenging times who shows growth because of that experience and is thriving, successful, happy, and making a positive contribution to others.

The Positively Powerful strategies set out in Chapter 5 support post-traumatic growth and becoming a Thriver.

---

22 Tedeschi, R.G., Shakespeare-Finch, J., Taku, K., and Calhoun, L.G. (2018). *Posttraumatic Growth: Theory, Research, and Applications.* Routledge.

5

Positively Powerful

The objective of these Positively Powerful strategies is to support your child's resilience when things get tough and to increase their positive and happy feelings of empowerment. Resilience means "bouncing back" from difficult experiences and the ability to feel happy and be successful, even after something difficult or bad has happened.[1] Becoming empowered is a process of becoming strong and feeling confident – allowing them to control their life and make good decisions. The Positively Powerful strategies will support your child in becoming a Thriver.

This chapter will provide you with insight into the seven Positively Powerful strategies, which each have two or three subcategories. Sections in this chapter provide suggestions on how to communicate about these strategies to your child. Short videos that your child can watch and other resources are on the Rise Above Bullying website.

Insight into Resilience

The National Scientific Council on the Developing Child, associated with the Center on the Developing Child at Harvard University, focuses on the science of early childhood and early brain development.[2] The following statement on the foundations of resilience is from their excellent Working Paper:[3]

> Multiple lines of research have identified a common set of factors that predispose children to positive outcomes in the face of significant adversity.

1 Center on the Developing Child. https://developingchild.harvard.edu (accessed 1 August 2024).
2 https://developingchild.harvard.edu (accessed 1 August 2024).
3 National Scientific Council on the Developing Child (2015). *Supportive relationships and active skill-building strengthen the foundations of resilience.* Working Paper No. 13. https://developingchild.harvard.edu/resources/supportive-relationships-and-active-skill-building-strengthen-the-foundations-of-resilience (accessed 1 August 2024).

Rise Above Bullying: Empower and Advocate for Your Child, First Edition. Nancy E. Willard.
© 2025 John Wiley & Sons, Inc. Published 2025 by John Wiley & Sons, Inc.

These factors encompass strengths that derive from the child, the family, peer and adult relationships, and the broader social environments that build and support sturdy brain architecture. When these positive influences are operating effectively, they "stack the scale" with positive weight and optimize resilience. When these positive factors are absent, disrupted, or undermined, there is little to counterbalance the negative effects of significant adversity, thus creating the conditions for poor outcomes and diminished life prospects. These counter-balancing factors include the following:

- The availability of at least one stable, caring, and supportive relationship between a child and the important adults in his or her life. These relationships begin in the family, but they can also include neighbors, providers of early care and education, teachers, social workers, or coaches, among many others.
- Helping children build a sense of mastery over their life circumstances. Those who believe in their own capacity to overcome hardships and guide their own destiny are far more likely to adapt positively to adversity.
- Children who develop strong executive function and self-regulation skills. These skills enable individuals to manage their own skills and emotions and develop and execute adaptive strategies to cope effectively with difficult circumstances.
- The supportive context of affirming faith or cultural traditions. Children who are solidly grounded within such traditions are more likely to respond effectively when challenged by a major stressor or severely disruptive experience.

The National Center for School Engagement conducted a study of high school students who had been bullied in elementary school.[4] The researchers identified three critical factors that increased the resilience of these students and led to successful outcomes in high school, despite the fact they were being bullied. These three factors were:

- A place of refuge where they could feel safe, appreciated, and challenged in a constructive way.
- Responsible adults who supported and sustained them and provided them examples of appropriate behavior.
- A sense of future possibility to persuade them that staying in school, despite the bullying, promised better things to come.

---

4 Seeley, K., Tombari, M., Bennett, L.J., and Dunkle, J.B. (2009) *Peer victimization in schools: a set of quantitative and qualitative studies of the connections among peer victimization, school engagement, truancy, school achievement, and other outcomes.* National Center for School Engagement. https://www.ojp.gov/ncjrs/virtual-library/abstracts/peer-victimization-schools-set-quantitative-and-qualitative-studies (accessed 1 August 2024).

Research into factors that promote resilience to bullying victimization is still in its infancy. However, a recent study by Hinduja and Patchin of the Cyberbullying Research Center explored the relationship between resilience and experience with bullying and cyberbullying.[5] The results demonstrated that resilience is a potent protective factor, both in preventing experience with bullying and mitigating its harmful effects.

A recent research study looked at three issues – family dynamics, peer support, and emotional regulation – in relation to cyberbullying. There is an interesting interplay between these factors. When family communication is positive and empathic, this appears to be both a protective factor against both being cyberbullied or engaging in cyberbullying. Peer support can also help young people endure negative situations and appears to provide protection against the negative effects of these situations. However, what healthy families and peer connections appear to facilitate is greater emotional regulation. The better able a teen is to regulate their emotions, the less likely they will be to be targeted by or engage in hurtful behavior.[6]

All of these protective factors are addressed by these Positively Powerful strategies.

Positively Powerful

The Positively Powerful strategies that will be presented in this chapter are:

- **Make Positive Connections.** Be a Good Friend. I make positive connections with good friends. Connect with Trusted Adults. The trusted adults in my life provide me with support.
- **Reach Out to Be Kind.** Be Kind to Others. I reach out to be kind to others as I know this makes us both feel happy. Act in Service. When I join with others to be of service, we can help to build a kind community.
- **Build My Strengths.** Be Proud. I take pride in who I am and what I am able to accomplish. Strengthen My Character. I use my character strengths every day and when things get tough. Embrace Failure. I try and sometimes I fail, which allows me the opportunity to learn.
- **Focus on the Good.** Find the Joys. I focus on the good things happening in my life. Be Thankful. I express my appreciation to others.

---

5 Hinduja, S. and Patchin, J. (2017). Cultivating youth resilience to prevent bullying and cyberbullying victimization. *Child Abuse & Neglect* 73: 51–62.
6 Arató, N., Zsidó, A.N., Rivnyák, A. et al. (2022). Risk and protective factors in cyberbullying: the role of family, social support, and emotion regulation. *International Journal of Bullying Prevention* 4: 160–173.

- **Be Mindful.** Practice Calmness. I take time during the day to achieve calmness and focus. Keep My Cool. I remain calm when things get tough.
- **Keep My Personal Power.** Hold Myself Tall. I hold myself tall and strong. Control My Thinking. I do not allow what happens to me to control how I think about myself or respond. Release and Let Go. I release and let go of my anger.
- **Think Things Through.** Think Things Through. I Think Things Through to decide what is best to do. Focus on My Future. I make goals to create my positive future.

Each of these Positively Powerful strategies will help your child's brain to form neural pathways that will help them to become more resilient and empowered. If they take the time to intentionally develop these inner strengths, this can help them recover from the challenges they have experienced, cope with new challenges, maintain their emotional well-being, and move forward to a successful life. They can become a Thriver.

The way to build these strengths is to maintain an intentional focus on the positive every day. The goal is to increase the amount of time that they are focused on the positive things happening in their life, the strengths they are building, and the successes they are having. Remember that, as described in Chapter 4, our brains tend to focus more on the negative than on the positive. This can result in the development of neural pathways that are always looking at situations from a negative perspective.

When your child intentionally focuses on these positive experiences, this will result in lasting positive changes in how their brain functions. By intentionally focusing on the positive, they are adding happier memories and building the neural pathways in their brain that will better support their positive future.

The Magic 5 : 1 Ratio

These Positively Powerful strategies have been demonstrated by the research to be effective. However, they will not work immediately. For these strategies to work will require constant intentional repetition for a period of time. Only then will they and you start to see positive results. The goal is to increase the amount of time that they are focused on the positive things happening in their life, the strengths they are building, and the successes they are having.

There appears to be a "magic formula." It is said that it takes five "positives" to undo one "negative." Every time your child has a negative experience or thought, they should strive to counter the negative neural pathways this may have established by focusing on five positive things. This will help your child start to see positive results.

The 40-day Experiment

A challenge in providing guidance to parents is that all children are different. They are different ages. Your children will have different levels in their willingness to engage in "new-fangled" ideas such as those presented in this chapter. If they are teens, they may be less likely to listen to you. A "one-size-fits-all" implementation approach to my guidance is not going work.

It is my hope that your child, you, and preferably your entire family, will try these strategies for at least 40 days. Below and on the Rise Above Bullying website, you will find a brief Happiness Survey. My recommendation is that you, and your child, and other family members complete this survey. Put your results in an envelope, not to be opened for 40 days. In 40 days, complete another Happiness Survey. Then, open the envelope to find your prior surveys and compare the differences.

This is the Happiness Survey:

Statement	Strongly disagree 1	Disagree 2	Agree 3	Strongly agree 4
I am pleased with the way I am				
I am satisfied with most everything in my life				
I am a happy person				
Usually other people are happy to be around me				
I feel that I am in control of my life				
I can do most things I want to do if I try				
I can work out my problems				
I reach out to help and be of service to others				
I have fun with other people				
Others are there for me if I am having a challenge				
Add up the numbers in the columns	Add up the 1s	Add up the 2s	Add up the 3s	Add up the 4s

Now, divide the total by 10. This is your current happiness score.

During this 40-day experiment, there are daily recommended activities that are set forth under these strategies. To keep your attention on the strategies for these 40 days, I recommend two approaches:

- **Keep a daily journal and engage in discussions.** As you will see in this chapter, it is suggested that you, your child, and other members of our family either take specific actions during the day, accomplish certain tasks, or reflect on what has happened. Pages that you can use to keep this journal are available on the Rise Above Bullying website. Download the pages, print them, and keep them in a folder. You each can complete the simple questions posed at dinner or bed time. If your child does not want to keep a journal, you can engage in the same activities by asking the questions that are set forth for the journal and having a discussion. The actual task of handwriting does appear to lead to increased effectiveness.

- There are three kinds of things to write in a journal: advanced planning; daily record of tasks that need to be accomplished every day; assessment of what happened that day. These are discussed throughout this chapter.

- **Use transitions strategies.** You, your child, and your family can also use transition times to remember to focus on certain positive actions. Transition times are the times when they (or you) are changing activities. For your child, transitions include leaving home to go to school or going from one class to another. For you, a transition time may be when you enter your place of employment. For both of you, a transition time could be if you enter a grocery store together. Sitting down to dinner is also a joint transition time, as is going out the door to get into the car to go some place. Specific things your child can do in transition times will be noted throughout this chapter.

Reflective Listening

Your use of an approach called reflective listening can help your child to know that they have been heard accurately and that they are supported.[7] Reflective listening is a special type of listening that is essentially telling the story of others. This requires paying close attention to the feelings the other is experiencing and the story behind or reasons for those feelings. Please recall that your child started to be able to identify both feelings and the reasons at a young age. Thus, the focus on "Tell My Story" and "Learn Their Story." Focusing on those feelings and reasons is the foundation of reflective listening. When you are engaging in reflective listening, you are learning the story of your child and reflecting what you are learning back to them.

When you engage in reflective listening with your child, or anyone else who is upset, you are letting them know that they are being heard and understood. You must focus solely on what they are feeling and thinking – and not on what you think about what they are feeling, thinking, or doing.

---

7 Katz, N. and McNulty, K. (1994). *Reflective listening*. https://www.maxwell.syr.edu/docs/default-source/ektron-files/reflective-listening-nk.pdf?sfvrsn=f1fa6672_5 (accessed 1 August 2024).

Reflective listening is a two-step process:

- Focusing on the other person's words, tone of voice, and body language to hear and understand how they are feeling and the reasons. Your focus is to "Learn Their Story."
- Responding to the other person by reflecting back your understanding of the feelings they are having and the reasons for those feelings.

There is a simple formula to reflective listening. This involves focusing on what the other has said and then reflecting this back to them as both an understanding of the feelings and reasons for those feelings. When they say something, especially when upset, seek to identify their story, both their feelings and the reasons for their feelings, and then reflect this back to them. "It sounds to me like you are feeling [name feeling] about [identify reason]. Can you help me understand more?" (Let them talk.) "So because [identify reason], you feel [name feeling]. (Let them talk.) "I think I understand better now. It really makes you feel [name emotion] because [identify reason]." This reflective approach needs to be followed after each statement of the other person until they have become calm.

As you read this, you may think this approach is rather formalistic. Try this the next time with your child or anyone else who has become upset. You will see this approach works like magic. When your child or any other person realizes you understand both their feelings and the reasons for their feelings, they will feel safer and their level of upset will decrease.

The benefits of reflective listening are significant. This lets the other person know that they have been heard, understood, cared for, and supported. This also allows you to check on the accuracy of your understandings and then to correct any of your misunderstandings. By allowing them to feel and talk, you are allowing them to move to a deeper understanding of their feelings and the reasons. After they become calm, you can both use the Think Things Through approach to problem solving that is described below.

Empowerment-building Strategies

The first four Positively Powerful strategies – Make Positive Connections, Reach Out to Be Kind, Build Your Strengths, and Focus on the Good – are the empowerment-building strategies. These are the activities that I recommend be a focus of daily journaling or questions. These are the key basic questions your child, you, and your family can journal about and you can discuss:

- Who did you have a positive connection with?
- How did you reach out to be kind?

- What did you do that you are proud of?
- What happened that made you feel good?

Make Positive Connections

Be a Good Friend. I make positive connections with good friends. Connect with Trusted Adults. The trusted adults in my life provide me with support.

Positive connections with both good friends and trusted adults are important for your child's emotional well-being and happiness. Young people who have good friends appear to experience less distress if treated badly. Having a close connection with a trusted adult is the foundation for youth resilience.

Be a Good Friend

Friendships Insight

Psychological research has found that stable, healthy friendships are crucial for our well-being and longevity. People who have friends and close confidants are more satisfied with their lives and less likely to suffer from depression.[8] In fact, psychological research from around the world shows that having strong social connections is one of the most reliable predictors of a long, healthy, and satisfying life.

Having a close friend to turn to when things are tough, such as when someone has been hurtful, provides strong protections. Research has clearly documented that young people who are bullied, but who have supportive friends, experience less distress.[9]

A recent study of the importance of adult friendships around the world began this introduction:[10]

Friendships enrich our lives in many ways. Friends give us both practical and emotional support when we need it. As a result, there are many

8 Choi, K.W., Stein, M.B., Nishimi, K.M. et al.; *23andMe Research Team; Major Depressive Disorder Working Group of the Psychiatric Genomics Consortium*; Breen, G., Koenen, K.C., and Smoller, J.W. (2020). An Exposure-Wide and Mendelian Randomization Approach to Identifying Modifiable Factors for the Prevention of Depression. *Am J Psychiatry* 177 (10): 944–954. https://doi.org/10.1176/appi.ajp.2020.19111158. Epub 2020 Aug 14. PMID: 32791893; PMCID: PMC9361193. *The American Journal of Psychiatry* 177 (10): 2020.

9 Salmivalli, C. (2010). Bullying and the peer group: A review. *Aggression and Violent Behavior* 15 (2): 112–120. https://doi.org/10.1016/j.avb.2009.08.007.

10 Lu, P., Oh, J., Leahy, K., and Chopic, W.J. (2021). Friendship importance around the world: links to cultural factors, health, and well-being. *Frontiers in Psychology.* https://doi.org/10.3389/fpsyg.2020.570839.

emotional and physical health benefits of friendships—the more people prioritize friendships, the happier and healthier they are ...

There is a reliable link between social support and mental and physical health across the lifespan, and one important source of support is our friends. Friends provide us with a strong sense of companionship, mitigate feelings of loneliness, and contribute to our self-esteem and life satisfaction. Perceiving greater support from friends is associated with a greater sense of purpose and control over one's life. In terms of predicting health, friendship occasionally predicts health to an equivalent and, in some cases, larger degree compared to spousal and parent–child relationships. Friends also help individuals institute healthy behaviors in their own lives ...

However, friendship is not universally good for individuals – depression and negative health behaviors can also spread through friend networks... .

In sum, friends play a significant role in people's mental and physical well-being, for better and for worse.

For young people, friendships are the first relationships that they have choice about. Friendships allow children to learn how to handle challenging interpersonal situations before they enter into closer personal relationships as teens and adults. Interacting with friends allows your child to build empathy for others and to practice seeking and providing support. Interactions with friends who share the same identity allows for the joint exploration of their shared identity.

High-quality friendships can protect young people from mental health issues – such as anxiety and depression. But there are also conditions where mental health struggles can harm friendships. Excessive self-disclosure about life's challenges can cause challenges in a friendship. If your child's friend is experiencing significant challenges, including depression, self-injury, or suicidal behavior, your child could take on these feelings and behaviors also.

Insight on Friendships to Share with Your Child

Provide your child with insight into the following or have them watch a short video on the Rise Above Bullying website:

- Having good friends can help you feel great about yourself and is also helpful if you are facing any challenges.
- To have good friends, you have to put in the effort. No one is going to come knocking on your door to ask you to be their friend.
- Be the friend that you want to have and treat people the way you want to be treated.
- The biggest barrier to finding new friends is fear of rejection. Focus on getting to know others better. If a friendship happens, this is great.
- The best way to find new friends is by engaging in activities that you are interested in.

- Give your friends space. Do not expect too much of your friend's time and attention.
- Realize that friendship break-ups happen. This is a normal part of life. Let go of your feelings of hurt by forgiving the other person.

These are questions for journal pages:

- **Advanced planning.** Think about what friendship means to you. What qualities would you like to have in a friend? Do you consistently act in this way with your friends and others? Conduct a friendship audit and create an action plan. Who are your current friends? What interests do you share? What are the strengths of these friendships? What are any weaknesses? How can you build on these strengths? How can you make new friends? Create an action plan to increase your positive friendships. Enjoy your interests to find new friends. What are you interested in and what do you like to do? Is there a club at school you might want to join or a class you might want to take? Is there an after-school center, program, or class you could go to?
- **Daily progress.** What friends did you have a positive connection with today?

Connect with Trusted Adults

Trusted Adults Insight

The importance of your child having positive connections with trusted adults both within and outside of your family cannot be overemphasized.[11] This is another statement is from the Harvard Center on the Developing Child's Working Paper.

> Decades of research in the behavioral and social sciences have produced a rich knowledge base that explains why some people develop the adaptive capacities to overcome significant adversity and others do not. Whether the burdens come from the hardships of poverty, the challenges of parental substance abuse or serious mental illness, the stresses of war, the threats of recurrent violence or chronic neglect, or a combination of factors, the single most common finding is that children who end up doing well have had at least one stable and committed relationship with a supportive parent, caregiver, or other adult. These relationships provide the personalized

---

11 Center on the Developing Child at Harvard University (2015). *Supportive Relationships and Active Skill-Building Strengthen the Foundations of Resilience*. Working Paper 13. https:// harvardcenter.wpenginepowered.com/wp-content/uploads/2015/05/The-Science-of-Resilience2.pdf (accessed 1 August 2024).

responsiveness, scaffolding, and protection that buffer children from developmental disruption. They also build key capacities – such as the ability to plan, monitor and regulate behavior, and adapt to changing circumstances – that enable children to respond to adversity and to thrive. This combination of supportive relationships, adaptive skill-building, and positive experiences constitutes the foundations of what is commonly called resilience.

The CDC has also identified "connectedness" as key to addressing the concerns of youth suicide, which is an identified risk for students being bullied and engaging in bullying.

> Review of studies to date suggests that connectedness affects STB (suicide thoughts and behavior) through one or more of the following routes: (1) expanding intergenerational social networks; (2) heightening opportunities for soliciting and activating assistance from others or systems (e.g., schools, families, or other social systems); (3) enhancing the likelihood that worrisome affect and behavior, including early signs of distress or more direct warning signs for suicidal behavior, will be noticed and proactively addressed by proximal systems (parents, peers, schools); (4) increasing exposure to positive coping and help-seeking norms; (5) increasing positive emotion and, as a consequence, cognitive flexibility and emotion regulation capacity; and (6) enhancing opportunities for experiencing belonging and utility in a community of others.[12]

Your child's trusted adult, including you, can also provide emotional support and help them Think Things Through. It is very important that your child has several trusted adults they can talk with who are outside of your immediate family. Many times, young people will not report bullying situations to the school. Often, they will also not tell their parent. They may fear you will overreact and your overreaction could make things worse. Of course, you want your child to come to you. But sometimes they might not. As a back-up, if your child has a trusted adult who is outside of your immediate family, your child may share their concerns with this adult first. This is why it is important that your child has some solid relationships with trusted adults who you also trust. Help your child connect with a trusted adult who is a Thriver, who faced challenges and has grown from those challenges.

---

12 Whitlock, J., Wyman, P.A., and Moore, S.R. (2014). Connectedness and suicide prevention in adolescents: pathways and implications. *Suicide and Life-threatening Behavior* 44 (3): 246–272. https://doi.org/10.1111/sltb.12071.

Some helpful standards for a trusted adult are:

- A trusted adult is someone who your child can talk to about anything and who they feel happy to be around.
- A trusted adult is someone they feel comfortable talking with about something that makes them feel uncomfortable or confused – or a problem they might be having.
- A trusted adult should be a good listener – someone who will listen to their opinions and ideas, seek to understand their perspective by asking questions. They will honor their feelings, rather than tell them to stop feeling the way they do.
- A trusted adult should help them Think Things Through and not immediately tell the young person their conclusion and directions about what they think the young person should do and will not immediately step in to "take care of things."

Insight on Connecting with Trusted Adults to Share with Your Child

Provide your child with insight into the following or have them watch a short video on the Rise Above Bullying website:

- Trusted adults are people you can turn to when you have a problem, when something bad is happening, when you have difficult questions you need to ask someone you can trust – as well as for the positive times.
- It is generally best if you are able to identify a number of trusted adults who you could talk to in different situations. Trusted adults can be family members and people outside of your family.
- If a trusted adult has been helpful, be sure to Be Thankful to this person.

These are questions for journal pages:

- **Advance planning.** Envision what you want in a trusted adult. Think of a conversation you had in the past with an adult where you walked away feeling that you were thoroughly heard and respected and the guidance and support you received made you feel empowered. What were the characteristics and qualities of the adult you spoke with that led you to feel heard and empowered? What did this adult do that made you feel heard and respected? What did this adult do that made you feel empowered? Conduct a trusted adult audit and create an action plan. Do you have a sufficient number of adults in your life you trust you can talk to about serious concerns? If not, go on a quest to find one or several trusted adults. Create an action plan to make a good connection with several trusted adults.
- **Daily progress.** What trusted adult did you have a positive connection with today?

Reach Out to Be Kind

> Be Kind to Others. I reach out to be kind to others as I know this makes us both feel happy. Act in Service. When I join with others to be of service, we can help to build a kind community.

There are many positive benefits to engaging in acts of kindness to others and engaging in acts of service. These benefits include better health, self-esteem, and optimism. Being kind to others also increases how well your child is accepted by peers. This makes the Reach Out to Be Kind strategy of highest importance if your child is being bullied.

Be Kind to Others

Kindness Insight

Research has identified that being kind to others results in a significant increase in feelings of happiness.[13] The Random Acts of Kindness Foundation provides great insight on kindness on their website.[14] The research they follow has documented the positive benefits of kindness. They have documented these positive benefits from engaging in kindness:

- Kindness is contagious. Witnessing kindness leads other people to be kind.
- Witnessing acts of kindness increases hormones that lead to better health, self-esteem, and optimism.
- Being kind helps people feel stronger, more energetic, calmer, less depressed, and leads to increased feelings of self-worth.
- When you are kind to another person, your brain's pleasure and reward centers light up, as if you were the recipient of the good deed.
- Being kind stimulates the production of feel-good and painkiller hormones and lowers stress hormones.
- Being kind can significantly increase positive moods and relationship satisfaction and decrease social avoidance in socially anxious individuals.[15]

---

13 Buchanan, K.E. and Bardi, A. (2010). Acts of kindness and acts of novelty affect life satisfaction. *The Journal of Social Psychology* 150 (3); Aknin, L.B., Dunn, E.W., and Norton, M.I. (2012). Happiness runs in a circular motion: evidence for a positive feedback loop between P, issue Prosocial spending and happiness. *Journal of Happiness Studies* 13 (2): 347–355.

14 https://www.randomactsofkindness.org (accessed 1 August 2024).

15 *Random Acts of Kindness (undated) The Science of Kindness.* https://www.randomactsofkindness.org/the-science-of-kindness (accessed 1 August 2024).

It has been found that being kind to others is associated with both academic achievement and social acceptance.[16] One study assessed the impact when students were encouraged to engage in daily acts of kindness. This study measured what is called "peer acceptance" – how well students were liked by peers.[17] As the researchers explained:

> Research suggests that goals for happiness, prosociality, and popularity may not only be compatible but also reciprocal. Happy people are more likely to engage in prosocial behavior and have satisfying friendships. Similarly, students who are well-liked by peers (i.e., sociometrically popular) are also helpful, cooperative, and emotionally well-adjusted. Past studies indicate that the link between happiness and prosociality is bidirectional – not only do happy people have the personal resources to do good for others, but prompting people to engage in prosocial behavior also increases well-being.

The theory of the researchers was that prosocial behavior has a strong positive association with peer acceptance, and this relationship is likely to be bidirectional. Children who feel accepted are more likely to do kind things for others, and, in turn, children who do kind things for others might gain increased acceptance by their peers. So they studied this.

The study focused on 9–11-year-old students. They measured students' life satisfaction and peer acceptance. They instructed one group of students to perform acts of kindness to others. Then, they took the same measurements. The students who were kind showed increases in life satisfaction. The level of peer acceptance of those students also increased significantly. As the researchers noted:

> Our study demonstrates that doing good for others benefits the givers, earning them not only improved well-being but also popularity. Considering the importance of happiness and peer acceptance in youth, it is noteworthy that we succeeded in increasing both among preadolescents through a simple prosocial activity. Similar to being happy, being well-liked by classmates has ramifications not only for the individual, but also for the community at large. For example, well-liked preadolescents exhibit more inclusive behaviors and less externalizing behaviors (i.e., less bullying) as teens. Thus, encouraging prosocial activities may have ripple effects beyond increasing

---

16 Caprara, C.V., Barabaranelli, C., Pastorelli, C. et al. (2000). Prosocial foundations of children's academic achievement. *Psychological Science* 11: 302–306.
17 Layous, K., Nelson, S.K., Oberle, E. et al. (2012). Kindness counts: prompting prosocial behavior in preadolescents boosts peer acceptance and well-being. *PLoS One* 7 (12).

the happiness and popularity of the doers. Furthermore, classrooms with an even distribution of popularity (i.e., no favorite children and no marginalized children) show better average mental health than stratified classrooms, suggesting that entire classrooms practicing prosocial behavior may reap benefits, as the liking of all classmates soars. Teachers and interventionists can build on our work by introducing intentional prosocial activities into classrooms and recommending that such activities be performed regularly and purposefully.[18]

Clearly, encouraging your child to Be Kind to Others every day is a very important way for them to gain the feeling that they are a Thriver – they can act in ways that make life better for others, even by just giving another person a reason to smile.

Insight on Kindness to Share with Your Child

Provide your child with insight into the following or have them watch a short video on the Rise Above Bullying website:

- One of the best ways you can improve your relationships with others, reduce the potential of being treated badly, and improve your own happiness is to intentionally Be Kind to Others frequently during the day. The intentional, daily practice of reaching out to be kind will help you create a "kindness shield" around you.
- Being kind to others can significant increase your happiness, help you feel stronger and less depressed, increase your feelings of self-worth, make you feel as good as the person you were kind to, and encourage other people to be kind, which contributes to establishing a kind community.
- The more you Reach Out to Be Kind to others, the more others will like and accept you.
- Strive to Reach Out to Be Kind to at least five students from outside of your social group every day. Strive to Reach Out to Be Kind to someone who has been hurtful to you in the past or their supporters, at a time when they are not being hurtful.
- Reach Out to be Kind using social media. Every time you use social media, make an intentional point of posting positive or supportive comments on the social media posts of others – especially if any person posts about some challenge they are having. Take the time to write something warm and supportive, even if this is just a few words or a friendly meme.
- Reach Out to be Kind during transitions. As you walk to a new class, Reach Out to Be Kind to a number of people. When you sit down in your new class, reflect on how you feel.

---

18 Layous et al. *Kindness counts.*

These are questions for journal pages:

- **Daily progress.** What did you do to be kind to others today both in person and using social media? How did this person respond? How did this make you feel?

Act in Service

Acting in Service to Others Insight

When young people engage in acts of service to their community, this results in many benefits, not only to the community, but also to the young person.[19] Sometimes, this service may be called "service learning," if this is an activity offered by the school. Other times, this may be referred to as "civic engagement" or "volunteering." One of the ways people who are Thrivers can be identified is that, because they have experienced challenges, they are very interested in acting in service to support others.

Acting in service can include activities such as volunteering in school, community, or political organizations. Acting in service can provide opportunities for social interaction that contribute to feelings of self-efficacy and can increase a young person's leadership skills. Being of service increases young people's feelings of well-being and results in better academic performance, reduced likelihood of engaging in risky behaviors, and greater likelihood of attending college. Young people who engage in service to others improve their problem-solving skills, their ability to work within a team, and ability to plan more effectively.

Young people are more likely to remain engaged when they can see that their participation is resulting in positive change. This helps them to realize that they are able to make contributions to society through their service. When young people engage in service, they gain a sense of personal satisfaction, knowing that they are making a difference in other peoples' lives. This allows them to gain more skills, learn more about themselves and their interests, and gain a connection to their community. Working with others who are also engaged in service allows them to make new friends. Acting in service also teaches them valuable skills that employers are looking for.

The more your child acts in service to others, the happier and more self-confident they will feel. If your child is feeling depressed because of what is happening to them in school, the absolutely best thing you can do is find a way they can Act in Service to others, especially in environments where they are working with other young people and where their activities will be appreciated.

One of the most fun ways your child can Act in Service is when you do this together as a family. As a family, you can decide what kind of organization you

---

19 Babey, S.H. and Wolstein, J. (2018). *Civic engagement among California high school teens.* UCLA Center for Health Policy Research.

would like to support. The times you spend with your child engaging in acts of service will become profoundly happy times.

Insight on Acting in Service to Share with Your Child

Provide your child with insight into the following or have them watch a short video on the Rise Above Bullying website:

- Acting in service to others is one of the best things you can do for yourself. This is also a great way to make life better for others.
- When you Act in Service this is a great way to make new friends, gain new skills, and learn more about yourself, as well as your community.
- You will have the opportunity to engage in activities that might end up being what you want to study and do for employment in your future.

These are questions for journal pages:

- **Advance planning.** What are your interests in life? How could you volunteer in your community in a way that fits with your interests? How could your acts in service help you to focus on your future?
- **Daily progress.** On the days when you have acted in service: What did you do to Act in Service? What did you learn? How did others respond? How did this make you feel?

Build My Strengths

> Be Proud. I take pride in who I am and what I am able to accomplish. Strengthen My Character. I use my character strengths every day and when things get tough. Embrace Failure. I try and sometimes I fail, which allows me the opportunity to learn.

Your child will become a Thriver, more resilient and empowered, when they are proud of their accomplishments, recognize and use their character strengths, and know that when they fail they have demonstrated that they are willing to try and are able to figure out what did not work.

Be Proud

Being Proud Insight

Oxford Languages provides two definitions of the word "proud":

- Feeling deep pleasure or satisfaction as a result of one's own achievements, qualities, or possessions or those of someone with whom one is closely associated.
- Having or showing a high or excessively high opinion of oneself or one's importance.

Obviously, the objective of the Be Proud strategy is to focus on the first definition, not the second. Sometimes, pride is associated with other not healthy self-conscious emotions, such exaggerated self-esteem, vanity, hubris, or the perception that you are superior to others. However, there are many positive aspects of feeling healthy pride. Being proud in a healthy way means you are feeling happy about what you have been able to accomplish. It is especially helpful if your child feels proud when they are kind to another, use a character strength, or try something that fails and not get upset by this.

Tracy, in her book *Pride: The Secret of Success* explains how pride plays a key role in the lives of most successful individuals.[20] The benefits of being proud in a healthy way include:

- Having self-confidence and a "can-do" attitude.
- Feeling good about yourself because of how your effort and hard work allowed you to accomplish something.
- Having a quiet belief in yourself that is grounded in competence, but has nothing to do with comparing yourself to others.
- Having an authentic, accurate understanding of your abilities.
- Expressing yourself in a socially positive way – not by bragging, but by being truly proud of your accomplishments.
- Motivating others to follow your leadership.
- Appreciating the accomplishments of others.[21]

To support your child in being a Thriver, encourage them to Be Proud of their accomplishments.

Insight on Being Proud to Share with Your Child

Provide your child with insight into the following or have them watch a short video on the Rise Above Bullying website:

- Some people think that having feelings of pride is not appropriate. In fact, pride is considered one of the seven deadly sins. The hurtful pride that causes concern is the self-centered, egotistical kind of pride where someone thinks they are better than everyone else.
- Healthy pride is the positive feelings you have about yourself when you have accomplished something that is important to you. Healthy pride is what all successful leaders in our society have. Feelings of healthy pride can significantly increase your happiness.

20 Tracy, J. (2016). *Pride: The Secret of Success*. HarperOne.
21 Seltzer, L.F. (2016). *8 crucial differences between healthy and unhealthy pride. Psychology Today*, September 28. https://www.psychologytoday.com/us/blog/evolution-the-self/201609/8-crucial-differences-between-healthy-and-unhealthy-pride (accessed 1 August 2024).

These are questions for journal pages:

- **Daily progress.** What did you do today that made you feel proud? Did you Reach Out to Be Kind to someone who is often excluded or to someone who has been hurtful to you in the past? Did you Act in Service that benefitted others? Did you use one of your key character strengths or a new character strength you are trying to build? Did you try to do and fail, but you embraced failure to figure out what you learned? Did you keep your cool when something bad happened? Did you focus on your future and engage in an action to support your future path?

Strengthen My Character

Character Strengths Insight

Two positive psychology researchers, Christopher Peterson and Martin Seligman, and a team of 55 social scientists from around the world engaged in a collaborative project to identify and classify the core human qualities that lead to goodness in human beings across cultures, nations, and beliefs. The strengths they identified are called Character Strengths.[22]

The VIA Institute on Character has a free Character Strengths Inventory for both adults and teens on its website.[23] These surveys will help both you and your child to identify your top Character Strengths. There is also a workbook for teens on the VIA Character website that you can purchase. There is a brief inventory on character strengths for younger children on the Rise Above Bullying website and a template you can use to create Build My Strengths cards. You can print these cards and have your younger child sort them into three piles: A lot like me. Sometimes like me. Not that much like me.

These are the VIA Character Strengths:

1) **Wisdom and knowledge** – cognitive strengths that entail the acquisition and use of knowledge.
   - Creativity. I like to think of new and better ways of doing things.
   - Curiosity. I am always asking questions and love to discover new things.
   - Critical thinking. I look at all sides of an issue to come up with the right answer.
   - Love of learning. I love to learn new things.
   - Wisdom. I am considered wise because I evaluate things from different perspectives.
2) **Courage** – emotional strengths that involve the exercise of will to accomplish goals in the face of opposition, external or internal.

---

22 Peterson, C. and Seligman, M. (2004). *Character Strengths and Virtues: A Handbook and Classification.* Oxford University Press.
23 http://viacharacter.org (accessed 1 August 2024).

- Bravery. I speak up for what is right, even if others do not agree with me.
- Persistence. I finish what I start, even if it becomes difficult.
- Integrity. I speak the truth and I take responsibility for my feelings and behaviors.
- Zest. I live life as an adventure, filled with excitement and energy.

3) **Humanity** – interpersonal strengths that involve tending to and befriending others.
   - Close relationships. I value the close relationships I have with others.
   - Kindness. I enjoy helping others, even if I do not know them well.
   - Social intelligence. I pay attention to the motives and feelings of others.

4) **Justice** – civic strengths that underlie healthy community life.
   - Teamwork. I always do my share and I work hard for the success of my group.
   - Fairness. I treat all people in a fair and just manner.
   - Leadership. I am good at providing leadership and direction when I am with a group of people.

5) **Temperance** – strengths that protect against excess.
   - Forgiveness. I am willing to forgive someone who has done something wrong.
   - Humility. I am humble and let my actions speak more than my words.
   - Prudence. I am careful about what I do and strive not to do things I might later regret.
   - Self-control. I pay attention and am always in control of what I do and say.

6) **Transcendence** – strengths that forge connections to the larger universe and provide meaning.
   - Appreciate excellence. I appreciate the beautiful and wonderful things in life.
   - Gratitude. I pay attention to the good things that happen to me and express my thanks.
   - Hope. I believe that good things are coming to me now.
   - Humor. I like to laugh, smile, and see the good in all situations.
   - Faith and purpose. I feel my life has a higher purpose that fits within the larger meaning of life.

One experiment the researchers did with this survey was to provide participants in a study with insight about their top five character strengths.[24] The participants were then asked to use one of their character strengths in a new way each day. This strategy was found to have excellent success in increasing the participants' level of happiness and decreasing their feelings of depression.

Everyone has different strengths. Your child's existing strengths can be strengthened through regular activities intentionally using their strengths. They can also be encouraged to build new strengths.

---

24 Seligman, M.E.P., Steen, T.A., Park, N., and Peterson, C. (2005). Positive psychology progress: empirical validation of interventions. *American Psychologist* 60 (5): 410–421. https://doi.org/10.1037/0003-066X.60.5.410.

One very important focus on your child's strengths is when these strengths are combined with problem-solving: Think Things Through. When your child needs to identify some strategies to respond to a situation, encourage them to think about strategies that use their strengths. Another strategy is to have copied the template for Build My Strengths cards. Then, when your child or your family is faced with a challenge, shuffle the cards and pull out several. Consider how using each of these strengths in the current situation might help.

A third strategy that is helpful to build new strengths is to pull out a strengths card for your family every morning. The goal for each member of your family will be to do something during the day that uses that strength.

Research that has focused on interventions grounded in character strengths has found a focus on such strengths results in significant increases in happiness, self-esteem, and life satisfaction, and a significant decrease in depression.[25] As your child recognizes their strengths, builds their strengths, learns new strengths, and recognizes strengths in others, this will increase their resilience and empowerment.[26]

Insight on Character Strengths to Share with Your Child

Provide your child with insight into the following or have them watch a short video on the Rise Above Bullying website:

- Character strengths are the core qualities that lead to goodness in human beings across cultures, nations, and beliefs. You can use this inventory to identify your primary character strengths.
- Everyone has different strengths. We can also develop new strengths. Whenever you intentionally use one of your strengths, this will increase your happiness.
- Each day pick one of your strengths to use in a new way. Or you can look over the list of strengths and pick a new strength that you want to build.
- You can use your strengths when things get tough. Think about and practice ways you can use each of your top strengths in situations where you are facing a challenge or are about to get upset.

These are questions for journal pages:

- **Advance planning.** What are your top character strengths? What strengths would you like to build?

---

25 Schutte, N.S. and Malouff, J.M. (2019). The impact of signature character strengths interventions: a meta-analysis. *Journal of Happiness Studies* 20: 1179–1196. https://doi.org/10.1007/s10902-018-9990-2.
26 Proctor, C., Tsukayama, E., Wood, A.M. et al. (2011). Strengths gym: the impact of a character strengths-based intervention on the life satisfaction and well-being of adolescents. *The Journal of Positive Psychology* 6: 377–388. https://doi.org/10.1080/17439760.2011.594079.

- **Daily progress.** What character strengths did you use today? What did you do that used this strength? How did this make you feel? Did you notice anyone else using a character strength that you admired?

Embrace Failure

Growth Mindset Insight

In her book, *Mindset: The New Psychology of Success,* Carol Dweck introduced the concept of fixed mindset and growth mindset to describe the underlying beliefs people have about learning and intelligence.[27] People who have a growth mindset believe that they and others can acquire any desired ability if they engage in the effort to do so. This includes their ability to gain effective skills to maintain positive personal relationships.

People who have a fixed mindset believe that abilities are mostly innate and cannot be changed. They interpret failure of themselves or others as the lack of basic abilities. They think that intelligence cannot be changed. They ignore constructive feedback and feel threatened by the success of their peers. They often blame outside factors for their failure. They tend to believe that their failure was not due to their lack of skill or determination, but rather the result of other people's actions.

Young people who have a growth mindset are more likely to continue working on an academic project, even if they have experienced failure. Their perception is that failure to accomplish an objective is not an indication of their personal failure. Rather this is viewed as motivation for them to try again so that they can continue to learn. They believe that everyone can get smarter if they work at it. They use constructive feedback to improve. They do not blame outside factors for their failures.

One person in our history who exemplified a growth mindset and embracing failure was Thomas Edison, who invented the lightbulb. He recognized failure as the way to learn what was not going to work. The following quote has been attributed to him:

> I never allow myself to become discouraged under any circumstances. I recall that after we had conducted thousands of experiments on a certain project without solving the problem, one of my associates, after we had conducted the crowning experiment and it had proved a failure, expressed discouragement and disgust over our having failed "to find out anything." I cheerily assured him that we had learned something. For we had learned

27 Dweck, C.S. (2006). *Mindset: The New Psychology of Success.* Random House.

for a certainty that the thing could not be done that way, and that we would have to try some other way. We sometimes learn a lot from our failures if we have put into the effort the best thought and work we are capable of.[28]

Your child can become a Thriver, more resilient and empowered, if they develop a growth mindset. One way you can support them in doing this is by providing the right kind of encouragement.[29] This encouragement will be really important in relation to your child's personal relationships. "Wow, you worked very hard to do that." "I know that what happened was upsetting to you. I could see that you were focused on remaining calm." "It is okay that you were not totally successful. Trying and failing helps us learn how to do things better." "What do you think you learned from this?" If you look online, you can find cool posters with growth mindset statements that you can print and put on your refrigerator.

Having a growth mindset if really important to reduce the potential your child will engage in retaliation against another if that other person has been hurtful to them. A study was done on this.[30] The researchers told students:

> Scientists have discovered that people do things mainly because of the thoughts and feelings that they have – thoughts and feelings that live in the brain and that can be changed. When you have a thought or a feeling, the pathways in your brain send signals to other parts of your brain that lead you to do one thing or another.. . . By changing their brain's pathways or their thoughts and feelings, people can actually change and improve how they behave after challenges and setbacks. So it's not that some people are "rejects" or that other people are "bad." Everyone's brain is a "work in progress."[31]

The study found that when the students learned about growth mindsets they:

- Did not engage in aggressive retaliation.
- Engaged in less aggression and acting out in class.
- Were less depressed.

---

28 Forbes, B.C. (1921). Why do so many men never amount to anything? *American Magazine* 91: 89.
29 Mueller, C.M. and Dweck, C.S. (1998). Intelligence praise can undermine motivation and performance. *Journal of Personality and Social Psychology* 75: 33–52. See also, Kamins, M. and Dweck, C.S. (1999). Person vs. process praise and criticism: implications for contingent self-worth and coping. *Developmental Psychology* 35: 835–847. Yousefi, H. and Khalkhali, V. (2020). The effects of mastery versus social-comparison praise on students' persistence: a role of fixed versus growth mindset. *Education Sciences and Psychology* 55 (1): 3–9.
30 Yeager, D.S., Trzesniewski, K.H., and Dweck, C.S. (2013). An implicit theories of personality intervention reduces adolescent aggression in response to victimization and exclusion. *Child Development* 84 (3): 970–988.
31 Yeager et al. *An implicit theories of personality intervention reduces adolescent aggression in response to victimization and exclusion.*

Insight on Growth Mindset to Share with Your Child

Provide your child with insight into the following or have them watch a short video on the Rise Above Bullying website:

- Our "mindset" is our way of perceiving things. Everyone has a mindset that shapes how they perceive the world and others around them. We may look at the world in a way that makes us feel strong and happy or in a way that makes us feel frustrated and weak.
- People with what is called a growth mindset know that the things that are happening to them can get better. They also know that they can change and get better. They keep trying, even when things are tough. People with a fixed mindset feel as if they are stuck with the way things or they are. So if things are not working the way they want, they are more likely to give up.
- When something is difficult, you may get into fixed mindset thinking. You may feel frustrated and think about quitting. This is when you can change your thinking to a growth mindset.
- There is a magical word that you can use to help maintain a growth mindset. That word is "yet." You can add the word "yet" onto the end of almost any sentence when you feel like you are failing. If you think "I cannot do this," you can change your statement to, "I have not been able to do this yet."
- If you have a growth mindset, you will see failure as the opportunity to have figured out what did not work. You can use failure to expand your abilities. "Well, that clearly did not work. What else could I try?"
- It is also important to know that others can change. You might think that someone who was hurtful to you will always be hurtful. When you know that you have the ability to change, you can figure out a positive way to respond.

These are questions for journal pages:

- **Advance planning.** Pay attention to your thinking. Does your thinking focus on growing into the future or are you more focused on what is happening now? Do you have fun with challenges, even though you know you might fail? Do you embrace your mistakes and failure because you know that you tried and have the opportunity to learn what will not work?
- **Daily progress.** Did you try to do something today and fail? If so, describe what happened, how you responded, and what you learned.

Focus on the Good

Find the Joys. I focus on the good things happening in my life. Be Thankful. I express my appreciation to others.

Maintaining a Focus on the Good in an excellent way for your child to overcome any harms that have occurred to them. Young people who have positive feelings about themselves are less likely to demonstrate perceived weakness that could lead to their being treated badly. They are also better able to avoid thinking badly of themselves if this occurs.

A consistent focus on the good things happening in their lives can help to support these positive feelings. Find the Joys is an internal process of feeling happy and joyful when good things happen. Be Thankful is an external process of expressing appreciation to others. However, because the research on these two processes is so closely linked, they will be discussed together.

Find the Joys and Be Thankful

Insight into Happiness and Gratitude

The Greater Good Science Center provides an excellent white paper on gratitude. It notes:

> Research suggests that gratitude may be associated with many benefits for individuals, including better physical and psychological health, increased happiness and life satisfaction, decreased materialism, and more.
>
> A handful of studies suggest that more grateful people may be healthier, and others suggest that scientifically designed practices to increase gratitude can also improve people's health and encourage them to adopt healthier habits.
>
> Many more studies have examined possible connections between gratitude and various elements of psychological well-being. In general, more grateful people are happier, more satisfied with their lives, less materialistic, and less likely to suffer from burnout. Additionally, some studies have found that gratitude practices, like keeping a "gratitude journal" or writing a letter of gratitude, can increase people's happiness and overall positive mood.
>
> In recent years, studies have examined gratitude's potential benefits for children and adolescents. For example, studies have found that more grateful adolescents are more interested and satisfied with their school lives, are more kind and helpful, and are more socially integrated. A few studies have found that gratitude journaling in the classroom can improve students' mood and that a curriculum designed to help students appreciate the benefits they have gained from others can successfully teach children to think more gratefully and to exhibit more grateful behavior (such as writing more thank you notes to their school's PTA).[32]

---

32 Allen, S. (2019). *The science of gratitude. A white paper prepared for the John Templeton Foundation by the Greater Good Science Center at UC Berkeley.* https://ggsc.berkeley.edu/images/uploads/GGSC-JTF_White_Paper-Gratitude-FINAL.pdf (accessed 1 August 2024).

Martin Seligman is the founder of positive psychology, a field of study that examines healthy ways of being, such as happiness, strength of character, and optimism. Please take the time to watch a video on his approach to flourishing.[33] In one of his studies, he asked adults to spend 5–10 minutes at the end of each day writing in detail about three things that went well that day, large or small, and also describing why they thought this happened.[34] Completing this exercise every day for one week led to increases in happiness that lasted for six months.

Rick Hanson, the author of *Hardwiring Happiness*, has outlined the research that demonstrates that it is possible for people to rewire their brain to be more happy.[35] The approach Hanson recommends involves an intentional focus on positive experiences to change our brain.

Please take the time to watch a TedTalk by Hanson called "Hardwiring Happiness."[36] Hanson calls this approach the HEAL method – Have, Enrich, Absorb, Link:

- **Step 1. Have a good experience.** Either notice a positive experience that is happening to you or create a positive experience for yourself.
- **Step 2. Enrich it.** Keep thinking about this experience for at least ten seconds or longer. Feel the positive experience in your body. Enjoy it. Think about how wonderful this is. Really take the time to feel happy.
- **Step 3. Absorb it.** Think about this positive experience as being absorbed – traveling deep into your mind and warming your heart. Bring the experience deeply into your being.
- **Step 4. Link positive and negative material.** This step is optional and likely will be a challenge for young people. Think about a negative experience or emotion, then sort of set this aside in your mind. Then, go through the first three steps of focusing on a happy emotion. Once you feel really happy, bring up the negative thought and seek to let the happy feelings overcome the negative feelings.

In a study that involved adult participants who took an online class to learn the HEAL method, the participants reported significant increases in positive

33 Seligman, M. (2012). *Flourishing – a new understanding of wellbeing*. Happiness & Its Causes (YouTube channel). https://www.youtube.com/watch?v=e0LbwEVnfJA (accessed 1 August 2024).

34 Seligman, M.E.P., Steen, T.A., Park, N., and Peterson, C. (2005). Positive psychology progress: empirical validation of interventions. *American Psychologist* 60 (5): 410–421. https://doi.org/10.1037/0003-066X.60.5.410.

35 Hanson, R. (2013). *Hardwiring Happiness: The New Brain Science of Contentment, Calm, and Confidence*. Harmony.

36 https://www.youtube.com/watch?v=jpuDyGgIeh0 (accessed 1 August 2024).

emotions and happiness and decreases in negative emotions. These happy feelings persisted two months after the course ended.[37]

Seligman also implemented an experiment with a thankfulness strategy in his research.[38] He asked people to write and personally deliver a letter of gratitude to someone who they thought they had not properly thanked for their kindness. The people immediately had a huge increase in their happiness scores. The happiness benefits lasted for a long time.

Insight on Focusing on Happiness and Gratitude to Impart to Your Child

Provide your child with insight into the following or have them watch a short video on the Rise Above Bullying website:

- Our brains naturally wire themselves to focus more on negative experiences than positive ones. This is because of all of those possible dangerous animals our ancestors faced. If primitive human did not quickly spot signs of the potential dangerous animal, they could become lunch. Unfortunately, if you have faced a lot of challenges, your brain may more frequently focus on negative things.
- The more you can focus on positive feelings, the less likely you will act in ways that demonstrate a perceived weakness that could lead to your being treated badly. Also, the more you focus on positive feelings, the less likely you will be to think badly about yourself if you experience a distressing situation or someone is hurtful.
- You can rewire your brain to be more happy. When you intentionally and frequently Focus on the Good by finding joys and being thankful, this will help your brain build neural pathways to support your greater happiness. As a result, more positive things are more likely to happen to you.
- A way to do this is to either notice a positive experience that is happening to you or create a positive experience for yourself. Keep thinking about this experience, taking the time to feel really happy, and then think about this positive experience as becoming absorbed into your being.
- As you are getting ready to leave one class for another, stop and think about one thing that happened in this class that made you feel good. Enrich this feeling and absorb it.
- If you experience something distressing, pull out a notebook and write down five recent positive experiences or things that made you happy. For each of

---

37 Hanson, R., Shapiro, S., Hutton-Thamm, E. et al. (2021). Learning to learn from positive experiences. *The Journal of Positive Psychology* 18 (1): 142–153. https://www.tandfonline.com/doi/full/10.1080/17439760.2021.2006759.

38 Seligman, M.E.P. (2011). *Flourish: A Visionary New Understanding of Happiness and Well-being.* Free Press.

these positive experiences, take a brief moment to enrich it and absorb it. Then, if you find yourself thinking about the negative incident again, look at what you wrote and intentionally shift back to positive thinking.

- The other strategy to increase your happiness is to say thank you, write a thank-you note, or write a post or comment on social media thanking someone who has done something helpful or kind to you.

These are questions for journal pages:

- **Daily progress.** What three to five things happened today that made you really happy? Did you express your thanks and appreciation to someone?

Personal Power Insight

The next three strategies are of great value for many reasons. However, a very important reason for implementing these strategies is to support your child in being able to respond to hurtful incidents in a positively powerful way that reduces the likelihood these incidents will continue and also reduces the harmful emotional impact of these experiences on your child. These strategies include Be Mindful, Keep Your Personal Power, and Think Things Through.

Hurtful behavior can essentially be considered a "power game," where a young person is seeking to gain "power points" by being hurtful. Young people who seek greater dominance are seeking additional "power points" by displaying their power to dictate who is to be considered acceptable and who is a "misfit." They also want to gain personal power from their admirers. They are hurtful to those who have lower social power and, thus, have fewer "power points." They also are hurtful to rivals for power. Young people who have both been treated badly and are hurtful are also seeking to gain some kind of power in their environment, where they are largely without power.

When young people overreact to being treated badly, this proves to the hurtful student and to all of the witnesses that the hurtful student has been successful in taking the their "power points." When young people gain and demonstrate greater personal power, they are less likely to be treated badly because they will present themselves in a more confident manner. They will also be less likely to react in a way that will result in a loss of their "power points." Rather than trigger and have an outburst, which only encourages the hurtful student, they will have a greater ability to remain calm, nonchalant, and simply walk away. When the student who is trying to gain "power points" does not receive a "reward" of causing the student they treated badly to visibly react badly, this can decrease this kind of hurtful treatment.

Be Mindful

> Practice Calmness. I take time during the day to achieve calmness and focus. Keep My Cool. I remain calm when things get tough.

The ability to self-regulate is an essential skill when one is treated badly. This can help your child remain calm so as not to reward the young person being hurtful by reacting in an upset manner. Self-regulation is also important to reduce the potential for impulsive retaliation. The frequent practice of being mindful creates the neural pathways that will increase your child's ability to keep their cool when things get tough. Thrivers have gained the ability to keep their cool in challenging situations.

Practice Calmness

Mindfulness Insight

Often young people who are treated badly overreact in response. When they over-react, this gives the one who was hurtful their reward. They were successful! The target's overreaction attracts more attention from witnesses. When a young person responds badly, this undermines their reputation. Sometimes, those who are treated badly may engage in retaliation. Because their overreaction usually is more disruptive than the original bullying they experienced, they end up being punished.

Self-regulation is a profoundly important component of resilience. The practice of mindfulness helps people achieve calmness and focus – which builds the capacity of their brain to better self-regulate.[39]

The University of California – Los Angeles Mindful Awareness Research Center is conducting a wide range of research studies on the benefits of mindfulness practice, including with young people. As stated on their website:

> Research in mindfulness has identified a wide range of benefits in different areas of psychological health, such as helping to decrease anxiety, depression, rumination, and emotional reactivity. Research has also shown mindfulness helps to increase well-being, positive affect, and concentration.
>
> Practicing mindfulness can also be helpful to foster physical health by improving immune system function, quality of sleep, as well as decreasing blood pressure. Structural and functional brain changes have also been documented in areas associated with attention, emotional regulation, empathy, and bodily awareness.

---

39 http://www.umassmed.edu/cfm (accessed 1 August 2024).

In addition to health, research has been made on the benefits of mindfulness in business and educational settings. In companies, results showed improved communication and work performance. In educational settings, mindfulness practices improved social-emotional skills, executive functions, and decreased test stress in students, as well as reduced stress and burnout in teachers.[40]

Research has documented effectiveness of mindfulness training and practice in addressing stress-related concerns of children and adolescents. Engaging in mindfulness activities documented positive results in improving their physical health, psychological well-being, social skills including emotional regulation, and academic performance.[41]

Insight on Mindfulness to Share with Your Child

Provide your child with insight into the following or have them watch a short video on the Rise Above Bullying website:

- When you practice being mindful it can help you become calm and focused.
- The more you intentionally practice being mindful, the more effectively you will prepare your brain so that it does not trigger when someone is hurtful or a challenging situation occurs.
- You can achieve greater mindfulness by routinely engaging in the practice of meditation. There several ways different ways you can engage in meditation. These include Clear Your Mind Meditation, Happiness Meditation, and Transition Calming.
- The following are the steps to for a Clear Your Mind Meditation:
  - **Be in a safe place.** Sit or lie in a safe place.
  - **Ground yourself.** If you are sitting, make sure your feet are on the floor. Whether sitting or lying, feel your energy go deep into the earth, grounding you there.
  - **Reduce input.** Close your eyes or gaze downward. This will help you focus on you, and not what is going on around you.

---

40 https://www.uclahealth.org/marc/research (accessed 1 August 2024).
41 Zenner, C., Herrnleben-Kurz, S., and Walach, H. (2014). Mindfulness-based interventions in youth organizations – a systematic review and meta-analysis. *Frontiers in Psychology* 5: 603. See also research noted at http://www.mindful.org/the-mindful-society/mindfulness-in-education-research-highlights (accessed 1 August 2024).

- **Breathe deeply.** Pay attention to your breathing. Take a slow breath in. Hold your breath for a short time. Release your breath out slowly. Keep repeating this.
- **Count down.** Envision that you are at the top of ten stairs. With each breath in and out, move down one stair. Feel your body relax as you move down each step.
- **Be there.** If your attention begins to wander, which it often will, gently return your thoughts to a focus on your breathing.
- **Back to focused.** When you are finished meditating, you can begin to wiggle your fingers and toes and then open your eyes.
- You might have challenges with the Clear Your Mind Meditation. It can be hard to think about nothing. The Happiness Meditation is a more active form of meditation. The change from the Clear Your Mind Meditation to the Happiness Meditation is at the Be There step. At this point instead of trying to keep your mind blank or clear, you will think about the four happiness-building Positively Powerful strategies. Like this:
  - **Make Positive Connections.** Think about someone you recently had a positive connection with, either a friend or trusted adult. Think about how great it felt being together.
  - **Reach Out to Be Kind.** Send loving thoughts to other people you care about.
  - **Build Your Strengths.** Think about something you did lately that used one of your character strengths or that you are proud of. Smile as you remember this.
  - **Focus on the Good.** Think about something that happened recently that made you feel really happy. Let your body feel the happiness of this memory.
- The last meditation strategy is Transition Calming. Do this Transition Calming practice every time you sit down in class at school or enter a new situation. When you sit down, close your eyes or gaze downward, and breathe slowly – taking a slow breath in, holding it briefly, and then releasing slowly. Take three to five slow breaths, then open your eyes or look up and be ready to learn.
- There are other ways to Be Mindful. You may take a yoga or a tai chi class, which is considered "movement mindfulness." You can also walk in nature, listen to calm music, play with a fidget tool, or read a book.

These are questions for journal pages:

- **Daily progress.** How many times did you practice being mindful today? Did you use the Clear Your Mind Meditation or the Happiness Meditation? Did you use Transition Calming every time you entered a new class or place?

Keep My Cool

Self-regulation Insight

Concerns of students who are not able to self-regulate and become disruptive are frequent in schools. These concerns appear to have increased with the ongoing contention that is evident in our society. This is a sad description of what is going on in many schools:[42]

> Schools across the country say they are seeing an uptick in disruptive behaviors. Some are obvious and visible, like students trashing bathrooms, fighting over social media posts, or running out of classrooms. Others are quieter calls for help, like students putting their head down and refusing to talk . . .
>
> The behavior issues are a reflection of the stress the pandemic placed on children, experts say, upending their education, schedules, and social lives. For students dealing with grief, mental health issues, or the layered effects of poverty and racism, big transitions can be even more challenging.
>
> Anxiety and chronic stress also trigger a child's "survival brain." ... While some students retreat, others feel like they are on high alert – turning a nudge in the hallway into cause for an outburst, for example. "You can get these really big reactions over really small things." ...
>
> Coupled with staff exhaustion, the behavior challenges are making school environments more tense than educators and students had anticipated – and underscoring how much support students need right now.

When a young person triggers and starts to become dysregulated, their hippocampus has sent warning signals to their amygdala, which has initiated a "fight, flight, or flee" response. This has resulted in the anterior cingulate cortex and prefrontal cortex becoming disconnected. Their amygdala is telling them, "You are not safe." Their ability to regulate their emotions and problem solve has been undermined. This interferes with their ability to process what anyone is trying to tell them. There is one thing – and only one thing – that can help them at this point. That is to regain the feeling of being safe.

Insight from Dan Seigel and Tina Payne Bryson's book, *The Whole Brain Child*, is really helpful in understanding and describing the process of becoming

---

42 Belsha, K. (2021). *Stress and short tempers: schools struggle with behavior as students return. Chalkbeat*, September 27. https://www.chalkbeat.org/2021/9/27/22691601/student-behavior-stress-trauma-return (accessed 1 August 2024).

dysregulated.[43] They call the process of becoming dysregulated "flipping your lid." You can explain this to your child by having them use their hand as a model of the brain to describe what happens when they trigger. The inner or downstairs brain is represented by their palm. The thumb represents the limbic system, with both the hippocampus and the amygdala. When they rest their thumb across their palm, this is about where the hippocampus and amygdala are in their brain. Curling their fingers over the top creates the anterior cingulate cortex and the prefrontal cortex. This is the upstairs brain, in its proper place. When they become dysregulated, their fingers flip up – they have "flipped their lid" – and can no longer regulate their emotions or solve problems.

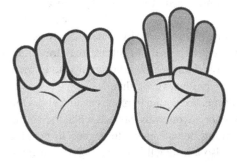

There are some defined stages to this process that are helpful to understand:[44]

- **Phase 1. Calm**. When young people are calm, they can focus and learn and engage in positive relationships with each other.
- **Phase 2. Trigger**. When a young person is triggering, they are in the process of losing their cool. Something has happened that has caused them to feel unsafe. Their amygdala is saying, "watch out – danger!". Their brain is beginning to lose the connection with their anterior cingulate cortex and prefrontal cortex, which is reducing their ability to regulate their emotions and to think. Their safety is rapidly becoming their only concern.
- **Phase 3. Escalate**. This stage can be very short. A young person can go from trigger to outburst in less than a minute. The most important issue to focus on is that the primary need of the young person at this time is to feel safe. At this stage, they have not yet lost full capacity to problem solve. Using reflective listening can be really helpful at this stage. "It appears that you are becoming upset because [identify reason]. How can I help?" Or you could say, "It looks like you don't feel safe because [identify reason]. How can I help you to feel safe?"

---

43 Siegel and Bryson. *The Whole Brain Child*.
44 Colvin, G. (2004). *Managing the Cycle of Acting-out Behavior in the Classroom*. Behavior Associates. I have slightly changed the stages from this source.

- **Phase 4. Outburst.** Obviously, this is the stage we want to avoid. This is when a young person has "flipped their lid." If a young person has become totally dys-regulated, both their safety, as well as that of others, is of concern. This is not an intentional choice to misbehave. At this point, a young person's anterior cingulate cortex and prefrontal cortex are primarily off-line. The key to effective de-escalation is to recognize that what the young person in this situation requires most of all is to regain the feeling that they are safe. Any reaction to them that continues their feelings of not being safe will not be effective. The strategies that absolutely must be avoided can be remembered by the acronym TACOS: Threats. Arguments. Criticism. Orders. Shaming. At this stage, reflective listening is still the most helpful approach to help your child regain the feeling that they are safe.
- **Phase 5. De-escalate.** At this point, the young person is beginning to calm down. They may need to engage in some physical activity. When they triggered and got agitated, their amygdala caused their body to release the stress hor-mones cortisol and adrenalin. It is important to get these hormones out of their system. Vigorous physical activity is the best way to do this.
- **Phase 6. Recovery.** At this point in time, the young person is again calm. One focus at this time needs to be on whether anyone was harmed when the young person became dysregulated. The young person needs to engage in positive actions to remedy this harm. This is also a time when the young person must Embrace Failure. They have been working on strategies to keep their cool. This time, those strategies failed. What can be learned from this failure? What other strategies to keep their cool might be helpful?

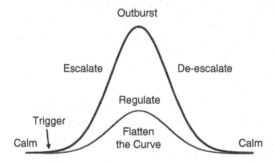

If your child is known to have challenges in self-regulation at home, when they are calm Think Things Through with them to identify several self-regulation strat-egies they can use at those times that they trigger. The goal is to collaborate with your child so your child can identify strategies they can use in the places where they are more likely to trigger which will lead to an outburst or if they have just started to trigger.

The goal is to "flatten the curve." Instead of triggering and this escalating, which will result in an outburst, the desired path is that when they trigger they immediately recognize this and take the steps they have identified to help them regulate to remain calm. This way they can avoid escalating up the curve to an outburst.

Have your child practice these strategies when they are not upset. Create a sign for on your refrigerator with the heading, Keep My Cool, with the strategies listed. Be Proud of your child's successes. Alternatively, your child may need to Embrace Failure. If they were not able to regulate at this time, they can use this as an opportunity to learn what did not work and to Think Things Through to identify some other self-regulation strategies.

If your child is having challenges with self-regulation at school, it is possible that school staff or environmental factors are triggering them. It is also possible that school staff are responding to them using the TACOS approach. Ask your child to describe how school staff are responding to them when they have triggered and are starting to get upset.

Think Things Through with your child to identify strategies they think would be helpful for them to use in different places at school. Can they walk away from the situation to get to a place where they can better self-regulate? Is there a calming place in the classroom or school they can go to? Do they need a "permission path" to leave an environment if they feel they are starting to trigger? Would some kind of a "code" that would communicate to a staff member that they feel they are about to trigger or have triggered be helpful?

Then, ask for a meeting for you and your child with key school staff, most likely the assistant principal and a counselor. Present your information about what seems to be triggering your child at school, including examples of how staff responded when they have triggered that were not helpful. Have your child present the strategies they think will help them to self-regulate if they have triggered. Discuss how the school can support your child in implementing these strategies. For younger students, a laminated card of "Keep My Cool" strategies could be placed on their desk.

Insight on Self-regulation to Share with Your Child

Provide your child with insight into the following or have them watch a short video on the Rise Above Bullying website:

- If you are faced with a challenging situation, it is exceptionally important that you are able to keep your cool to remain calm. Failure to effectively keep your cool could lead you to engage in an outburst that could cause harm to you or others. When you frequently practice meditation, this will help to create the neural pathways in your brain that will allow you to keep your cool more effectively. This is why frequent practice to Be Mindful is so important.
- Your brain is always on alert for threats to your safety. Your hippocampus plays a key role in this. This is where your past memories are processed. This includes memories of negative experiences you have had in the past. You may be in a situation that is not really much of a threat at this time, but your past negative

memories may be accessed and will trigger your amygdala telling you that you are not safe. Your stored, unconscious negative memories may cause you to overreact to the current situation, even if at this point in time you actually are safe. If a student who is frequently hurtful to you passes you in the hall and looks sideways at you making a stupid face, you may trigger. You may also trigger if your classroom becomes too noisy or for other reasons that relate to how you are interacting in the world.

- You may actually not be safe. But if you do not keep your cool, you will have a harder time responding and this could result in even more challenges. When you are able to keep your cool, you are better able to get yourself out of danger.

- If you frequently fail to keep your cool and often become disruptive, this will have a very damaging impact on your reputation, friendships, and ability to learn effectively.

- When you know that there is a higher risk you will trigger and become disruptive in certain situations, this knowledge gives you the power to change what could happen.

- There are six stages in a situation that lead you to lose your cool and become disruptive. These are:
  - **Calm.** You feel calm and relaxed.
  - **Trigger.** Something happens that triggers you and you start to feel upset.
  - **Escalate.** You become increasingly upset.
  - **Outburst.** You are now out of control and engage in disruptive behavior.
  - **De-escalate.** You now feel confused and embarrassed.
  - **Recovery.** The time it takes for you to calm down and regain the ability to resume activities.

- The goal is to flatten the curve. When you trigger, this is the time to take specific steps to keep your cool so that you do not become more escalated and have an outburst. You want to go from calm, to trigger, to keep your cool, and back to calm.

These are questions for journal pages:

- **Advance planning.**
  - First, identify what situations commonly trigger you. Is there a person who treats you with disrespect who causes you to trigger? Do you feel immediately triggered if a teacher calls on you in math class? Is the cafeteria just too loud? Write down what situations are more likely to cause you to trigger.
  - Next, Think Things Through about what helps you to keep your cool when you have triggered. Write down the things you know can help you keep your cool. This could be walking away, playing with a fidget toy, or watching a fun video on your computer. Once you have developed a list of what you can do to better keep your cool, you will need to talk to the school to get permission to take these steps if you are about to trigger or have triggered.

- If something bad happens, there are four important immediate steps to take. The first of these is to keep your cool by taking deep breaths to remain calm. The next three steps will be added as the background for these steps is discussed.
- After you have gotten yourself out of the immediate situation, you may need to engage in some physical activity. When you triggered and started to get agitated, your amygdala caused your body to release cortisol and adrenalin. It is important to get these hormones out of your system. Physical activity is the way to do this.
- It is very likely that you are going to fail from time to time. Embrace Failure to identify what did not work so that you can try a different approach the next time.
- After a situation like this, take the time to connect with a trusted adult. Share what happened and your thoughts to get feedback on your thinking and plans for the future.

- **Assessment.** Whenever you have been triggered, write out what happened and how you handled the situation. Did you escalate and engage in an outburst or were you able to keep your cool? Note specifically what happened before you triggered so that you can be alert to when this might happen again. Do a self-evaluation of your effectiveness. Embrace Failure and decide whether there are strategies you might want to change in the future. Release and Let Go of any anger. If you were able to keep your cool, congratulate yourself. Be Proud!

Keep My Personal Power

Hold Myself Tall. I hold myself tall and strong. Control My Thinking. I do not allow what happens to me to control how I think about myself or respond. Release and Let Go. I release and let go of my anger.

To effectively address the concerns of hurtful behavior directed at, and sometimes by, young people, it is necessary to increase their level of personal power. This can be addressed both by a focus on two strategies at that moment: Hold Myself Tall and Control My Thinking. It is also helpful when they can Release and Let Go of their anger at the other person at a later date. When they remain angry, this does not allow them to keep their personal Power.

Hold Myself Tall

Powerful Presence Insight

In humans and other animals, standing tall with a very open posture indicates high power, whereas hunching over with arms crossed over your chest indicates lower power. If you maintain physical posture that demonstrates that you feel that you lack personal power, others will think of you as less powerful.

(As an alternative term, you can encourage your child to "Stand Tall." I use the term Hold Myself Tall because not all children are able to easily stand.)

Research conducted by Amy Cuddy, a professor at the Harvard School of Business, has demonstrated that adopting a pose that indicates power – a "power pose" – can result in increased feelings of confidence.[45] An excellent TedTalk by Cuddy on power posing provides greater insight into this, as does her book, *Presence*.

Cuddy did an experiment where she had one group of college students in the business school hold themselves tall in a power position for a period of time. Another group of students held themselves in a powerless position. These students were then interviewed by a very assertive person, as though they were applying for a job. Their interviews were video-taped. People who knew nothing about what the students did before their interview judged the performance of the students on videos. These judges strongly favored the students who had held themselves tall before the job interviews.

What this study demonstrated is that simply holding a "power pose" before a challenging interpersonal relationship task allowed students to increase their effective performance. Cuddy's research has also demonstrated that it is possible to "fake it" by assuming a power pose, which will then help a person "make it" by feeling more confident.

It is helpful to watch the popular "Let It Go" music video from the movie *Frozen*.[46] Have your child note how powerless Elsa appears in the first part of the video. Then, note when she holds herself tall and proud. Have your child practice "feeling small" and "holding themself tall."

Insight on Powerful Presence to Share with Your Child

Provide your child with insight into the following or have them watch a short video on the Rise Above Bullying website:

• Watch Cuddy's TedTalk with your older child or watch the "Let It Go" music video with your younger child. Encourage your child to try this experiment: Have them hold themself small in a position that indicates they feel they have no power – shoulders hunched, arms crossed, head down. Ask how this makes them feel. Now encourage them to stand up tall or hold themself tall. Shoulders back. Head held high. Arms out to their side or over their head in a celebration pose, like they just won a race. Ask how this makes them feel.

45 Cuddy, A. (2012). *Your body language may shape who you are*. TedTalk, June. https://www.ted.com/talks/amy_cuddy_your_body_language_may_shape_who_you_are?language=en (accessed 1 August 2024);Cuddy, A. (2016). *Presence: Bringing Your Boldest Self to Your Biggest Challenges*. Little, Brown & Company.
46 https://www.youtube.com/watch?v=L0MK7qz13bU (accessed 1 August 2024).

- Every morning, before they leave your house, encourage them to hold themself tall for a few minutes in a position of personal physical power. If you drive them to school, when they are leaving your car, remind them to hold themselves tall. (As noted, you can also use the term Stand Tall.)
- Remind your child to hold themself tall whenever they come into school or leave one class to go to another. Also, they should remember to hold themself tall whenever they are in an area where they previously have experienced any challenges.
- If something bad happens, there are four important immediate steps to take. The first of these is to keep your cool by taking deep breaths to remain calm. Then, keep your personal power by holding yourself tall. This will increase your feelings of personal power, which will help you to feel more safe.

These are questions for journal pages:

- **Daily practice.** Did you hold yourself tall before leaving your house, when going into school, and when leaving class to go to another?
- **Assessment.** Did something challenging happen? Write about what happened and how you handled the situation. Did you hold yourself tall? Do a self-evaluation of your effectiveness. Embrace Failure and decide whether there are strategies you might want to change in the future. Release and Let Go of any anger.
- If you kept your cool and held yourself tall, congratulate yourself. Be Proud!

Control My Thinking

Rational Thinking Insight

Your child will never be able to control when someone might treat them badly or if other bad things might happen to them. But they do have the ability to control their thinking about how they feel about themselves and how they respond in these challenging situations. This way they can keep their personal power.

Rational thinking is an old theory. Perhaps the first statement of this strategy is from the ancient Stoic philosophers, as set forth by Epictetus, who in the first century CE said: "Men are disturbed not by things, but by the views which they take of them."[47]

A psychologist, Albert Ellis, developed a theory called Rational Emotive Behavioral Therapy (REBT). The essence of this theory is that harmful consequences are not just caused by the adversities that happen to us, but also by our

---

47 For more on Epictetus, see https://plato.stanford.edu/entries/epictetus (accessed 1 August 2024).

beliefs about those adversities.[48] While we cannot control what might happen, we can control our beliefs. Ellis developed the A-B-C model:

- A is the Adversity or bad thing that happened.
- C is the Consequence of how you feel or respond.

But A is not solely responsible for C.

- B is your belief – this is what you think or believe about A, not merely that A happened.

Thus, $A + B = C$. While it is not possible to change A, it is possible to be in control of B, and thus have greater control over the C. Translation: We do not always have control over what happens to us. But we do have the ability to control what we think of ourselves and how we respond.

Insight on Controlling Their Thinking to Share with Your Child

Provide your child with insight into the following or have them watch a short video on the Rise Above Bullying website:

- You will never be able to control when or if someone might treat you badly. You will never be able to control whether or if other bad things might happen to you. You do have the ability to control your thinking about how you feel about yourself and how you respond in these challenging situations.
- If you are ever in a situation where someone has been hurtful or find yourself thinking about a past situation that occurred, think to yourself, "I will not give that person the power to control what I think about myself or how I respond."
- If something bad happens, there are four important immediate steps to take. The first of these is to keep your cool by taking deep breaths to remain calm. Then, keep your personal power by holding yourself tall. At the same time, control your thinking by thinking to yourself, "I cannot control what happens to me. I can control how I respond."

These are questions for journal pages:

- **Assessment.** Did something challenging happen? Write out what happened and how you handled the situation. Did you control your thinking? Do a self-evaluation of your effectiveness. Embrace Failure and decide whether there are strategies you might want to change in the future. Release and Let Go of

---

48 Ellis, A. (1994). *Reason and Emotion in Psychotherapy: Comprehensive Method of Treating Human Disturbances,* rev. and updated. Citadel Press; Ellis, A. (2003). Early theories and practices of rational emotive behavior theory and how they have been augmented and revised during the last three decades. *Journal of Rational-Emotive & Cognitive-Behavior Therapy* 21 (3/4).

any anger. If you kept your cool, held yourself tall, and controlled your thinking, congratulate yourself. Be Proud!

Release and Let Go

Forgiveness Insight

The other term that could be used for Release and Let Go is that of "forgiveness." However, the concept of forgiveness can be somewhat challenging. If someone has caused us harm, like bullying us, the idea of forgiving this person can be a challenge. To forgive someone feels like letting them off the hook for something bad that they did. However, as every religion appears to endorse the positive outcomes of forgiveness, there is also an obvious benefit of forgiveness.

Forgiveness has been noted as a way to resolve anger and other negative emotions.[49] Resolving this anger will result in better emotional well-being. Forgiveness is a way to restore hope for the future.

The negative health effects of not forgiving include increased depression and anxiety, social isolation, and even physical health concerns associated with stress. Not forgiving someone means that you are holding onto the anger over what happened and what the other person did. This can also lead to constantly thinking about what happened, which continues the harmful impacts of toxic stress. Not forgiving prevents people from moving on with their lives. Studies have shown that engaging in forgiveness leads both to a reduction of anger and an increase in hope.

In a recent study on the relationship between forgiveness, anger, hope, and psychological health resulted in the following conclusion:

> Forgivers experience greater psychological health (lower anxiety and depression and greater self-esteem) indirectly through reduced anger and improved hope for the future.... This finding allows researchers and clinicians to have greater confidence in making the claim that forgiveness reduces anger and restores hope, leading to greater health. Unforgiveness may continue to entrap victims in emotional prison, but forgiveness not only helps victims overcome anger but also helps them find freedom to explore new possibilities for the better future. The restoration of freedom seems to be one of the paradoxes of forgiveness that forgivers experience when they make a courageous decision to let go of the past and move on.[50]

49 Kim, J.J., Payne, E.S., and Tracy, E.L. (2022). Indirect effects of forgiveness on psychological health through anger and hope: a parallel mediation analysis. *Journal of Religion and Health* 61 (5): 3729–3746. https://doi.org/10.1007/s10943-022-01518-4. Enright, R.D. and Fitzgibbons, R.P. (2015). *Forgiveness Therapy: An Empirical Guide for Resolving Anger and Restoring Hope.* American Psychological Association.
50 Kim et al. *Indirect effects of forgiveness on psychological health through anger and hope: a parallel mediation analysis.*

Insight on Forgiveness to Share with Your Child

Provide your child with insight into the following or have them watch a short video on the Rise Above Bullying website:

- You have been hurt by the actions or words of another. This has left you with feelings of resentment and anger – sometimes even hatred. But if you hold on to your pain, you are the one who will suffer. When you hold onto your pain and anger, this means that the other person has some of your "power points." They have succeeded in making you feel bad. How can you stop their success? By releasing and letting go so that you no longer carry the anger within you.

- Release and Let Go is a form of forgiveness. However, sometimes it is hard to think about forgiveness. This feels like you are letting someone who has engaged in wrongdoing off the hook. You might think that they are the one who should tell you they are sorry and ask for your forgiveness. Releasing and letting go does not mean excusing the harm that was done to you. This also does not require making up with the person who harmed you. In fact, releasing and letting go does not require that you have any interactions with this person. Releasing and letting go is something you are doing for yourself, so you can be happier.

- Being hurt by someone can cause you to feel anger and sadness. If you keep thinking about what happened this will continue to fill your body with negative feelings. These negative feelings can crowd out any positive feelings. You might bring your anger into other activities in your life. You may be so focused on the wrongs that happened that you cannot enjoy the present and the good things happening now. When you Release and Let Go of your anger, this will open the door to hope for your future.

- Releasing and letting go is about you letting go of your anger and deciding to move on with hope in your life. This process relates to Control My Thinking. You could not control what happened to you. You can control how you feel about yourself and what actions you take. You cannot make another person tell you they are sorry. But you can let go of your anger, so that you are more happy. Some steps you can take to Release and Let Go are:
  - Think Things Through. Identify what happened and the person who caused this harm. Acknowledge how this made you feel and recognize how these negative feelings are impacting other aspects of your life.
  - Choose to Release and Let Go of your anger. This will allow you to release the control and power that the hurtful person has had in your life. By releasing and letting go, you are taking back your personal power. It is helpful if you Release and Let Go while you are being mindful.
  - After you have released and let go, pay close attention to Find the Joys by focusing on the good things that are happening in your life.

These are questions for journal pages:

- **Assessment.** If you decided to Release and Let Go, write about this. Write out what your thinking was and how you handled the situation. You could even write a Release and Let Go commitment statement in your journal.

Think Things Through

> Think Things Through. I think things through to decide what is best to do. Focus on My Future. I make goals to create my positive future.

When young people gain effective problem-solving skills they are more resilient in figuring out how to respond if they are faced with any kind of a challenge. When they Think Things Through, this is the opposite of acting without thinking. When they focus on their future, by creating goals and planning their actions, this is a very effective strategy to overcome any harms and move forward in their life. Thrivers can Think Things Through and maintain a focus on their future.

Think Things Through

Problem-solving Insight

Some young people who are bullied often lack critically important problem-solving skills, especially in interpersonal relationships. When they gain greater problem-solving skills – that is, when they learn how to think of their own solutions to problems, consequences to their actions, and how they and others feel about things – they are less likely to engage in risky behavior and are more resilient in figuring out how to respond if someone is hurtful to them.

Myrna Shure, author of several *I Can Problem Solve* books, has done significant work focused on supporting young people in effective problem-solving.[51] Four key interpersonal cognitive problem-solving skills she identified are:

- **Means–ends thinking.** Reach a stated goal by planning a step-by-step action plan to reach that goal.
- **Alternative solution thinking.** Identify different possible solutions to a stated problem.

---

51 Dr. Shure's books include:Shure, M.B. (1992). *I Can Problem Solve (ICPS): An Interpersonal Cognitive Problem Solving Program*. Research Press; (1996). *Raising a Thinking Child Workbook*. Shure, M.B, Holt: (republished by Research Press, 2000).

- **Consequence thinking.** Consider what might happen if they were to take certain actions.
- **Weighing pros and cons.** Consider what might happen that could be good or bad to decide whether or how to carry out an act.

There is an excellent problem-solving intervention approach for young people who are having challenges called collaborative problem-solving. This process engages adults in participatory problem-solving with a young person. The key part of this process is that the young person comes up with the strategies to try. The adult does not dictate their expectations and strategies. You can learn more about two strategies, Collaborative Problem Solving and Lives in the Balance, at these two websites.[52] Also, many school counselors are now using an approach called "solutions focused counseling." Solutions focused counseling is a strengths based approach that focuses on building strengths and resilience in students by empowering students to identify strategies to address their challenges.[53] You can recommend these approaches to your child's school. Research has documented excellent effectiveness.

When your child knows how to effectively solve problems, this provides the foundation for success in school, higher education, family life, and in their employment. These are the steps that are necessary to engage in effective problem-solving:

- **What is the situation?** Step back from the situation and think about what has happened to make sure you have a clear understanding. Make sure you are paying close attention to the present situation and that your thinking is not controlled by memories you have stored in your hippocampus.
- **Do I need to remedy any harm?** Carefully consider whether you have engaged in any actions that might have contributed to a challenging situation by being harmful to another. If so, identifying a strategy to remedy this harm is necessary.
- **What do I want to accomplish?** Determine what you would like to achieve or what outcome you desire.
- **What strategies could I use?** Identify several different strategies you could take to resolve the problem that are in accord with your values and uses one of your primary character strengths.
- **For each strategy, what might happen?** Think about and try to predict or envision what might happen if you used each of those strategies.

52 https://thinkkids.org; https://livesinthebalance.org (accessed 1 August 2024).
53 Sabella, R.A. (2020). *Solution-Focused School Counseling: The Missing Manual.* Independently Published. Murphy, J.J. (2023). *Solution-focused counseling in schools*, 4e. American Counseling Association.

- **What is my best choice?** After thinking through what might happen as a consequence of each strategy you thought of, then weight the pros and cons to decide which strategy would be the best to try first.
- **How should I proceed?** Determine what steps to take to accomplish this strategy.
- **Did this work?** Evaluate your effectiveness. Realize that the first thing you try might not work. Embrace Failure. The fact that the first thing you tried did not work is totally okay. You learned what would not work.
- **What else could or should I do?** Repeat this process if the first strategy did not achieve your desired goal or if you learned something that leads you to decide that some other action is necessary.

Insight on Problem Solving to Share with Your Child

Provide your child with insight into the following or have them watch a short video on the Rise Above Bullying website:

- When you gain effective problem-solving skills you can become more resilient in figuring out how to respond if you are facing any kind of a challenge. Thinking things through is the opposite of acting without thinking. Share with them the Think Things Through process outlined above.
- Sometimes thinking things through all by yourself can be a challenge. You can also use the Think Things Through process with a good friend or a trusted adult. If either your friend or the trusted adult starts to tell you what to do, stop them and tell them you want their help thinking through a number of strategies and that you need to be in charge of deciding what to do.
- If something bad happens, there are four important immediate steps to take. The first of these is to keep your cool by taking deep breaths to remain calm. Then, keep your personal power by holding yourself tall. At the same time, control your reaction by thinking to yourself, "I cannot control what happens to me. I can control how I respond." The last step is to think to yourself, "I got this. I can Think Things Through to decide what is best to do."

These are questions for journal pages:

- **Write in your journal.** At the end of the day, think about what happened during the day and whether you faced a situation where you needed to engage in effective problem-solving. If this happened, write about what happened and how you used the Think Things Through strategy. Do a self-evaluation of your effectiveness. Decide whether there are strategies you might want to change in the future. If something challenging happened and you kept your cool, held yourself tall, controlled your thinking, and thought things through, congratulate yourself. Be Proud!

Focus on My Future

Future Directed Thinking Insight

Recall from the Introduction the information from the National Center for School Engagement study of high school students who had been bullied in elementary school.[54] The researchers identified three critical factors that increased the resilience of these students and led to successful outcomes in high school, despite the fact they were being bullied. One of the factors was a sense of future possibility that promised better things to come.

A new effective, intervention approach for adults suffering from depression incorporates this kind of future-thinking approach. It is called Future Directed Therapy (FDT).[55] As explained by Jennice Vilhauer, author of *Think Forward to Thrive*, who developed this approach:

> The theoretical model of human behavior behind FDT is based on three primary concepts: (1) The desire to thrive is the primary drive of all human beings because it promotes the evolutionary process. (2) Thought and behavior are limited resources that humans utilize to promote their thriving. (3) Preparing for the future is essential to thriving and much of human functioning has evolved for the purpose of creating the future.[56]

Essentially, the FDT process involves helping people understand how their thinking actually produces the future and how they can develop more positive thinking patterns. Additionally, participants are guided to develop practical skills for creating and achieving goals, planning, problem solving, learning to take action, and effectively dealing with obstacles or disappointments. This is a strategy to assist people in becoming a Thriver.

The Focus on My Future strategy can be used to support your child to develop goals and develop strategies with a focus on their positive future.

54 Seeley, K., Tombari, M.L., PhD Laurie J. Bennett, L.J. and Dunkle, J.D (2009). *Peer victimization in schools: a set of quantitative and qualitative studies of the connections among peer victimization, school engagement, truancy, school achievement, and other outcomes*. National Center for School Engagement. https://schoolengagement.org/wp-content/uploads/2021/02/PeerVictimizationinSchoolsExecutiveSummary1.pdf (accessed 1 August 2024).

55 Vilhauer, J. (2023). *Think Forward to Thrive: How to Use the Mind's Power of Anticipation to Transcend Your Past and Transform Your Life*. WMI Press; http://futuredirectedtherapy.com (accessed 1 August 2024).

56 Vilhauer, J., Young, S., and Kealoha, C. (2011). Treating major depression by creating positive expectations for the future: a pilot study for the effectiveness of future directed therapy (FDT) on symptom severity and quality of life. *CNS Neuroscience & Therapeutics* 2011: 1–8. http://futuredirectedtherapy.com/wp-content/uploads/2011/05/FDT-and-MDD-CNS-published-version.pdf (accessed 1 August 2024).

A popular goal-setting approach is called SMART. To make sure goals are clear and reachable, each one should be: **S**pecific. **M**easurable. **A**chievable. **R**elevant. **T**ime Based.[57] Some professionals have suggested an expansion to be SMARTER, by including **E**valuated and **R**eviewed.[58]

There have been other changes in the terms. Because this has happened, I will take the liberty to set forth the Positively Powerful version of the SMARTER acronym.

When thinking about goals, Vishen Lakhiani recommend thinking in terms of how what you would like to accomplish will be in service to others. Keeping in line with the SMARTER acronym, I am going to shift "S" to relate to "Service-oriented" and incorporate the ideas of "specific" into "Measurable." Lakhiani has also identified concerns about a focus on "Achievable" goals.[59] If your child only selects goals they perceive are "achievable," they may be limiting themself to lower standards based on what they currently think they are able to accomplish. The "A" goal will be changed to "Ambitious." The first "R" will shift from Relevant to Resilient, as this will focus on how your child can use the resilience they have gained to move forward. The last "R" word has been shifted to "Revise," as this incorporates the concept of embracing failure and thinking things through to revise your path.

Thus, the Positively Powerful SMARTER approach to establishing goals that Focus on My Future is:

- **Service-oriented.** Think of goals that also include how what you want to do will be of service to others. Instead of thinking that you want to be an auto mechanic, think of how you want to use your mechanical skills to ensure that people are driving safe and reliable vehicles. Instead of thinking that you want to be a teacher, think of how you want to help children learn and grow. Instead of thinking that you want to be a doctor or a nurse, think of how you want to help others be healthy. What do you want to do that is in service to others?
- **Measurable.** Think about your goals in a way that enables you to track your progress. Part of establishing a measurable goal is thinking things through so you know what you want to accomplish, and what things you will need to do to accomplish these objectives. How will you determine whether you are achieving success?
- **Ambitious.** Your goal should stretch your abilities and require you to reach higher to do greater things. When you set an ambitious goal you are going to have to be comfortable with embracing failure. Remember that Edison set an ambitious goal of inventing a light bulb. He was very comfortable with

---

57 Drucker, P.F. (1954). *The Practice of Management.* HarperCollins.

58 Mind Tools Content Team. (n.d.). *SMART Goals.* https://www.mindtools.com/a4wo118/ smart-goals (accessed 1 August 2024).

59 Lakhiani, V. (2020). *The Buddha and the Badass: The Secret Spiritual Art of Succeeding at Work.* Rodale Books.

embracing failure, as are all inventors. If you are not quite sure you are ready to be really ambitious, set a goal that is reasonably ambitious. Will your goal require you to expand your insight and abilities and help you to achieve a goal that is really important for both you and for others in society?

- **Resilient.** When bad things happen, you have to be resilient in response. Being resilient means you can focus on the strengths you have gained when bad things have happened. What have you learned from your life experiences and what are the strengths you have gained by dealing with challenges that you can build on to create a positive future for yourself and for others?

- **Time-based.** Having a target date or time is helpful when setting goals. This will help you to focus on what you need to do to move forward in a timely manner to achieve a deadline by a specified time. The time-based activities can be both for your larger goal and for the action steps you need to take to accomplish this goal.

- **Evaluated.** An important step in thinking things through is determining whether what you did was successful. This is where the component of "Evaluated" comes into play. When you periodically evaluate your goal or actions you have taken to achieve this goal, this allows you to stay on track – or perhaps to revise. When you evaluate your goal or action steps, you may have to Embrace Failure.

- **Revised.** You may or may not need to revise your overall goal. If things are working fine, keep with your goal. However, life changes. As you grow older you may have different thoughts about your goals. It is perfectly appropriate to revise your goal or the actions you are taking to achieve a goal.

Insight on Goal Setting to Share with Your Child

Provide your child with insight into the following or have them watch a short video on the Rise Above Bullying website:

- In studies of young people who had been bullied, and who as they became older were successful and happy, one thing which was identified that really helped them was a sense of future possibility that promised better things to come. Focus on your future is an important strategy to overcome and move past any harm from what has occurred.

- To focus on your future requires that you identify goals and develop plans for how to accomplish those goals. There is a popular goal setting approach called SMART or SMARTER. You may have learned about this at school. However, the Positively Powerful Focus on My Future SMARTER has some different words and tasks. Explain the process as described above.

These are questions for journal pages:

- **Advance planning.** Go through the Positively Powerful Focus on My Future SMARTER process to identify a goal. Then, Think Things Through to create an action plan. To create an action plan, create a list of actions you will need to take to accomplish your goal, establish a timeline for each action, identify what resources or supports you will need and where you can obtain these, and monitor your progress.
- **Assessment.** Identify an action you took to reach your goal. Have you learned anything that may require that you revise a goal or a planned action?

6

Positively Powerful Strategies for Those Being Treated Badly

The Positively Powerful strategies have been created to support young people who are currently being bullied to gain the resilience and empowerment to:

- Reduce the likelihood that others will be hurtful to them.
- Increase their effectiveness in responding if someone is hurtful.
- Reduce the potential that being treated badly will cause them significant emotional distress.
- Increase the likelihood that others will step in to help them.

This chapter will provide you with guidance on how these strategies can be used by your child who is being bullied. Recall the statement from Taylor Swift from the Introduction. This is an example of the empowerment of someone who experienced being bullied. Taylor, with the loving support of her family, became a Thriver. You and your child can watch a YouTube video where she discussed the bullying and how she responded.[1]

Understand Hurtful Behavior as a Power Game

Recall the discussion from Chapter 5 on bullying as a strategy to obtain "power points." This chapter will expand and apply the Positively Powerful strategies presented in the last chapter to strategies to both reduce the potential someone is hurtful and to respond in a positively powerful way if this does occur to minimize or prevent any lasting harm.

---

1 Taylor Swift bullied at school. Taylor Music (YouTube channel). https://youtu.be/K_j3rj-ATP8 (accessed 1 August 2024).

Rise Above Bullying: Empower and Advocate for Your Child, First Edition. Nancy E. Willard.
© 2025 John Wiley & Sons, Inc. Published 2025 by John Wiley & Sons, Inc.

What Young People Think

First, some background insight that may be helpful. While it is true that some young people think those who are hurtful are "cool" and "popular," the vast majority of young people do not like to see people being hurtful to others. There are clear survey data that demonstrate this. Recall the PISA survey mentioned in Chapter 3.[2] In addition to asking about experiences of being bullied, the survey asked students about five bullying-related attitudes. PISA asked students whether they "strongly disagree," "disagree," "agree," or "strongly agree" with the following statements, with the following results:

- It irritates me when nobody defends bullied students – 81% agreed or strongly agreed.
- It is a good thing to help students who cannot defend themselves – 88% agreed or strongly agreed.
- It is a wrong thing to join in bullying – 88% agreed or strongly agreed.
- I feel bad seeing other students bullied – 87% agreed or strongly agreed.
- I like it when someone stands up for other students who are being bullied – 90% agreed or strongly agreed.

In the 2015 survey I conducted asked teens what they thought when they saw someone being hurtful.[3] The vast majority, 89%, said they really did not like to see this happen. This response is virtually identical to the PISA findings.

Show this data to your child and encourage them to recognize that if someone is being hurtful to them, they should realize that 9 of the 10 students who see that this is happening really do not like to see this. It may help if your child understands that the challenge these disapproving students most often face is that they are too afraid of the power of the person who is being hurtful. While they do not like seeing someone being bullied, they do not think it is safe for them to step in to help. Because most are afraid to express their disapproval, the witnesses may think that other students support what is happening.

The survey I conducted also found that students truly admire other students who:

- Are respectful and kind to others.
- Reach out to help someone who has been treated badly.
- Try to include those who have been excluded.
- Tell someone being hurtful to stop.

---

2 Organization for Economic Cooperation and Development (OECD). (2020), "Bullying", in PISA 2018 Results (Volume III): What School Life Means for Students' Lives, OECD Publishing, Paris, https://doi.org/10.1787/cd52fb72-en.
3 Willard, N. (2016) Embrace Civility Student Survey. https://www.embracecivility.org/wp-content/uploadsnew/ECSSFullReportfull.pdf (accessed 1 August 2024).

- Help someone who was hurtful decide to make things right.
- Help other students resolve an argument or conflict.
- Were treated badly, but stood tall and responded in a positive way.
- Were hurtful, but stopped and made things right.
- Tell an adult if a situation is serious.

Students clearly did not admire those who:

- Think it is cool to put others down.
- Say disrespectful and hurtful things to others.
- Laugh when seeing someone being treated badly.
- Support their friend in being hurtful.
- Engage in battles with those they perceive as rivals.
- Create drama to get attention.
- Encourage the exclusion of students they consider different.
- Join in when someone else is being hurtful.

My survey did show that students tend to have mixed feelings about those who ignore hurtful situations. This is likely due to messages they have received about not getting involved. Certainly, ignoring a hurtful situation is far better than supporting the person who is being hurtful or laughing. However, as students learn that there are ways they can respond to be helpful that are also safe, this will hopefully change. Positive ways that young people can step in to help when they witness someone being hurtful are discussed in Chapter 10.

In addition, students appear to have mixed feelings about retaliation. The likely reason for this is that, in some parts of society, retaliation is considered to be acceptable. Retaliation is discussed Chapter 7.

Positively Powerful Strategies

Your child can use the Positively Powerful strategies if they are experiencing bullying. The following is how these strategies can support your child in becoming more resilient and empowered despite the fact that they are being bullied. This will be followed by specific recommendations on the Positively Powerful strategies they can use when someone has been hurtful.

Make Positive Connections

Having a good friend can make a huge difference in your child's emotional well-being. Their friend's support can help them to get through these hurtful situations. Their friend can help them to understand that the other person is the one with the problem, not them. Your child's friend can also help them to Think Things Through to figure out what they can do in response to this situation.

Having some trusted adults is also helpful. It is assumed that you are one of your child's trusted adults. However, as I discussed in Chapter 5, it is very important that your child have some trusted adults they can talk with who are outside of your immediate family.

Your child's trusted adults, including you, can also provide emotional support and help them Think Things Through. It is important that your child find trusted adults who they can trust will support their desires for how to respond and will not immediately step in to "take care of things."

Please remember, being bullied is an experience of having someone seek to take your personal power away. Make sure that you do not further seek to take your child's personal power by immediately jumping in to tell them what to do. Assuming you have good connections with your child's other trusted adults, please communicate this caution also to them. Of course, if your child might be exhibiting significant emotional distress, taking the step to get them professional help is advised. Otherwise, seeking to support your child in deciding how they want to handle the situation is advised.

Reach Out to Be Kind

The Reach Out to Be Kind strategy is the most powerfully positive approach your child can use to reduce the likelihood that others will treat them badly. The absolute best thing that can happen if someone is hurtful to your child is for another student to tell the one being hurtful to stop. If your child maintains a consistent approach of reaching out to be kind to others, both in their school and online, this will increase their peer acceptance. This may also increase the likelihood that a student will step in to help your child if they see someone treating them badly.

Encourage your child to Reach Out to Be Kind to at least five students who are not within their social group every day while at school. Additionally, encourage your child to develop a consistent habit of looking for the opportunity to post a kind comment to several digital friends every time they use social media. Ideally, every time your child checks their social media, they will take a minute to post five supportive and kind comments, not just "likes," on the postings of others. Encourage your child to pay attention to what starts to happen when they do this.

A more sophisticated Reach Out to Be Kind strategy your child could try is to identify the more socially powerful students who are consistently kind and respectful in their school. Socially powerful, kind, and respectful students are ones most likely to feel that they are sufficiently powerful to safely be able to publicly tell a hurtful student to stop. If your child reaches out to be kind to these types of students, this could potentially increase the likelihood they will step in to help.

Another more sophisticated reaching out to be kind strategy is to be kind to a person who sometimes treats them badly – at a time when this person is not being hurtful. Likely, these should be very short comments, like "Nice job on that answer" or simple kind acts like holding the door open. This could help to reduce the potential this person will be hurtful to them in the future. Reaching out to be kind to the friends of the student who is being hurtful could also potentially increase the likelihood they will tell their friend to stop.

Build My Strengths

When your child builds their strengths, they will feel more powerful. When your child takes the time to Be Proud of what they accomplished, this builds their "power points." When your child identifies their strongest character strengths – "These are my strengths" – this provides them with a feeling of effectiveness. When they use their character strengths, this will increase their feelings of personal power. When they feel more powerful, this will increase the likelihood they will present themself as a person who has personal pride, which translates to personal power.

The other benefit of knowing their greatest character strengths is that they can combine Build My Strengths with Think Things Through. You can engage in valuable discussions with your child about this. If they are facing any challenge, they can Think Things Through to identify strategies they could use to respond that use their character strengths. This will give your child greater confidence.

As your child is learning more effective strategies to reduce the likelihood they will be treated badly and to respond effectively to situations if they have been treated badly, they may fail. This is the key place where the magic word "yet" can help. They are developing strategies to respond more effectively. Those strategies have not been effective *yet*. When they Embrace Failure they can identify what has not worked, and then Think Things Through to figure out some better strategies given what they have learned.

Focus on the Good

The wonderful power of focusing on the good is that this strategy will increase your child's happiness. This will also increase their ability to keep their personal power, especially when things get tough. The student who bullies your child wants your child to feel bad. This is how this student takes your child's "power points." When your child daily practices focusing on the good, this creates neural pathways that will increase your child's happiness. This will reduce the power of the other student to be able to cause your child to feel bad.

Be Mindful

The student who treats your child badly wants your child to overreact and to appear weak and helpless. If your child publicly overreacts and shows that they are upset, this rewards the student who is engaging in bullying. This also attracts the attention of other students. These other students are able to see that the hurtful student caused your child to lose control – to lose their "power points." In the minds of those who are hurtful, this proves their power over your child to others. When your child has the ability to keep their cool by not overreacting when someone is hurtful to them, they can better keep their personal power.

Being mindful and practicing calmness on a daily basis is of exceptional importance. The daily practice of meditation using all three meditation methods will help to form the neural pathways in your child's brain so that when they need to keep their cool in a challenging situation, they can more effectively do so. This is why including this daily mindfulness practice is so important.

Keep My Personal Power

When your child can keep their personal power by holding themself tall, others are much less likely to even think of being hurtful to them. Think about how your child appears when walking or moving down the hall at school. Does your child convey the appearance of a young person who has personal power? Or does your child walk or move through the school with their head down and shoulders hunched – "feeling small?"

When your child can control their thinking they can choose not to give any power to others to make them feel bad, and this also allows them to keep their personal power. Releasing and letting go is an important strategy after someone has been hurtful. Your child cannot change what happened. If they hold onto the pain of this incident, the only person they are harming is themselves.

Think Things Through

Sometimes, when someone is being hurtful, your child will have to quickly Think Things Through to figure out how to get out of this situation. Then, after your child has gotten away, it will be necessary to Think Things Through to decide whether there is anything they need to do in response to what happened.

It will be really helpful if you and your child could collaboratively Think Things Through in advance to plan strategies that use their strengths for common situations when someone is hurtful. Your child may also need to Think Things Through to identify any ways they may be behaving that appear to be resulting in other students treating them badly. While not blaming themselves, they can identify some ways that use their strengths to change their behavior. In addition, if your child has been hurtful to another, they must Think Things Through to identify their motivations and determine how they can remedy the harm.

Positively Powerful in Hurtful Situations

The following is the combined process to use the Positively Powerful strategies to respond in those situations where someone has been hurtful to them:

- **Keep My Cool.** Things just got tough. Your child should breathe deeply and slowly to keep their cool. It is very important that they do not show a negative reaction.
- **Hold Myself Tall.** Your child should immediately hold themselves tall. This is a way to both demonstrate to others that they have personal power and help them to feel more powerful. Even if they do not currently feel powerful, holding themselves tall will cause them to feel more powerful. They can "fake it" by holding themselves tall, which will help them "make it" by feeling more powerful.
- **Control My Thinking.** Your child should immediately think to themselves, "I am worthy. I deserve respect. I choose not to give that person the power to make me feel bad. That person is showing who they are, not who I am." It is likely helpful if your child remembers that the vast majority of other students do not like to see people being hurtful. Even if these other students are not brave enough to stand up to the one engaged in bullying, they are not thinking bad thoughts about your child.
- **Think Things Through.** Your child will need to quickly decide what to do at this immediate point in time. Options will vary based on the people, situation, and environment. Your child could:
  - **Ignore this person.** If your child chooses to simply ignore this person, they should basically ignore what happened, hold themselves tall, with their head high, and move away with pride. If they are in a place where they cannot leave, they could envision the other person as being not present and try to start a conversation with someone else.
  - **Calmly tell this person to stop.** Your child might choose to calmly, but firmly, tell this person to stop. They should not get into an argument. If this person continues to be hurtful, they should move away holding themselves tall.
  - **Ask a kind question.** Your child could possibly ask a kind question, such as: "Are you having a bad day? Is there something I could do to help?" Or they could ask, "Have I done something hurtful to you? If so, I am sorry." Reacting

by being kind to the person who is being hurtful to you may help to shift the dynamics and will have a favorable impact on any witnesses.

 – **Go to a safe place.** If your child can, they should hold themselves tall and go to a place where there is a school staff member who would be in a position to witness and step in to stop any continuing harm. However, your child should not look like they are complaining to that staff member. This could be interpreted as "tattling." They should just go to a place where there is an adult who would likely see if the hurtful behavior continues and would step in to help.

 – **Capture and report.** If the hurtful behavior is on social media, your child should capture an image of the post and report abuse to the site. They should keep their hands off the keyboard until they are calm and have thought things through about how to respond. When or if your child does post, they need to make sure they appear calm and logical. They must show no signs that they are upset.

 – **Own it and fix it.** If your child has been hurtful to this other student, your child needs to own and fix what they have done. More on this in Chapter 7.

- **Make a Positive Connection to Think Things Through.** As soon as possible, your child should connect with you, a friend, or another trusted adult to receive support. At this time, your child and you, their friend, or other trusted adult can collaboratively Think Things Through about what additional responses might be necessary. Many times, you or another adult may want to step in to protect your child. This could also take your child's personal power away. Your child should ask you or another trusted adult to first try to help them by providing "invisible guidance." Invisible guidance is assistance provided to help them to respond on their own – without anyone knowing that someone else is helping them. A friend can also provide invisible guidance. It is especially effective for you, a friend, or another trusted adult to provide invisible guidance in online situations. You, their friend, or other adult can be sitting right there with them as they craft an online response.

- **Keep My Personal Power**. Documenting what happened is a very important action that will be helpful to allow your child to keep their personal power. Your child should write down what happened, where this occurred, and who else was present. They should specifically note if any staff member witnessed this and what this staff member did. If your child did not do this at the time, work with them on this documentation when they get home from school. If you do eventually report the situation to the school, this immediate documentation will be really helpful. You and your child should make sure to capture and save any hurtful material posted on social media.

- **Control Their Thinking and Release and Let Go.** Your child must remember that they could not control what happened to them. But they do have the ability to control what they think about themselves and how they respond. Likely, at this point in time, thinking about "forgiveness" will not be a wise or possible.

But finding a way to Release and Let Go of the pain of what happened in the future by focusing on their positive connections and strengths will be helpful.

- **Focus on the Good.** Encourage your child to think about five recent things that happened that made them feel really good. Alternatively, they could take out a pen and paper and write down five happy things at that time. Your child should take the time to enrich and absorb these good feelings. If your child starts to feel bad, encourage them to look at their list of good things.

Engaging in Conflict Resolution

It is helpful for your child to have skills in conflict resolution. Effective conflict resolution is grounded in the ability to Think Things Through with another person to achieve a positive resolution. Initially, your child must be able to "Tell Their Story" by clearly identifying how they are feeling and the reasons. "I am feeling [name emotion] because [identify reason]." They also need empathy to identify how the other person might be feeling and the reasons – to "Learn the Story" of the other person. Having this insight then provides the foundation for effective reflective listening. "I sense that you are feeling [name feeling] because [identify reason]."

Effective conflict resolution involves these steps:

- **Keep their cool.** Hopefully, this will enable the other young person to also remain or become calm.
- **Respectfully initiate.** Start by saying, "When you [identify action], this makes me feel [name emotion]. Can we talk about this so that we can move past this and maintain a positive relationship?"
- **Reflectively listen.** When the other person responds, your child should respond in a way that reflects how this other person feels and the reason using reflective listening. You child should seek to "Learn The Story" of the other person and then reflect this back to them. "It sounds like you are feeling [name emotion], because [identify reason]. Am I understanding this properly? My reaction to what you have said is [name emotion and identify reason]." It will be helpful if your child can continue to respond to this other young person's statements in a reflective manner. This is the best way to support that young person in feeling heard, being able to express their feelings and reasons, and achieving a resolution.
- **Respectfully disengage, if necessary.** If these communications have not resulted in a clearing of the air so the other person is also calm, it is best at this point for your child to say, "I am not sure we can resolve this conflict at this time. Hopefully, we can talk in the future to do so." Then, walk away holding themselves tall.

- **Collaboratively Think Things Through.** If the discussion has allowed the emotions and reasons to be clear and both are calm, it is time to shift to jointly thinking things through. "What could we do so that we both feel good and appreciate each other?" Your child could suggest some strategies and invite the other to suggest strategies. The discussion could also reflect on thinking about what might happen if that strategy were to be selected.
- **Resolve.** Your child could then suggest a possible resolution. "Why don't we try to [describe strategy]. If this does not work, we can talk again."

After any situation where your child has engaged in conflict resolution with another young person, it will be really helpful for your child to frequently intentionally Reach Out to Be Kind to that young person. This will help to create positive feelings that will continue the resolution of the conflict.

Responding to Hurtful Acts That Were Not Intended to Cause Harm

Your child may experience a time when someone says or does something hurtful, but it appears that there was not an intent to be hurtful.[4] Nevertheless, your child may feel bad because of what this person said or did. As discussed, this may be considered a microaggression, although the term "aggression" is likely not appropriate. If your child is a member of a minority identity group, what the other person said or did or the way your child feels may be related to their status as a minority. However, microaggressions can occur to anyone when they feel a hurtful impact, but it does not appear the other person intended to be hurtful.

As mentioned earlier, when your child feels upset by something another person said or did that does not appear to be intended to be hurtful, but did have a hurtful impact on your child, the first thing your child needs to do is to Think Things Through. The first step in thinking things through is to make sure that you have an accurate understanding of the situation. Your child's reaction may be based on what just happened or may be based on negative situations or messages from the past, the memories of which are stored in their unconscious. Your child is advised to ask themselves, "Is my reaction to what this person said or did based on what they actually said or did, or is my reaction based on my past experiences or messages I have received?"

After your child engages in this analysis, they have a decision to make: Should they have the serenity to Release and Let Go because the situation is not that

---

4 Lilienfeld, S.O. (2017). Microaggressions: strong claims, inadequate evidence. *Perspectives on Psychological Science* 12: 138–169.

serious or because trying to communicate with this other person might cause greater concerns? Or should they have the courage and strength to respectfully approach this person?

If your child decides to respectfully approach this other person, this should be done in a conflict resolution manner, with a slight twist on how this is introduced to the other person. Remember, this other person does not, at the start, realize that there is a conflict or that they did something that was perceived by your child as being hurtful. Initiating the conversation can proceed like this: "Hey I would like to talk with you. I do not think that when you said or did [identify action] you were intending to be hurtful. However, when you [identify action] I felt [name emotion] because [identify reason]. I would like talk with you about this because I would like to have a positive relationship with you. Can we talk?"

Following this, your child is advised to use the above conflict-resolution and reflective-listening approach to engage with the other person. The reason it is really important for your child to respond with reflective listening is that they just essentially challenged this other person as being hurtful. Reflective listening will support a positive reaction by this other person if their first response has been negative. This is the best way to allow the other person to feel as though they have been heard and reduces the potential they will become angry.

If your child does decide to respectfully approach the other person, this is either going to work or not work. If the other person becomes angry and it does not appear that a positive resolution is possible, your child can say, "I am sorry, I was just hoping to bring this to your attention to see if we could discuss it so we could maintain a positive relationship. But that appears to not be possible at this time, so I will just wish you a good day. Maybe we can talk in the future." And walk away holding themselves tall.

If your child is able to achieve a positive resolution, they could say, "I knew there was a risk approaching you about this. I want to thank you for how you responded." The best thing to do after this, to maintain the positive resolution, is for your child to intentionally Reach Out to Be Kind to this other person with some frequency.

Assert-with-care Communications

The following is a creative strategy you and your child might want to follow. It is a strategy to communicate with the student who is being hurtful. This approach may also be effective if a school staff member is being hurtful to your child. Keep in mind though that this approach might not work. Your child should have the controlling voice over whether this strategy should be attempted. Embracing failure may be necessary.

This assert-with-care communication should not be done face to face. This should be done using private digital messaging. There are several reasons for this:

- **Collaboratively Think Things Through.** Your child, with you by their side providing "invisible guidance," can take the time to write a message carefully before it is sent. Your child, again with your invisible guidance, can also take time to carefully write a response if the other student responds. If the situation involves a hurtful staff member, you and your child should decide whether the message should come from you or your child.
- **Private communications.** Communicating with this student privately, hopefully without this student's supportive friends being around, might open up an avenue for resolution. If this student responds in a hurtful manner, your child is not yet again in a public place with someone saying disparaging things in front of witnesses. However, this student could share your child's message. This is why your child has to be really careful about what they write.
- **Digital evidence.** Digital communications are retained in a digital format. If your child or you can obtain digital evidence that points to the fact that this student or staff member was hurtful, this can be really powerful. These private digital messages can be saved and shown to your child's principal and others who are brought into the resolution. The principal can also share these communications with this student's parents. This is a great way to get beyond the "my child would never do that" parental response.

The fact that digital communications are retained in a digital format is why this approach could be very effective – and is the most important reason you and your child need to be really careful in what is written and sent. There is an old adage from the early days of the internet that, when you post or send something, you should think about how it would feel if what you sent or posted appeared on the front page of the newspaper. Because, unbeknownst to the person you are communicating with, you intend to use any helpful evidence you obtain to show to others to get the hurtful behavior to stop, your child's or your communications must always be calm and respectful.

If you can gain digital evidence to support your claim that this student or staff member is being hurtful to your child, this can be very helpful in getting the behavior to stop. This can be especially helpful if this hurtful student is one who school staff does not think causes problems or is a staff member.

Digital Communications to a Hurtful Student

Start your message to a student like this: "Today you [describe what happened]. If I have done anything to you that has caused you to treat me like this, please let me know and I will stop and apologize. I just want you to stop treating me in this way."

If this student made a mistake and did not intend to be hurtful or was sorry afterwards, reaching out in this way could very well lead this student to decide to

make things right. Note that in your child's first communication they have indicated an appropriate path. It is likely best if your child uses a reflective listening
approach in response to the reply by this other student.

If this student does not correct what your child said about what happened, then
you have obtained evidence from this student of what happened. If the student
denies this happened, indicate that others saw this and repeat again your request
that they stop doing this. "There were other students who saw what you did. I am
just asking that you stop."

If this student intends to continue to be hurtful, your child will likely get a hurtful message back. Your child must realize in advance that this may occur and not
overreact by sending an aggressive message in response. The fact that your child
respectfully tried to read out and received aggression in response also will be very
helpful evidence to share with the school.

Do not continue these messages beyond two or three messages. Either this
approach will work quickly or it will not work at all. If this approach does not
seem to be working, your child should end the communications by saying, "Well,
I just thought I would respectfully try to get this to stop, but this does not appear
to be working. So I will stop messaging you."

If the student continues to send hurtful messages your child should not respond,
but should definitely save the messages. In addition, after these communications,
your child should keep watch for this student's public posts. If this student publicly posts anything about your child after this, be sure to capture this as an image
and file an abuse report with the site or app.

After communicating in this way, you and your child will have evidence to document that what happened and this student's response to your child's calm and
respectful request that the other student stop being hurtful. Your child will be able
to demonstrate that they calmly and respectfully asked this other student to stop.

It is also possible that these communications will help to resolve the problem. If
these communications are effective, the best thing to do after this, to maintain the
positive resolution, is for your child to intentionally Reach Out to Be Kind to this
other person with some frequency. Your child must always keep in mind that it
may be necessary to share these communications with the principal. Therefore,
your child's messages must always be totally respectful.

Digital Communications to a Hurtful Staff Member

Depending on the staff member and the situation, it may be best that you initiate
the message to them. Alternatively, your child might want to do this. Again, be
absolutely, totally respectful in all of your communications. You want to be able to
show that you are communicating with this staff member in a respectful manner,
despite the fact you think they are being hurtful to your child.

An initial message from you could be: "I was told that today you [describe what
happened]. It would help me to know your thoughts on what is happening and

why. If there are some things my child is doing in your class that are being disruptive, I would appreciate knowing. We will work on some strategies to address this. Please help me understand why you appear to be treating my child in this hurtful manner. My child is really sad and upset and does not want to come to school. I am interested in your thoughts on what is happening and how this can be addressed. Thanks in advance."

Recall that there appear to be two primary reasons why school staff members are hurtful to students. One is that they are having challenges maintaining positive behavior in the classroom. Your child's behavior may be an initiating cause of how they are being treated by this staff member. However, even if your child has challenges in their behavior, there is no justification for the staff member to treat them in a hurtful manner. The other possible challenge is that the staff member is being hurtful in a way that is grounded in inappropriate bias. Either way, you should be able to obtain some evidence of the basis upon which the staff member is treating your child from their response.

The staff member may respond using some forms of rationalizations, as were discussed in Chapter 2. Most common would be statements such as: "Your child is [describe behavior]. I was merely correcting his/her/their behavior." "I am just maintaining appropriate behavior in the classroom." "Your child is overreacting." "I was just joking."

Your next response must incorporate the principles of reflective listening, as discussed in Chapter 5. "Based on your response, it seems to me that you are [identify emotion you perceive the staff member is expressing] because [reflect back the reason or reasons that were provided]. Can you help me understand how [describe hurtful behavior of the staff member] is helpful in dealing with this situation?" You might have several rounds of back-and-forth communications. In every message you send, continue the same reflective pattern: "You are feeling [identify emotion] because [describe reason]. Can you help me understand how you think [describe their behavior] is helpful?"

These communications may help to clear up what is happening. If not, after several exchanges, you can end with a message that suggests further discussions with the principal. Remember, because showing these messages to a principal may be necessary to get the situation resolved, it is imperative that your communications be totally respectful.

Start a Positivity Ripple

Remember one key to positivity through a Focus on the Good – a focus on five positive experiences can help to undo the harm of one negative experience. If your child overreacts after someone treats them badly, they lose power to the person who was hurtful. But if your child goes positively powerful they can gain even greater personal power.

A story of an amazing incident demonstrates the power of responding being treated badly in a positively powerful manner. A high school student, Caitlin Prater-Haacke, was under attack at school and on social media. Instead of getting into an argument online or feeling really bad, she got a batch of Post-it notes and some markers. She spent the weekend writing positive messages on those Post-it notes. On Monday, she placed these positive-message Post-it notes on every locker in her school.[5] Think in terms of personal power. Who won this power struggle? Who got the most "power points?" Who is the Thriver? Caitlin's TedTalk and story would be good for you and your child to read and watch.[6]

Your child can create a "positivity ripple." Think of when you toss a small stone into water. The impact of the stone sends ripples across the surface of the water. These ripples go far beyond where the stone entered. Your child can create a ripple of positivity and also inspire positivity in others. Because one good act often inspires countless others, the results of that positivity will likely ripple back to your child.

These are some ways your child could start a positivity ripple after they have been treated badly:

- **Thankful or gratitude meme.** Your child can find and post a meme on their social media profile about thankfulness or gratitude. Then, your child can publicly note the things they are thankful for and the people they are grateful to have in their life. Start with this statement, "I learned today that there needs to be more positivity in the world." Your child can also ask others to add in the comments the things and people they are thankful for.
- **Positivity through personal messaging.** Encourage your child to send a personal message to five or more of their friends. Write this to them: "I am starting a positivity ripple. Please write to five or more of your friends and tell them what you appreciate about them. What I appreciate about you is [describe]. Let us see how far we can make this positivity ripple spread." This positivity ripple can also be done in person by writing notes to five people. However, likely it is more powerful to do this on social media, because many others are more likely to see this.

---

5 Grainger, C. (2014). Student responds to bullying with positive Post-its, school punishes her for littering. *Toronto Sun*, October 7. https://torontosun.com/2014/10/07/student-responds-to-bullying-with-positive-post-its-school-punishes-her-for-littering (accessed 1 August 2024).
6 Haake, C. (2015). How one teen took a stand against bullying (and ended up going viral) with a Post-it note. *Teen Vogue*, June 8; Haake, C. (2015). How to make positivity stick. Tedx Talks (YouTube channel). https://youtu.be/cElB84gf6uc (accessed 1 August 2024).

What your child will accomplish by taking either of these steps is twofold: it will create a shift in the focus of their thinking to good friends and good things that are happening for them for which they are grateful, and it will demonstrate to anyone who sees these postings that the student who was hurtful did not gain any "power points" from them. Your child is publicly demonstrating that they have the ability to Rise Above Bullying and contribute to positive things happening in the world.

7

Positively Powerful Strategies for Those Being Hurtful

Stop, Own It, and Fix It

No child is perfect. They all make mistakes. Sometimes, they act in a way that others perceive as being hurtful when they really did not intend to be hurtful. Sometimes, they trigger and overreact and in doing so are hurtful to others. Sometimes, they are just plain hurtful. Sometimes, someone has been hurtful to them and they retaliated.

In all of these kinds of situations, generally what we as parents hope is that our child quickly accepts personal responsibility and takes steps to make things right. These are the issues that will be discussed in this chapter.

Basis of Hurtful Behavior

The reasons why a young person may be hurtful can vary. The most common motives for being hurtful were discussed in Chapter 2. If your child is engaging in hurtful behavior, ask your child about their motives using this list as a start. This analysis may help your child find the best path to accept personal responsibility and take steps to make things right. The following are the three most common motivations.

Feel Out of Control

Sometimes young people treat others badly because they are feeling out of control in their own lives. These young people are the "hurt people hurting people" who were discussed in Chapter 1. They may be angry, feel powerless, and want to gain

Rise Above Bullying: Empower and Advocate for Your Child, First Edition. Nancy E. Willard.
© 2025 John Wiley & Sons, Inc. Published 2025 by John Wiley & Sons, Inc.

some level of control. Others may have frequently been hurtful to them, so they are hurtful back.

These young people may have experienced significant challenges in their lives and, as a result, they trigger. This then grows to an outburst – and while they are out of control they are hurtful. If they continue on this path, they will not have a happy or successful life.

If this describes your child, the Positively Powerful strategies in Chapter 5 will assist you in supporting your child to overcome these challenges and changing their behavior. It is very important to get the hurt that is being directed at your child to stop.

Retaliation – Often Impulsive

Other times, young people are hurtful directly in response to someone being hurtful to them. Often this retaliation is impulsive, but other times it is planned. These young people can also bring their friends into these retaliatory acts.

Want to Be Considered "Popular" and "Cool"

Some young people are striving to be at the top of the school's "social ladder." These young people were discussed in Chapter 2. They think that putting down and excluding those who some might consider to be "misfits" is a way for them to gain social status and power. Other times, they are hurtful to those who they consider to be "rivals" for a romantic interest, place on the team, or other desired outcome. They think that others will respect them if they demonstrate their power over others in this way. These young people may not even think they are being hurtful. They may rationalize that they are just maintaining "social order."

Two Types of Leadership

If your child is being hurtful in an effort to improve their social status, it is necessary to consider the behavior of those who want to be perceived as leaders – those seeking higher social status. Not every young person wants to be a "leader." Many young people are really not all that focused on where they are on the "social ladder" of their school. They are perfectly okay with just doing their own thing.

However, some young people do have a strong interest in being considered a leader. They desire a higher social status. If your child wants to be perceived to be a leader, what kind of a leader will they be? If your child is more of a follower, what kind of a leader will your child choose to follow?

From the business research literature, we can learn that there are two paths people can take to achieve a position of leadership. These two different strategies are called "dominance" and "prestige."[1] This is a helpful description:

> Dominance and prestige represent evolved strategies used to navigate social hierarchies. Dominance is a strategy through which people gain and maintain social rank by using coercion, intimidation, and power. Prestige is a strategy through which people gain and maintain social rank by displaying valued knowledge and skills and earning respect.[2]

Employees may act in compliance with dominance leaders and view them as powerful. They may be respected and even admired. But they are not liked. Prestige leaders who focus on building positive community in their businesses gain respect by displaying knowledge, skill, and talent and engaging in actions as a compassionate leader of their community. People look up to these kinds of compassionate leaders.

Young people also display these differences in leadership style. Ask your child to consider those students who are perceived as leaders in their school. Which students who are considered leaders by some regularly put down and exclude others? Which students engage in battles with rivals for athletic positions or dating partners? Which students demonstrate leadership by being consistently kind and respectful to other students? Which students are contributing to a positive school community? Is your child considered a leader in their social group? What kind of a leader is your child? Is your child following the leadership of another student? What kind of a leadership approach is used by the student whose leadership your child is following?

Rationalizations

Rationalizations, discussed in Chapter 2, are the excuses people tell themselves or others to justify that their behavior was appropriate – even when it clearly was not.[3] Students who are hurtful frequently use these rationalizations.

- **Spin it.** "I was just joking around." "It was a prank."
- **Deny personal responsibility.** "Someone else started it." "It wasn't my fault."

1 Cheng, J.T., Tracy, J.L., Foulsham, T. et al. (2013). Two ways to the top: evidence that dominance and prestige are distinct yet viable avenues to social rank and influence. *Journal of Personality and Social Psychology* 104: 103–125.

2 Maner, J.K. (2017). Dominance and prestige: a tale of two hierarchies. *Current Directions in Psychological Science* 26 (6): 096372141771432. https://doi.org/10.1177/0963721417714323.

3 Bandura, A. (1991). Social cognition theory of moral thought and action. In: *Handbook of moral behavior and development*, vol. 1 (ed. W.M. Kurtines and J.L. Gewirtz), 45–96. Lawrence Erlbaum.

- **Deny the harm.** "What happened wasn't that bad." "They are just overreacting."
- **Blame the other.** "They deserved it." "They do not belong here." "If they would stop [describe behavior], this would not happen."

Discuss with your child how people create rationalizations as excuses for their hurtful behavior. Be on the lookout for examples of people using excuses to rationalize hurtful behavior. Pay attention to news stories. Especially when some leader in our society is accused of doing something inappropriate, it is probable that they will create rationalizations to excuse their behavior.

If your child has been hurtful, listen carefully. You will likely hear one or more of the rationalizations above. In using these rationalizations, your child can try to maintain that what they did was appropriate or excusable.

You can respond by saying something like, "That sounds to me like an excuse. You know that our family's values are to treat others with respect. In this situation, you acted in a way that is not in line with our family's values. In order to try to rationalize that what you did was okay, you are creating an excuse. Can you tell me which kind of rationalization you used? Did you try to spin it, deny you had any responsibility, deny the harm, or blame the other person?" As your child tries to explain, engage in reflective listening so that they can hear your identification of their emotions and the reasons. As your child "tells their story" are they rationalizing that it was okay for them to do something that is not in accord with your family's values?

Be Positively Powerful Strategies

If your child is about to be hurtful or has been hurtful, they will hopefully choose to Stop, Own It, and Fix It. This is how the Positively Powerful strategies relate to this choice.

Make Positive Connections

In Chapter 4, insight was shared on how, during their teen years, your child can be highly influenced by their peers. They are going through a process of deciding what their personal values are and how their relationships with others are supporting those values. Do a friendship assessment with your child that considers the values of their friends. These are some questions you can ask your child:

- "Do your current friends share your personal values and our family's values on how others should be treated?"
- "If your friend is being hurtful, will you join in and support your friend?"
- "If your friend is being hurtful, how could you encourage your friend to be more kind to others?"

Reach Out to Be Kind

If your child frequently or occasionally treats others badly, the practice of reaching out to be kind can be really helpful to shift the way they interact with others. In discussions with your child, especially focus on how they feel when they Reach Out to Be Kind. Ask your child to think about how people respond to them when they were kind. Even the simple practice of holding the door open for someone will likely yield a smile and thanks in return.

Strive to increase your child's engagement in acts in service to others. This will engage them in positive activities with others where they will receive positive feedback for the positive efforts they are making.

Build My Strengths

When your child focuses on their character strengths and doing what makes them proud to be them, they are less likely to want to try to take power from others by being hurtful to them. There will be times when your child makes a mistake and is hurtful. When your child embraces failure, they can realize that they were hurtful and what they need to do is accept personal responsibility and remedy the harm.

Focus on the Good

When your child focuses on the good and are thankful for what is happening in their life, they will be less inclined to want to mess up those positive feelings by being hurtful to someone.

Be Mindful

Often times, young people are hurtful to others because something hurtful has happened to them. If your child cannot keep their cool, they may trigger and act fast in a hurtful way without thinking.

Taking times during the day to Practice Calmness through mediation can help your child build the neural pathways to support their ability to remain calm. When your child knows how to keep their cool when something starts to trigger them, this will enable them to stop themself from being hurtful when something hurtful has happened to them.

Keep My Personal Power

When your child keeps their personal power by holding themselves tall and controlling their thinking, they will feel less inclined to strive to take someone else's power by treating them badly. When they Release and Let Go of their anger, they are less likely to respond to others in an angry way.

Think Things Through

Have frequent conversations with your child, encouraging them to Think Things Through about their personal values. Every time you hear of an incident where someone has been hurtful, ask your child why they would choose to not be hurtful. The Think Things Through strategy can be very helpful if someone has been hurtful to them and they need to figure out how they can respond in a positively powerful manner, rather than being hurtful back.

Stop

The approach I recommend when a young person has been hurtful is to encourage them to Stop, Own It, and Fix It.

Focus on Your Personal Values

Underlying a decision to Stop, Own It, and Fix It are your child's personal values. Ask your child why they would choose not to be hurtful to another. These are the kinds of questions you can ask:

- "How you would feel if someone did this to you or someone you care about?"
- "How would you feel about yourself because of how this reflects on you?"
- "Is it against your personal values and our family's values to be hurtful to others?"
- "How would another person feel if you are hurtful to them?"
- "What would the people who deeply care about you think about your hurtful actions?"
- "What would your friends think about your actions if you were hurtful?" (If their friends would be supportive or encourage them, then it is time to find a new set of friends.)
- "How would being hurtful damage your reputation, relationships, and opportunities?"
- "If you are hurtful to someone, do you think you might or should get into trouble at school?"

All of these reasons are good reasons to not be hurtful. Just like everyone has different character strengths, we all also have different reasons why we would not want to be hurtful to others.

Avoid Retaliation

Why would your child choose not to be hurtful to someone who has been hurtful to them? Is their original thinking in response to the above questions still valid? Do these reasons still reflect their personal values? Help your child recognize that if someone is hurtful to them, they have the power to respond in a powerfully positive manner, rather than doing something that will reflect badly on them by being hurtful to others.

There are some who will tell your child that if someone is hurtful to them and they do not fight back, they are a wimp. Remember, this is the thinking that gets young people sent to die in battle – just to protect the dignity of their country's leaders.

Think about what might happen in school. The danger for anyone who is being treated badly is that, if they retaliate, they are often the ones who end up getting into trouble. Very often those who are being hurtful engage in subtle hurtful acts that are not obvious to school staff. The pain of experiencing these hurtful acts builds up until the targeted student triggers and engages in retaliation. The student who was being treated badly and retaliated then gets punished because their response caused a substantial disruption.

If someone has treated your child badly and they feel like retaliating, this is a strategy they can use to avoid retaliating and still keep their personal power:

- **Keep Their Cool.** As your child increases their self-regulation skills they will be less likely to engage in impulsive action in response to being treated badly. Keeping their cool helps your child to give themself the time to Think Things Through, rather than acting without thinking. "I can keep my cool when things get tough."
- **Keep Their Personal Power.** By recognizing that they cannot control what happens to them, they can only control how they respond, they realize that they can maintain control of their actions and not act in a way that is against their personal values or could get them into trouble. "If someone is hurtful, I will hold myself tall and remain in control of how I think about myself and act."
- **Embrace Failure.** Embracing failure also means knowing that not only can you change, but other people also can change. Just because someone was hurtful does not mean they will continue to be hurtful. When your child knows that people can change they can understand that holding out for a more positive resolution is a better path. "If I respond in a positive manner, this can help the other student to change and not be hurtful to me in the future."
- **Release and Let Go.** If someone has harmed your child and they hold on to the feelings of hurt, this person will continue to keep your child's personal power. By acknowledging the pain that they felt, but deciding to Release and Let Go of this pain, they can keep their personal power.

- **Think Things Through.** When your child can Think Things Through to figure out what to do if someone has been hurtful, this helps them to identify a positive response.
- **Make a Positive Connection.** When your child connects with a good friend or trusted adult this will facilitate obtaining personal support. "I can make a positive connection with a good friend or trusted adult who will provide me with support."

Own It and Fix It

If your child has made a mistake and was hurtful to someone, help them to realize they can change, make better choices, and make things better. They can Own It and Fix It. If they Own It and Fix It, this will reduce the potential that this other person will retaliate against them. In addition, this will help to repair any damage they did to their reputation by being hurtful.

In the survey I conducted in 2015, the majority of students admired those who had been hurtful but who then took actions to Own It and Fix It. Ask your child: "If you knew someone who was hurtful and they owned it and fixed it by accepting personal responsibility and taking steps to remedy the harm, what would you think about this person?"

The bottom line is that if your child was hurtful to another, they also harmed themself. By owning it and fixing it they are both remedying the harm they caused to another and the harm they caused to themself. Here is a way your child can Own It and Fix It:

- **Embrace Failure.** When your child embraces failure, they realize that they can change. They know they can learn from their mistakes and make better choices. They can make things better for someone they treated badly.
- **Think Things Through.** Your child can Think Things Through about the actions they took and any rationalizations they might have made. Did they think of this as just a joke, when it really was not? Did they think that since everybody does this it is okay for them to be hurtful? Did someone else encourage them? Have they suggested to others that what they did was not that bad? Did they think this person deserved to be treated badly? After your child considers the rationalizations they made for their actions, encourage them to dig deeper and think about what is going on inside of them. Figure out what their motivations were that led them to treat someone badly. Are they also being treated badly? Did they follow the lead of another young person who was being hurtful and who encouraged them to join in? Were they trying to get attention? Were they retaliating? Did they act without thinking?

- **Embrace Failure.** Encourage your child to Own It by embracing failure and acknowledging that what they did was wrong. Even if they were retaliating because someone treated them badly, their hurtful response was also wrong. If they accept personal responsibility that what they did was wrong, hopefully the other person will also accept personal responsibility. Embracing failure and accepting personal responsibility is a challenge for many.
- **Think Things Through and Reach Out to Be Kind.** Fix It by taking steps to make things right. This can include a number of actions, so it is necessary to Think Things Through to figure out how best to Fix It. Acknowledging to the other person that what they did was wrong and telling the person they were hurtful to that they are sorry is the one of the best ways to Reach Out to Be Kind to this person who they harmed.
- **Make a Positive Connection.** Your child can make positive connections by telling their friends and trusted adults how they made a mistake, but they stopped, owned it, and fixed it and that they are making a personal commitment not to be hurtful again.
- **Be Proud.** When your child owns it and fixes it they should absolutely Be Proud.

8

Positively Powerful Strategies for Close Relationships

Enhancing Important Relationships in a Positively Powerful Way

Healthy relationships are important for everyone. This is why Make Positive Connections is the first strategy in the Positively Powerful strategies.

Healthy close relationships include relationships with best friends, as well as dating partners.[1] Healthy close relationships provide your child with opportunities for many positive experiences that affect their well-being. It takes energy, time, and care to develop and maintain healthy close relationships. Unfortunately, relationship break-ups can be followed by bullying.

During your child's teen years, they will become strongly focused on forming close relationships with both friends and dating partners. Relationships made during these years can be very special. However, as your child grows and discovers who they are and the path they want to take in their life, these relationships will also change. Sometimes, they will end.

Your child is in learning mode. They are learning how to form, grow, change, and end close relationships. The lessons they learn during their teen years can help them form, grow, change, and end close relationships in a happy and healthy manner throughout their life.

---

1 Centers for Disease Control (2024). Dating matters. https://www.cdc.gov/intimate-partner-violence/php/datingmatters/?CDC_AAref_Val=https://www.cdc.gov/violenceprevention/intimatepartnerviolence/datingmatters/index.html. Insight in this chapter was derived from the excellent resources on this site. This insight was expanded to address both close friendships and dating relationships (accessed 1 August 2024).

Foundations of Close Relationships

Your child's emotional health and well-being depends heavily on their ability to form close relationships. Healthy relationships start with effective communication, honesty, respect, sharing, and trust. A healthy relationship should be based on the belief that both members of the relationship are equally in a position of control. Decision making about issues related to the relationship should be shared equally.

In healthy relationships, it is important that your child to maintains the freedom to be themself. Sometimes, when young people start to date they want to spend all of their time with their new friend or partner. It is important they maintain their individual identity and continue to do the things they enjoy with people other than a close friend or dating partner. It is important they also spend time with family and other friends. These family members and other friends can be a valuable source of support, especially if they experience difficult or stressful times in their relationship or if their relationship ends.

Establishing mutually acceptable boundaries is important in any relationship. Romantic partners should never pressure the other to do things they have not agreed to do. Mutual respect means not only giving respect to a partner, but also expecting respect for oneself.

Sometimes, when teens want to be in a relationship with someone, they are hurtful to others who they perceive also might also want a close relationship with this person. Bullying or hurtful "drama" is often based on dating relationship desires. A person who is hurtful to others to gain a relationship with your child is not a good choice for your child. This person is demonstrating that they can and will be hurtful to achieve what they want. This will likely include being hurtful and controlling over your child to get what they want.

Healthy or Unhealthy Relationships

Communication: Essential to Healthy Relationships

A healthy relationship cannot exist without effective communication. Effective communication is necessary to make decisions that help the relationship to grow, solve problems, and resolve conflict. Effective communication is a shared responsibility that involves both sending and receiving messages. Communication in relationships can sometimes become complicated. Communication about really important issues is generally best done face to face. In this way, both people are able to better understand what the other is saying and to communicate their own thoughts.

In today's age of digital communications things have changed. Many teens spend a lot of time communicating with friends and dating partners via messaging. This form of communication can have some heightened risks because their ability to notice non-verbal cues has been eliminated.

Characteristics of Healthy Relationships

These are the characteristics of healthy relationships:

> Being caring and loyal. Trusting their friend. Communicating their feelings and desires. Supporting their friend during challenging times. Holding shared beliefs and values. Sharing common interests and goals. Recognizing and respecting differences in each other. Accepting and respecting each other's needs. Being honest with each other. Listening to each other. Using respectful language. Understanding the other person's wishes and feelings. Being willing to compromise. Enjoying being with each other. Laughing together.

Evidence of an Unhealthy Relationship

The evidence that your child is involved with someone in an unhealthy relationship is when this other person:

> Makes degrading and insulting comments. Ignores their interests. Tries to isolate them and prevent them from spending time with family and other friends. Tries to dominate, control, and direct their activities. Engages in threats and intimidation. Encourages them to participate in unwanted, harmful, or illegal behavior. Is physically abusive, such as slapping, pushing, or punching them. Demands nude images, which may then be shared with others. Engages in sexual assault, including unwanted touching or coerced sex. Takes or controls their money or their spending. Exploits them to get what they want. Is hurtful, then loving, hurtful, then loving.

I have created a relationship assessment that is on the Rise Above Bullying website. If you have concerns about the quality of a relationship your child is in, you might provide this to your child and suggest they complete it. Your child could then talk with you or another trusted adult or a friend about what this assessment indicates.

Consent

Consent is an important concept in any close relationship. This includes both a close friendship and dating relationship. For any joint activity your child intends to engage in with their close friend or dating partner, consent is necessary. Consent must be:

- **Informed.** Make sure both fully understand all of aspects of the "who," "what," "when," "where," and "how."
- **Freely given.** Neither your child's friend or partner, nor your child, should pressure, trick, or threaten the other into saying "yes" or pretend they have said "yes"

when they know the other cannot or did not do so. If your child feels that someone is trying to coerce them, this is a clear sign of an unhealthy relationship.

- **Active.** Consent should be active and understandable – a clear, positive expression of agreement. Passive resistance should not be presumed to be consent.
- **Reversible.** If someone says "yes," but then changes their mind and says "no," it is necessary for the friend or partner to respect the "no" and stop.

Times of Difficulty

Young people who form close relationships generally start out with very good intentions. Sometimes, disagreements and conflicts will arise. Conflicts are not necessarily negative. Your child and their friend or partner can both grow and gain new skills through the process of resolving conflict.

If your child is experiencing a difficult time in their friendship or partnership and they need to communicate with their friend or partner about an issue of concern, encourage your child to take time to Think Things Through about how they really feel and why. Help your child to decide what is negotiable and what is not. Help your child know when to compromise and when they should stand their ground. The conflict resolution approach in Chapter 6 is how your child can seek to address conflict with a close friend or dating partner.

Sometimes, problems arise in friendships or partnerships because the people in the relationship have different expectations for the relationship, have become distracted with other activities, or are interested in walking a different path that will interfere with continuing the relationship.

Relationship Break-ups

Relationship break-ups are a normal part of life, especially for teens. This is because teens are exploring who they are, what their personal values are, and what their future path will be. For a time, their values and interests may match those of their friend or partner. But this can change. When this changes, relationships frequently come to an end. A relationship may also come to an end when it is unhealthy or when one person is hurtful to the other. Or a relationship may come to an end because the two young people are simply choosing to walk a path that is not in line with this relationship.

When close relationships come to an end, both friends or partners will go through a period of grief, due to their loss. Five stages of grief have been found to be universal. These stages are experienced by people from across many cultures at a time of loss. If your child breaks up, they will grieve the loss of their friendship or partnership. You and your child should expect this to happen.

Everyone grieves differently. Some grieve in a more external manner. Others process things more internally. People spend different lengths of time working through each stage of grief. They also feel each stage at different levels of intensity. The five stages do not happen in any specific order. Your child may find themself going back and forth between different stages.

The fact that people go through these grief stages in a different manner can increase challenges if they must be present in the same physical location. This can also be challenging if they have mutual friends. If one of them is in a state of anger and the other in a state of denial or bargaining, conflict is likely.

The five stages of grief are:

- **Denial and isolation.** The first reaction to a loss situation is to deny the reality of the situation. "This is not happening, this cannot be happening." This is a normal reaction to handle overwhelming emotions. For most people, this stage is a temporary response. Denial helps to avoid the immediate pain.
- **Anger.** In this stage, the reality of what has happened is more evident and the pain is present. The response to this pain is anger. Acting on their anger can cause even greater concerns. Your child's anger most likely will be directed at the person they have broken up with. It may also be directed at others who they think might have played a role. The greatest danger at the anger stage in this digital age is if the partners shared nude images. Often, in anger, these images are shared with others. This is a very good reason to encourage your child not to share such images or, if they do share, to make sure the image does not show their face or can be traced back to them. If your child has such images of their former partner, make sure that they know that the sharing of a nude image of anyone under 18 can be considered to be a crime.
- **Bargaining.** There is often a desire to seek to regain some level of control by engaging in "If only" thinking. "If only I had [fill in the blank] this would not have happened."
- **Depression.** At the depression stage, your child will feel sadness and regret. This is the stage when they are coming to accept the reality of what has happened. They are preparing for the separation to be real.
- **Acceptance.** At this point in time, your child will feel more calm and will have accepted the reality of what happened. They are not necessarily happy, but they will have accepted the pain of loss and will be ready to move on.

Be Positively Powerful Strategies

These are the Positively Powerful strategies to grieve the loss of a friendship or partnership:

- **Make Positive Connections.** Encourage your child to connect with other friends and be open to meeting new people. Support them in engaging in new activities to meet new people. It is best not to seek to form a new dating relationship while they are still grieving. They need to reach the point of acceptance.

- **Reach Out to Be Kind.** Talk with your child about acknowledging any hurtful actions they took that led to the end of the relationship. Encourage them to apologize, if possible. Also encourage them to practice something to say about what happened if someone asks that will not cause any further harm to their former close friend or partner. Encourage your child to find a new way they can engage in acts of service, which will greatly help to get through the grieving process.
- **Build Your Strengths.** When a relationship ends, this can lead a young person to feel as though they have failed. By embracing failure they can accept that people can change. This includes both them and others. Encourage your child to think about their key strengths and how they can use these strengths to move forward into new positive relationships. Encourage them also to reflect on the valuable things they learned because of this relationship.
- **Focus on the Good.** Help your child keep themselves busy doing things that they enjoy. Whenever they feel stuck in the grieving process, encourage them to note the positive things that are happening in their life and be thankful.
- **Keep Your Cool.** While it is understandable that your child is angry, encourage them not to act on that anger and engage in attack. Whenever they begin to feel upset, deep breathing to keep their cool can help.
- **Control Your Thinking and Release and Let Go.** While your child cannot control what happens, they can keep their personal power by controlling their thinking about how they feel about themself. Encourage your child to Release and Let Go of their feelings of hurt and anger, so that they can keep their personal power and move on.
- **Think Things Through.** Encourage your child to consider whether there are any patterns in their actions or selection of friends or partners that they want to change. Encourage them to Think Things Through to decide what they are going to do to move on – that will bring them greater happiness.

Disrupted Relationships

If your child has experienced a disrupted relationship in the past with a family member or with peers, it is likely they will have greater difficulties forming close friendships or partnerships. Because of the prior challenges they faced, sad memories are stored in their brain and their neural pathways are wired more for protection than positive connections. Fortunately, it is possible for your child to create happier memories and rewire the neural pathways to allow for the formation of positive close friendships and dating partnerships.

To do so, it is helpful for you and your child to have a better understanding of the dynamics. When they have had a disrupted relationship, the negative memories in their brain and their neural pathways became wired in a way that will likely cause them to not trust others. The underlying message they may believe about themself is that they are unlovable. They may believe that the reason they are being treated badly is because there is something wrong with them. When their neural pathways have wired themselves to see themself as unlovable, they will see evidence of this in their interactions with others. They likely will have a subconscious fear of rejection.

One key thing your child must watch for is their interpretation of their interactions with others. They need to be able to realize that their brain may interpret nice or neutral actions with another person in a negative manner. They may also be more likely to trigger and overreact when things do not go their way. It is also possible that they will become involved with someone who also had a disrupted relationship in their past. This will double the challenges.

Remember the primary message of this book. Your child can rewire their brain! Your child can change. So can others. Your child has the ability to rewire the neural pathways in their brain so that they can form close friendships and dating partnerships. This is how to use the Positively Powerful strategies to become a Thriver:

- **Make Positive Connections.** As noted before, the best way for your child to make friends is by engaging in activities they enjoy. They may need your support to find ways to engage in these activities so they can make new friends.
- **Reach Out to Be Kind.** The intentional, daily practice of reaching out to be kind will help to create a "kindness shield" around your child. Because of how your child is kindly treating others, others will respond with kindness. This will help your child to demonstrate to themself that they are truly not unlovable. Acting in service is another powerful strategy to build their feelings that they are lovable and can do loving things for others.
- **Build My Strengths.** When your child is proud of their accomplishments and focuses on using and building their character strengths, they will feel more secure and lovable. They also can embrace the failures that may have occurred in the past by realizing that both they and others can change.
- **Focus on the Good.** For every time your child felt let down, that an important person was not there for them, that they were treated badly, this created a negative neural pathway. The best way to rewire their brain is to make a consistent and intentional practice of finding the joys and being thankful for the good things that are happening in their life, as this is the best way for them to become happier and more secure.
- **Be Mindful.** Because of your child's experiences, they will be more likely to trigger and engage in an outburst. Taking the time every day to Practice Calmness through active meditation is essential to build the neural pathways to reduce the potential this will occur. When they know how to keep their cool,

they can stop themselves from triggering and overreacting when they feel that someone they are in relationship with has let them down.

- **Keep Their Positive Power.** Everyone deserves to be treated with respect and kindness. If your child is in a close relationship that is not healthy they may need help removing themself from this relationship. They must control their thinking by realizing that the past disruptive relationships they were in were something that happened to them that they could not control. But they can control their thinking and realize that they are a loving and lovable person. They will also need to Release and Let Go the pain that was caused by these prior disruptive relationships. For as long as they hold onto the pain of what happened to them in the past, they have given over their personal power to another. Help them to find meditations online that specifically focus on letting go of negative "cords" your child might have with any person who let them down.
- **Think Things Through.** The important first step in thinking things through is having an accurate understanding of the full situation. Because of what your child has experienced, they may have greater difficulties in doing this because their perspective of the current situation may be guided by the memories of past hurtful relationships. A friend or a trusted adult can help them to Think Things Through to gain an accurate understanding of the current situation. They can also Think Things Through to identify some positive strategies to move forward in a positive manner.

9

Positively Powerful on Social Media

Positive Empowerment When Using Social Media

The Positively Powerful strategies can also support your child's positive engagement with others when using digital communications and social media.

Your child's use of the internet and social media offers significant benefits for their social, educational, and creative activities. Social media allows them to creatively demonstrate their personal identity and maintain ongoing connections with friends and with those who share their interests. Most teens rely on digital devices to watch videos, download music, play games, and communicate with friends. Most are also using the internet daily to help with their school work.

There are ways your child might use social media that could negatively impact their well-being or lead to them being treated badly or treating others badly. The positives and cautions associated with internet use are discussed in this chapter.

Historical Background

When young people first started to use the internet the 2000s, the initial concerns related to their ability to access pornography and the ability of sexual predators to gain access to them. These were actual concerns, but only for a minority of youth. The "techie quick fix" solution to these concerns was filtering software – which technically sophisticated teens were and are easily able to get around.

Rise Above Bullying: Empower and Advocate for Your Child, First Edition. Nancy E. Willard.
© 2025 John Wiley & Sons, Inc. Published 2025 by John Wiley & Sons, Inc.

In the 2000s, I was asked to testify before the Children's Online Protection Act Commission addressing these concerns. I took along Dr. Seuss's book, *Oh the Places You'll Go* and read to them in classic kindergarten teacher style:

> You'll look up and down streets. Look 'em over with care. About some you will say, "I don't choose to go there." With your head full of brains and your shoes full of feet, You're too smart to go down those not-so-good streets.[1]

One group suggested that my testimony "presented the most compelling case – educate children, parents, teachers, librarians, and other community members as a means of reducing exposure to inappropriate sexual contacts or materials."[2] You can read my written testimony on my website.[3]

In 2007, my two books, *Cyberbullying and Cyberthreats: Responding to the Challenge of Online Social Aggression, Threats, and Distress* and *Cyber-Safe Kids, Cyber-Savvy Teens: Helping Young People Learn to Use the Internet Safely and Responsibly*, were published.[4] My book *Cyber Savvy: Embracing Digital Safety and Civility* was published in 2011.[5]

My thinking has always been that adults need to make sure that the use of digital technologies by younger children happens in safe places. By the time they are teens and are venturing out into the social media world, we need to make sure their heads are full of brains (knowledge) and their shoes are full of feet (skills), so that they can choose not to go down those not-so-good digital streets and can use these technologies and social media effectively, safely, and responsibly.

The more recent concerns are about use of social media by teens causing harm to their mental health. Especially coming out of the pandemic, there have been many news articles noting that children and teens are suffering greater emotional

---

1 Seuss, D. (1990). *Oh, the Places You'll Go!* Random: House.
2 Online Policy Group (2000). Action: legislation and policymaking: filtering: United States 2000: COPA Commission Hearing III. http://www.onlinepolicy.org/action/legpolicy/copahearing3.htm (accessed 1 August 2024).
3 Willard, N. (2000). Choosing not to go down the not-so-good cyberstreets. https://www.embracecivility.org/wp-content/uploadsnew/2011/10/Cyberstreets.pdf (accessed 1 August 2024). This testimony was to a different audience, but is the same testimony.
4 Willard, N. (2007). *Cyberbullying and Cyberthreats: Responding to the Challenge of Online Social Cruelty, Threats, and. Distress.* Research Press. Willard, N. (2007). *Cyber-safe Kids, Cyber-savvy Teens: Helping Young People Learn to Use the Internet Safely and Responsibly.* Jossey Bass.
5 Willard, N. (2011). *Cyber Savvy: Embracing Digital Safety and Civility.* Corwin Press.

concerns. Many of these articles talk about social media as the major cause of the concerns.[6]

There has been an increase in youth use of digital technologies and there has been an increase in youth mental health concerns. But proving that use of social media is causing this increase in mental health concerns is simply not possible with the research methodologies that are being used. There are a lot of other things happening in our society that can also cause mental health concerns in young people, especially those who are within minority identity groups.

There are risks to social media use and also benefits.[7] As you will see if you read this helpful article, what these professionals from the American Psychological Association are recommending is exactly what I recommended in 2000:

> Research suggests that setting limits and boundaries around social media, combined with discussion and coaching from adults, is the best way to promote positive outcomes for youth. Parents should talk to kids often about social media and technology and also use strategies like limiting the amount of time kids can use devices and removing devices from the bedroom at night. Caregivers should also keep an eye out for problematic behaviors, such as strong cravings to use social media, an inability to stop, and lying or sneaking around in order to use devices when they aren't allowed.
>
> In helping to set boundaries around social media, it's important that parents don't simply limit access to devices, Alvord added. "Removing devices can feel punitive. Instead, parents should focus on encouraging kids to spend time with other activities they find valuable, such as movement and art activities they enjoy," she said. "When kids are spending more time on those things, they're less likely to be stuck on social media."[8]

A minority of young people are at greater risk online. It is important that we continue to pay attention to the concerns faced by these young people. What has been found in research is that teens who are depressed or anxious about other things going on in their life appear to be more likely to also be engaging in unhealthy use of social media. Young people who use social media for a lot of time have been found to be more depressed than those who do not use it much or not

---

6 Richtel, M., Pearson, C. and Levenson, M. (2023). Surgeon general warns that social media may harm children and adolescents. *New York Times*, May 23.

7 APA Health advisory on social media use in adolescence. https://www.apa.org/topics/social-media-internet/health-advisory-adolescent-social-media-use (accessed 1 August 2024).

8 Weir, K. (2023). Social media brings benefits and risks to teens. Psychology can help identify a path forward. *American Psychological Association* 54 (6): 46.

at all. The question remains: Are depressed young people using social media more than those who are not depressed or does overuse of social media cause such depression? Rather than thinking that addictive internet use is "caused by" the internet, addictive internet use may be evidence of mental health concerns.

While not the sole cause of mental health concerns, there are legitimate concerns about the impact of social media on the mental health of teens, especially of girls. Boys often spend time playing digital games. Girls are more likely to spend time on posting images of themselves and looking at images posted by others. Females, both girls and women, have historically always been judged more based on appearance. Social comparison is a very significant factor on social media.

After a teen boy stops playing a game, he rarely is stressed about what happened in the game or thinks about what might happen the next time he plays. When a teen girl posts an image on social media, she is often worried about what others will have to say about her image. Even when not using social media, she may continue to be worried about what is happening related to her post. Again, do not think of this in terms of "the internet is causing her to be overly focused on her appearance and what others are saying about her." Rather, consider what insecurities or lack of positive relationships this young girl might be experiencing – the concerns of which appear to be manifesting in her online activities.

The Good News

Multiple research studies have demonstrated that the vast majority of today's young people are making good choices online and when using cell phones.[9] Most are effectively handling the negative situations that occasionally occur and are not overly distressed by these situations. Most do not like seeing people engage in hurtful online behavior.

While, from time to time, young people may face situations involving online risk, such risk rarely results in serious harm. Sometimes young people make mistakes that could be prevented if they more fully understood the risks and employed effective strategies to avoid and respond to these negative situations. It is also quite clear that young people who feel unsafe or marginalized in their community or even family, especially for those who are sexual minorities, have been able to find online communities where they feel welcomed and supported.

---

9 Haddock, A., Ward, N., Yu, R., and O'Dea, N. (2022 Oct 27). Positive Effects of Digital Technology Use by Adolescents: A Scoping Review of the Literature. *Int J Environ Res Public Health* 19 (21, 14009): https://doi.org/10.3390/ijerph192114009. PMID: 36360887; PMCID: PMC9658971.

Your objective as a parent must be to ensure that your child becomes cyber savvy. Cyber-savvy young people:

- **Keep their lives in balance.** They balance use of social media with other activities. This especially includes in person activities with others.
- **Keep themselves safe.** They understand the risks. They know how to avoid getting into risky situations, to detect whether they are at risk, and to effectively respond.
- **Present a positive image.** They present themselves online as someone who makes positive choices.
- **Respect others.** They respect the rights, privacy, and property of others and treat others with civility.
- **Take responsibility for the well-being of others.** They help others and report serious concerns to a responsible adult.

Active and Positive Parenting

Research has found that the children of parents who are actively and positively involved in their social media lives demonstrated fewer online risk behaviors.[10] Further, it has been found that cyberbullied teens whose parents were actively and positively involved were less emotionally distressed and better able to respond effectively to these incidents.

One strategy to be positively engaged with your child about their social media activities is this: Every time you interact with your child about their digital activities, be sure you make positive statements about their good choices. From your child's perspective, interactions with you related to social media activities will "feel good." Thus, your child will be more inclined to want to share aspects of their digital life with you. "You appear to be making such good choices on social media." "I am glad you recognized this as a concern. What are some of the ways you think this concern can be addressed? You usually have really good ideas."

Through the Years

Guide your approach based on the age of your child:

- When children are young, it is the parent's responsibility to make sure their internet use is in a safe online environment and that they engage in safe

---

10 American Psychological Association. (2023) Keeping teens safe on social media: What parents should know to protect their kids. APA.net, May 9. https://www.apa.org/topics/social-media-internet/social-media-parent-tips (accessed 1 August 2024).

communications. Children who still believe in unicorns cannot be expected to protect themselves online. To them, the internet is more of a "magic box." Parents must ensure that their use is safe.

- By third grade, young people can begin to grasp essential concepts about how the internet and social media functions, which provides the ability for them to take on more personal responsibility for good decision making.
- By middle school, many tweens will be able to take on even more personal responsibility for good decision making. Many tweens want to jump into social media environments with teens. This shift needs to be made carefully, based on an understanding of your child's social-emotional maturity.
- The most important thing for parents of teens to know is that the "biological imperative" of every teen is to learn to make their own decisions and resolve their own problems. It is necessary for your child to learn to independently make safe and responsible choices using social media – which requires practice in doing so. Your important role is to support your child in becoming independent. This will involve "teachable moments" and the need to Embrace Failure when they have made mistakes.

General Guidelines

These are important general guidelines for parents:

- **Express appreciation.** Frequently express your appreciation about your child's positive internet and social media interactions. "What a good decision you made ..."
- **Warn against impulsivity.** Warn against impulsive actions using the internet and social media. "Always remember, anything you send or post can easily become public." Tell your child that it is especially dangerous to ever send or post anything if they are upset or angry – because this is when mistakes are most often made. "If you are ever really upset, turn off your cell phone or walk away from the computer. Wait until you have calmed down before you do anything."
- **Never overreact and work in partnership.** Never overreact if your child reports an online concern. You want your child to feel comfortable reporting such concerns. Your first comment must be positive. "You are smart to realize this is a problem you should tell me about." Then, indicate a commitment to work in partnership to respond. "Let us figure out what is happening and work together to find a way to fix this."
- **Use reflective listening.** Use a reflective listening approach when your child expresses a concern related to the internet or social media. This will help your child to feel more supported – and more willing to share.

- **Use logical consequences and require remedy of harm.** If your child has engaged in risky, inappropriate, or harmful behavior, impose a logical consequence that will focus your child's attention on why this action has caused or could cause harm to them or to someone else. Support your child to Stop, Own It, and Fix It. Require that your child remedy any harm. "What were you thinking? What do you think has happened – or could happen as the result of your actions? How would you feel if someone did this to you? What can you do to make things better?"
- **Pay attention to possible red flags.** Red flags include appearing emotionally upset during or after use, disturbed relationships with family members or friends, spending too much time online, engaging in excessively secretive behavior when using technologies, and making subtle comments about online concerns. If any red flags are evident, pay closer attention and carefully try to engage your child in discussion using reflective listening.
- **Encourage caring for others.** Encourage your child to help others directly or report to you or another responsible adult if they witness someone being harmed or at risk online. "It is important to make sure everyone is safe online. If you see someone is being hurt or making a bad choice, reach out to help. If the problem is serious, tell me or another adult."
- **Educate yourself.** Educate yourself on issues of profiling and advertising. Point out to your child the strategies sites use to obtain their demographic and interest information and digital advertising strategies.

Cyber-safe Kids

These are recommended strategies for parents of younger children:

- **Create a fenced online play yard.** Limit your child's access to sites you have selected as appropriate. As your child grows, make these decisions together. Look for family safety features or technologies that allow you to limit your child's access to selected sites, control who they can communicate with privately, manage time spent online, and review the history file. You can also create a "fenced play yard" using bookmarking and a combined parent/child email address.
- **Know their online friends.** Make sure you personally know everyone your child communicates with through e-mail, messaging, and any other form of personal communications. Limit communication with strangers to general areas of safe, moderated children's sites.
- **Safe username and password.** Help your child create a safe and fun username and a safe password. Make sure your child knows to never disclose their password to anyone other than you. Use your e-mail address for any site registrations.

- **Keep it public.** Keep your family computer in a public place in your house so you can remain engaged in what your child is doing. Your child should know that everything they do online is open to your review. Make use of technical tools. When you provide a cell phone to your child, implement the safety and security features provided by the company.
- **Select safe sites.** If you want to allow your child to participate in a social networking environment, select safe sites that are designed for children, not for those over the age of 13.

Cyber-savvy Teens

These are general guidelines for parents of tweens and teens:

- Tweens and teens will not stay in "electronically fenced play yards." Most teens will view monitoring software as intrusiveness that is an indication that you do not trust them. Use of monitoring might be an appropriate, short-term logical consequence if your child's use of technologies has been highly inappropriate. In other words, they lost your trust and your use of monitoring software will allow them to rebuild this trust.
- Pay attention to what your child is doing online, but balance your supervision with your child's emerging legitimate interests in personal privacy. Remember, if your child feels you are overly intrusive, it is exceptionally easy to find a way to go behind your back. Positive interactions, both face to face and online, will be more effective in encouraging your child to share.
- Implement the use of cell-phone safety and security features provided by your cell phone provider that are appropriate to your child's age and demonstration of personal responsibility. Work with your child to make sure they understand the reasons for these protections.
- Discuss issues of responsible cell-phone use, including responsible texting and issues around the capture or sending of nude images. Show your child how easy it is for anyone to forward or post something they have sent digitally.
- Make sure your child turns off their cell phone and computer when going to bed. If there are any problems associated with this, use the security features that allow you to control time of use or remove the cell phone from their bedroom.

Many tweens and almost all teens are actively engaged in social networking. These guidelines are recommended:

- It is best not to allow tweens to register on social networking sites for users over the age of 13. Make this decision based on your child's maturity.
- When you decide to allow your child to start social networking, go through the settings with your child to make sure that only accepted friends can see your child's profile.

- At first, insist that your child only establish friendship links with people they know and trust. Review all of their social media friends to make sure this is the case. As your child gains experience, allow your child more freedom to exercise their own good choices.
- If your child is younger, or if your child has a habit of not making good choices, it is likely best that you have your child's login password, so you can review everything that is happening. For most young people, the best way to supervise is to create your own profile and friend your child. This way you can regularly review what is happening, including materials posted and friends added.
- Advise your child that you will regularly review their profile, and if any material is posted that is not safe or not in accord with your family's values, you will place restrictions on their use. As your child gains experience and demonstrates good decision making, you can back off this review.

Do Not Let Them Tell You That You Are Not Good Enough

Capturing Your Eyeballs and E-wallet

It is important that you and your child understand the underlying mechanism of how social media companies are funded – because the way this happens can have a potentially harmful emotional impact on your child.

Do social media companies charge you for their services? No. How then are they making money? Advertisers. What do advertisers want? They want to "capture your child's eyeballs" so that they will "open their e-wallet" (or more likely your e-wallet) to purchase their product or service. Advertisers know that teens have significant spending power on their own. They also know that teens influence their parents' spending. Advertisers may also be organizations that want to encourage your child to support their activities or support their cause.

Advertisers know that if they want to influence your child's purchasing, they have to engage with your child on social media. Sit down with your child while on their favorite social media site and look over the ads. The terms such as "Sponsored" or "Promoted" are indicators of advertisements. Advertisers want your child to click on the link to "See more" or "Learn more." They also really would like your child to "share" advertisements with your friends.

Social media sites want your child to spend lots of time on their site so they can show them lots of advertisements that are specifically directed to what they are interested in. In other words, they basically want your child to become "addicted" to spending lots of time on their site. Any time your child spends having fun with friends in person is time away from their advertisements.

Social media sites also want your child to have lots of "friends." This is because they also want your child to become an unpaid "influencer." They hope that your child will share advertisements or their thoughts about what they purchased with others. This is why social media sites are constantly pressuring your child to add new friends. Make sure your child understands this.

Influencer Marketing

Advertisers use an approach called "influencer marketing."[11] They look for people who have a strong social media presence, with lots of followers and consistent posts that attract attention. The companies then enter into a contract with this influential person. The influencer agrees to act as a regular "face" for the company's product or service. Companies believe that an influencer has the power to affect purchasing decisions because of their ongoing relationship with their audience. They know that your child can be influenced because the influencer will be even more likely to "capture their eyeballs." Another term for "influenced" is "manipulated." Teens really do not want to be "manipulated." Using the term "manipulated" can transmit a helpful perspective to your child.

Data Collection and Advertising Strategies

Social media companies have a robust system to collect data about your child (and you).[12] They follow and track everything your child does on their site, including what posts and advertisements they look at. The amount of data they collect about every user is massive. This includes demographics, interests, friends, friends' interests, the pages or groups your child is following, the news they are reading, and more. They can even track your child's physical location when they access the site using their cell phone.

Social media sites not only track your child when they are using one of their sites, they also gather data about your child from many other sites that they might visit. Many of those sites have installed an invisible pixel from the social media companies. When you visit these websites, the pixel sends information back to the social media companies they are advertising on. Then, advertisers can use this

---

11 Geyser, W. (2024). What is influencer marketing? – the ultimate guide for 2024. Influencer Marketing Hub, January 30. https://influencermarketinghub.com/influencer-marketing (accessed 1 August 2024).

12 Newberry, C. (2022). Social media data collection: why and how you should do it. HootSuite, January 24. https://blog.hootsuite.com/social-media-data-collection/#:~:text=Social%20 media%20data%20is%20any,post%20publicly%20on%20social%20media (accessed 1 August 2024).

information about your child to decide what "sponsored" ads they will see. This is how one site explained marketing pixels to website owners:

> Marketing pixels, aka tracking pixels, are essentially these tiny snippets of code that allow you to gather information about visitors on a website – how they browse, what type of ads they click on, etc. This behavior data helps you, as a marketer, send the user paid ads that are likely to be most interesting to them. Tracking pixels are also used to measure a marketing campaign's performance, track conversions, and build an audience base.... As we mentioned before, pixels allow you to better understand your user's online behaviors and shopping patterns. By using pixels, marketers are able to track useful metrics like digital ad impressions, email opens, sales conversions, and pretty much any other type of activity related to their campaign. They also extend the impressions on a potential customer by showing them related paid ads even after they have left your website. A win–win situation.[13]

Your child needs to be fully aware that everywhere they go online is tracked and that data goes into a database to determine what advertisements will be sent to them.

Pain or Anger Points

There is another marketing technique that advertisers often use that your child must be able to recognize – because this technique could make your child feel bad about themself or make them angry. The marketing technique involves triggering your child's amygdala to get them to focus and pay attention – to "capture their eyeballs." Unfortunately, they often try to do this by creating fear or anger.

Realize that social media companies and advertisers have extensive teams of researchers whose sole focus is on strategies to keep teens using social media, clicking on links for more information, making purchases, and sharing information about their purchases with their friends.

Many marketers use what are called "pain points." Their advertisement will suggest what problem they think your child has that their product or service can provide a solution for. Advertisers know that teens are very interested in what their peers think about them. They try to create a "pain point" by making it appear that if your child does not have the right body image, clothes, shoes, or "whatever" that other teens will not like them. They will not be considered to be "cool."

---

13 Digital Marketer (2019). What is a tracking pixel – explained in 800 words or less. Digital Marketer, September 17. https://www.digitalmarketer.com/blog/what-is-tracking-pixel/#:~:text= Marketing%20pixels%2C%20aka%20tracking%20pixels,be%20most%20interesting%20to%20them (accessed 1 August 2024).

The companies are striving to push your child's "pain point" to convince your child that their product or service will take care of this pain.

What the advertisers try to do is make your child feel a "pain point" – that they are not "good enough" – and then try to sell them their product or service as the way to resolve their pain. The following is from a blog on How to Market to Teenagers: Tips for Developing a Successful Campaign:

Understand Teen Pain Points

When marketing your small business specifically to teenagers, it's critical to know any pain points that make your product or service a must-have for teens. Carefully study teen influencers who have audiences similar to your target clients. Through them you should be able to develop a better under-standing of the pain points your target audience has.

For example, let us say you are an online clothing retailer. Visit social media platforms like TikTok, Instagram, and Twitter to see how teen influ-encers express their opinions about style and self-expression. See which common themes come up and how they relate to (and can be solved or soothed by) your product or service.

It's important, however, to go beyond just finding out what the pain points are. Go deeper to understand why certain issues matter, and what emotions, desires, fears, or insecurities may be underneath the surface. Even if a pain point does not directly relate to your product, speaking to these struggles publicly can help you connect with your teenage audience on an emotional level.[14]

It is very important that your child learns to notice the advertising messages that make them feel "not good enough." Your child has to keep their "head full of brains" so that the efforts of social media sites and advertisers do not lead them to feel badly about themself. The social media sites and advertisers are trying to manipulate your child to think that their product or service is just what they need to be considered "popular" and "cool."

Another very concerning pain point for some advertisers is anger. Social media sites and advertisers, including organizations that are promoting hurtful values in our society, also know that your child will spend lots of time looking at the kinds of information that makes them angry. Social media sites have said that there is no place for hate on their site. Do not let these statements fool you. There are, unfor-tunately, too many organizations and news providers that are using social media

---

14 Waldenback, L. (2024). How to Market to Teenagers: Tips for Developing a Successful Campaign. allBusiness, May 13. https://www.allbusiness.com/how-to-market-to-teenagers (accessed 1 August 2024).

sites to strive to get more people involved in activities that divide us as people. These organizations and news media companies are trying to gain your child's attention by making them angry using their pain points and then take them down a "rabbit hole" to additional similar material.[15]

Adding These Two Practices Together

Depending on how your child uses social media, much of what your child looks at online is going to be recorded and used to direct advertising to them. Advertisers are also very likely to seek to get your child's attention by pushing on their "pain points." Organizations and others may also try to influence your child's attitudes and behavior on social or political issues.

These are some examples: Say that your child would really like to have some of those top-notch running shoes – that cost a minor fortune. They spend some time looking at those shoes online. They might even place some shoes on a "wish list." All of their actions are recorded by the marketing pixels on those websites.

The next time they go on their favorite social media site, guess what is going to appear in their feed? Lots of "sponsored" ads for running shoes that will convey the pain-point message that unless they have these kinds of expensive shoes, they will not be considered "cool."

Perhaps your child is overweight. They might do some research on websites for what they can do to lose weight. Those websites might have social media pixels. The next time they go on their favorite social media site, they will likely see lots of "sponsored" ads for weight-loss products or services. These ads will have carefully crafted text and images that trip your child's pain point about being overweight. Then, they will present their product or service as the way to solve your child's pain.

Perhaps your child is interested in events or issues that are happening in their community, our country, or the world. They may see a "sponsored" advertisement that directs them to respond to a poll or read an article about some event or issue. This poll or article may then provide them with insight that is designed to make them mad. If they click on "Read more," this will alert the organization that sponsored the advertisement that they have an interest in this issue. The next time they use social media, even more advertisements related to this issue will be in their feed. The more your child gets angry and clicks to read more, the more material designed to make them angry will appear in their feed.

Can you see how badly these tracking and advertising practices can make your child feel about themself?

---

15 Kang, C. and Singer, N. (2023) Meta accused by states of using features to lure children to Instagram and Facebook. *New York Times*, October 24. https://www.nytimes.com/2023/10/24/technology/states-lawsuit-children-instagram-facebook.html (accessed 1 August 2024).

Help Your Child to Keep Their Personal Power

There is really nothing you or your child are going to be able to do about the way they are tracked and profiled on social media. There are some things they can do to control any advertisements or sites that are making them feel "not good enough" or are making them angry. On most social media sites, there are three dots at the upper right corner of all ads. Your child can click on a link that tells the site to stop sending these kinds of ads to them. Encourage your child to regularly click on the links to direct social media sites to not send them any of the ads that they perceive are communicating to them that they are "not good enough." I will note that my personal experience is that this strategy does not work very effectively.

Most often your child is going to have to come to you to obtain access to your "e-wallet" to make a purchase. Every time this happens, this provides a "teachable moment" to discuss with your child what they are seeing in advertisements. You can use these moments to empower your child to become a wise consumer.

- Think Things Through to use the internet to conduct research and make good decisions about their purchases for products or services.
- Make Positive Connections with companies and sites that are supporting everyone to become the best they can be.
- Keep Their Cool if they see information online that might make them angry or feel bad about themselves.
- Keep Their Personal Power by recognizing when a company is trying to manipulate them by suggesting they are "not good enough." Decline to purchase from companies that use this advertising approach. Click on the three dots to see if this can make such ads go away.

Think Before You Post

Remember, What You Do Reflects on You

When your child uses social media, anything they post or send is recorded in a digital format. What they post or send can be widely disseminated, without their control. This is true even if they post on a social media page they have designated as "private" or if they have messaged just one friend. If what they have posted or sent goes public, this can affect their reputation, relationships, and opportunities – in a good way or a bad way – depending on what they posted or sent.

Encourage your child to always remember that what they post or send will reflect on them – perhaps for a very long time. Your child must keep their cool. If your child is upset, it is really important they keep their hands off their digital device until they have become calm. They should be careful not to post or send without thinking things through.

Recognize that there are different kinds of personal information your child might post or send that have different risks associated with such disclosure.

- **Personal interest information.** This includes information about them, their interests, and the activities they are engaged in. This is generally safe to share on their social media page, within safe online community groups, or send to friends.
- **Personal contact information.** This includes your child's address, phone numbers, and e-mail address. This information could make it easier for an unsafe person to find your child. This information should not be posted or shared without your permission.
- **Financial identity information.** This includes any personal identification or financial account information. This information can be used for identity theft. This information should only be shared on secure websites when making a purchase, with your permission.
- **Sensitive or damaging personal material about your child.** This includes material that can make your child appear vulnerable, demonstrate that they make bad choices, or that they want to be kept secret. This information could be used to manipulate them or disseminated to harm their reputation, relationships, and opportunities. This information should generally not be posted or shared publicly or privately. However, there are times when this kind of sensitive information may be shared, with care, on a secure professional emotional support site.
- **Sensitive or damaging personal material about others.** This includes material that your child could post that might harm the reputation, relationships, and opportunities of others. This information should never be shared in a digital format, publicly or privately. One exception to this is if your child becomes aware that someone is seriously distressed and may be considering engaging in actions that could cause harm to themselves or others. In this situation, your child should absolutely provide information about this to a responsible adult who is in a position to step in to help.
- **Damaging information about your child posted by others.** This is information that could harm your child's reputation, relationships, and opportunities. Make sure your child knows to capture an image of this information so they have documented what has happened. They should tell this person to take the information down and save all communications. They should also file an abuse report with the site and tell you so that you can work together to address the situation.
- **Threats.** Make sure your child knows to never post material that someone else might think is a threat. Realize that teens have been arrested and prosecuted for posting material they claim was a joke, but that others saw as a threat. Your child should always report to a responsible adult if someone has posted information that could be a threat, even if they are not sure whether the threat is credible.

- **Sexual images.** Make sure your child understands that if they send a sexual image of themselves, this creates a high probability that at any time, totally outside of their control, that image will be distributed publicly. This will damage their reputation, relationships, and opportunities. While they may think that the person they send this image to will respect their privacy, remind them that close personal relationships often end. When a relationship ends, anger is a predictable reaction. When a person is angry and has a sexual image of the other person, posting this or sending it to others is something that often happens. If your child receives a sexual image from another, they absolutely must not send it further. Especially if your child is over the age of 18, they must be exceptionally careful. Asking for or sending these sexual images of someone who is under 18 can be considered trafficking in child pornography. Teens have been arrested and prosecuted for exchanging sexual images. When your child becomes an older teen or young adult, they are likely to share sexual images. Ask them to research "safer sexting" to find ways that they can send such images that will reduce the likelihood of the ability of others to identify them in such images.

Positively Powerful Strategies

Encourage your child to Think Things Through about their personal values and image they want to present of themself to others via social media. Do they want others to look up to them and respect their values? What image of themself do they think will best serve them for what they want to do in the future? If they want to go to college, get a great job, or attract a wonderful partner, what personal standards do they intend to follow at this time so that anyone looking at the history of their online presence will see evidence of the high quality person they are?

Keep Your Life in Balance

Avoid Addictive Use of Social Media

The addictive use of social media is a concern for some teens. Your child will experience greater happiness if they keep their use of social media in balance with other important life activities – time with friends, activities they enjoy, homework, helping out at home, and time in nature.

Remember, the social media companies strive to make your child become as addicted as possible – to serve their financial interests. Also remember that research has documented that teens who spent a great amount of time using social media are more depressed and anxious than teens who keep their lives in balance.

A major reason why your child might spend too much time using social media is "Fear Of Missing Out" (FOMO). Your child may have FOMO that, if they do not check their social media frequently, they will not be absolutely up to date on what is happening with their friends.

Indicators that your child's use of social media might be out of balance include:

- Feeling depressed or anxious, especially about things that are happening on social media.
- Spending more time using social media than they had planned or failing in their attempt to cut back on their use.
- Burying their head in a cell phone when they are with other people.
- Using social media late into the night, when they should be sleeping.
- Being preoccupied with and thinking about what they could be doing online when they are not online.
- Experiencing nervousness or anxiety when they are not able to check their social media.
- Neglecting or losing interest in school or their favorite activities.
- Excessively sharing posts on social media.
- Being angry when their friends are not as engaged on social media as they are.
- Arguing with you about time limits or sneaking around these limits.

Positively Powerful Strategies

Discuss the above indicators with your child. Does your child think their use of social media may be out of balance?

- Encourage your child to Think Things Through to decide what their personal standards are for how they will keep their life in balance. What strategies will they use to make sure they are following their personal standards?
- You and your child could make a list of the things they enjoy doing in the real world and the people they enjoy spending time with in person. You can support them as they strive to increase the times they do these things and get together with these people.
- Your child might want to set time limits for themself. They could use the timer on their cell phone when they start. They should stop when the timer goes off.
- Good sleep is really important to your child's well-being. This is where your decision that their cell phone needs to be out of their bedroom at night can possibly help your child. If your child's friends are engaging in too much posting and messaging at night and you make the decision that your child's cell phone should not be in their room, this actually can make things easier for your child. If your child's friends ask why they are not interacting in social media, they can blame you. If you have a good relationship with the parents of your child's closest friends, you can discuss the concerns of their need for sleep. If you all make the decision that cell phones are not in bedrooms at night, this will be easier for every child.

Connect Safely

Interact Safely with Others Online Interact Safely with Friends, Friends of Friends, Acquaintances, and Strangers

There are differences between public and private communications on social media in terms of the kinds of people your child may interact with. There are differences in the risks associated with these interactions. Have a discussion with your child about the kinds of people they should interact with using social media. As your child grows older, they will increase their interactions with people on social media who they do not know in person. Your child will be communicating with their known friends. The other kinds of people they may interact with may include:

- **Friends of friends.** Friends of friends are people who a personal friend of your child knows well in person and can vouch for.
- **Acquaintances.** Acquaintances are people who your child has met in person, but really does not know very well.
- **Strangers.** Strangers are people who neither your child nor any of their friends know in person.

People who your child communicates with on social media who they do not know well or do not know at all are likely to be entirely safe. One of the wonders of the internet is your child's ability to connect with other people from throughout the world who share their interests.

However, it is also possible that your child could communicate online with someone who presents concerns. Realize that the concern is not "online strangers." A person who presents concerns could be a friend, an acquaintance, a friend of a friend, or a stranger.

Many social media sites suggest that users send "friend" requests to people who have an established a friendship link with one of their friends. Your child must realize that their friend may have established a friendship link with someone who is actually a stranger. Before your child responds to a friendship request, they should check with their known friend to see if they really know this person in person.

As discussed above, social media sites want your child to have lots of friends. This way your child can become an unpaid influencer when they share advertisements with their friends. They love it when teens think they are really "cool" they are because of how many friends they have. Anyone can have a lot of friends on social media. They just have to not really care who they have friended.

When your child becomes an older teen or young adult, they will establish many more friendship links with acquaintances and strangers. These are most often people who they meet in social media communities where they share an interest. They may go to a community or school event, meet someone there, and decide to become friends on social media.

Your child must recognize that, when they are interacting with people who they do not know well in person, this person could tell them things about themselves that are not accurate. It will be more difficult detecting this because of the lack of an in-person connection.

Detecting and Avoiding Dangerous People Online

Your child may communicate with a person online who is dangerous and presents a threat to their safety. This person may be seeking to entrap your child into sexual activities or sex trafficking. They may be trying to recruit your child to join in a group that encourages hate activities. Your child may be at risk or a friend of your child may be at risk. It is important that your child knows the danger signs, both to protect themselves and to watch out for the safety of their friends.

You and your child might think that the people who present danger will show this by doing something that immediately makes your child feel uncomfortable, like immediately asking them to send a sexual image. Sometimes, dangerous people do act just like this. Savvy teens can usually detect and avoid these kinds of dangerous people quite quickly.

The far more dangerous people start their relationships by being overly friendly. They will work very hard to become your child's new best friend. They will seek to convince your child that they are the most amazing person they have ever met. They will frequently tell your child how wonderful they are.

Your child must be extremely wary of anyone who offers them gifts or opportunities, keeps telling them how wonderful they are, always takes their side, and tries to distance them from their other friends and your family. A person who behaves like this is trying to manipulate your child.

This process is called "grooming." Your child is being groomed to do something that would otherwise be against their values. It is generally only after a dangerous person has taken the time to form a relationship with a young person that they will start to engage in behavior that would more obviously raise concerns – but by this time, your child may have become "hooked." This is from a recent *Washington Post* article:

> A how-to guide circulated on Telegram offers tips on how to groom girls who are "emotionally weak/vulnerable."
>
> "Gain her trust, make her feel comfortable doing anything for you, make her want to cut for you by getting to her emotions and making it seem like you are the only person she could ever need in her life," it advises.

Another guide advises how some target girls who have eating disorders or bipolar disorder to lure them into further unsafe and unhealthy behaviors.[16]

The dangerous person may have convinced your child to send them a sexual image. Then, they will threaten to publicly post this image if your child does not do other things they want your child to do. This is called "sextortion." A Federal Bureau of Investigation website provides some helpful resources.[17] Please take the time to review this site with your child. Remind your child that while they are likely smart enough to not get manipulated, a friend of theirs may not be. Their insight could be very valuable to protect a friend.

Most hate group recruitment occurs in online gaming sites. Recruiters for hate groups look for young people who feel alienated and alone. They use the same grooming strategies to make your child feel that someone cares about them. The US Government Accountability Office released a new report in 2024 that provides insight into this concern: *Online Extremism: More Complete Information Needed about Hate Crimes That Occur on the Internet.*[18]

If your child is interacting with someone online who makes them feel even a bit uncomfortable, they need to do the digital version of "walk away." Your child will need to leave the room (the site or page) and lock their door (block the person). If this person tries to "follow them" (will not stop trying to communicate) or threatens them, they are even more unsafe. This is when your child must know to report the concern to a responsible adult, which may be law enforcement.

If your child suspects they have been interacting with a dangerous person online, it is imperative that they tell you. Even if your child has been sufficiently savvy to detect the risks and get away from a possibly dangerous person, other teens might not be so savvy and attentive to the concerns. You and your child's reporting could help those teens at higher risk.

If your child becomes aware that a dangerous person is communicating with a friend, they can seek to convince their friend to take these protection steps. However, their friend may have become "hooked." Advise your child that it is really important that they tell you, a responsible adult at school, or law enforcement. This is necessary to protect the safety of their friend.

---

16 Boburg, S., Verma, P., and Dehghanpoor, C. (2024) On popular online platforms, predatory groups coerce children into self-harm. *Washington Post*, March 13. https://www. washingtonpost.com/investigations/interactive/2024/764-predator-discord-telegram (accessed 1 August 2024).

17 https://www.fbi.gov/how-we-can-help-you/scams-and-safety/common-scams-and-crimes/ sextortion (accessed 1 August 2024).

18 US Government Accountability Office (2024). Online extremism: more complete information needed about hate crimes that occur on the internet. Gao.gov, January 12. https:// www.gao.gov/products/gao-24-105553 (accessed 1 August 2024).

In the footnotes there are links to news stories that I strongly encourage you to read with your child before they are allowed to engage in any social media activities. From *ABC News:* "Parents of teenager who died by suicide after sextortion scam urge 'tough' conversations with children";[19] from *NPR*, "Right-wing hate groups are recruiting video gamers";[20] and from the *Washington Post*, "On popular online platforms, predatory groups coerce children into self-harm."[21]

After reading these articles, ask your child these questions: What kinds of young people do these predators and hate-mongers target? How are connections made? What is the strategy that these predators and hate-mongers use to groom young people? What should you do if you think you have gotten entrapped? What should you do if you think a friend of yours has gotten entrapped? Do you think it is important to tell an adult even if you or a friend have engaged in actions that were not wise?

Meeting in Person

If your child is older and has gotten to know someone online, they may want to arrange to meet in person. This may be a friend of a friend, an acquaintance, or even a stranger. There are important safety steps your child should take if they plan to meet in person with someone they have gotten to know through social media. Make it clear to your child that you need to be involved in this decision. Please realize that if you "just say no," it is quite possible that your older child will simply go behind your back. These safety steps include:

- **Make sure you and your child know enough about this person to assess their safety.** Your child should only arrange for a meeting if they have communicated for some time with this person – enough time to be able to get a good sense of their personal values. Ask your child to share with you the profiles, pages, and communications they have had with this person.
- **Plan a meeting in a public place with their trusted friends present.** The public place could be at the mall or a coffee shop. In addition to having their friends present, it is advisable to have you close by.

---

19 Barr, L. (2023). Parents of teenager who died by suicide after sextortion scam urge 'tough' conversations with children. ABC News, May 3. https://abcnews.go.com/US/parents-teenager-died-by-suicide-after-sextortion-scam-urge/story?id=99047305 (accessed 1 August 2024).
20 Kamenetz, A. (2018). Right-wing hate groups are recruiting video gamers. NPR, November 5. https://www.npr.org/2018/11/05/660642531/right-wing-hate-groups-are-recruiting-video-gamers (accessed 1 August 2024).
21 Boburg, Verma, and Dehghanpoor, On popular online platforms, predatory groups coerce children into self-harm.

- **Have an escape plan.** With your child, create a "code word" that they can text to their friends or to you that communicates "get me out of here."
- **Never leave the public place with this person.** Your child should take time after this meeting to Think Things Through, talk with you and their friends about what they learned, and determine how they want this relationship to progress.

Protect Your Face and Friends

Use Social Media Safely and Responsibly

Social media sites have Terms of Use to which all users agree when they establish a profile on the site. These Terms of Use prohibit actions that could cause harm to others or the site. Social media sites also have protective features that give users control over who can access their information or send messages. These sites and apps also have abuse-report systems and ways to block people your child does not want to interact with.

Review these terms and the abuse report system with your child to make sure they know how to use these protection tools to protect themself and their friends. Some companies are more diligent than others.

Sometimes, teens do not want to report abuse. They think that something bad might happen to them if the person who is being abusive finds out they have filed this kind of a report. There are several reasons why it is safe to file an abuse report:

- Abuse reports are confidential. Unless your child is reporting a private message, no one will know they reported.
- Many sites use artificial intelligence approaches to detect and remove objectionable material. Someone's material could be removed without anyone reporting.
- If the harmful material has been publicly posted, anyone can report.

All of these factors mean that the person who was reported on will not know who reported the abuse. This means it is safe to report abuse if someone is being hurtful to your child or to anyone else.

Read with Your Eyes Open

Assess the Credibility of Information and Trustworthiness of People

When your child accesses information online, it may be accurate or not. When your child interacts with people on social media, they could be trustworthy or not. The steps to assess the credibility of information and the trustworthiness of people are similar.

Concerns associated with dangerous people online were discussed above. The material in this section provides greater insight. Any individual, organization, or company can post information online. The intentions of posting such information may vary. There is no way to be entirely certain of the credibility or accuracy of any information posted online, especially with any activities associated with politics or social issues. There are well-documented efforts to post and push the dissemination of inaccurate information.

It is important to understand the dangers in relying on appearance, high ranking in search returns, number of followers, or numbers of tweets as a basis to assess credibility. All of these factors can be manipulated. These are some helpful steps for when your child seeks to assess the credibility of information or trustworthiness of people:

- **Determine the importance.** Determine how important it is that the information is credible and safe. The importance of determining credibility and safety will vary. Determining the time of a movie is less important than assessing the accuracy of medical information. How important is it that they assess the safety of a person? If they are just interacting with them online, this may present fewer concerns than if they are thinking of meeting in person.
- **Identify the path.** Identify the path to the information. Did they look for this information using a search engine? Did this information "pop" onto their feed? It is probable the information they search for using good search terms has higher credibility. Do they have a logical connection to a person through a mutual friend? Did this person just pop onto their social media page with a friend request? A person who just "popped" onto their social media page presents more concerns regarding safety.
- **Evaluate the source.** Evaluate the source of the information. Is this information from a credible news organization? If they are reading information from a news source that may have bias, they should check with a number of news sources before making a final determination of credibility. How did they first come in contact with a person? If they are interacting with someone who they do not know in person, they should keep in mind that there are challenges in evaluating their safety simply because they lack the ability to effectively check them out.
- **Look for potential of bias.** Look for evidence of interest and potential bias in the information itself. Have they read critically? Seek to identify signs of potential bias of information. Especially note any signs of hatred toward certain groups or individuals. Have they considered this person critically? Seek to assess the values held by someone they may be interacting with. Consider whether the values of the other person are in accord with their own values.

- **Watch out for manipulation.** Look for evidence of attempted manipulation. Is the information being presented in a way that is seeking to encourage them to take some action to support whoever is providing the information? Are they being asked to commit to an issue or action? Is this commitment to actions that supports a just and positive society or does this appear to be an effort to create hatred and divide society? As discussed earlier, dangerous people online are most likely to be overly friendly and manipulative so they can become your child's new best friend.
- **Assess consistency.** Determine the consistency of the information. Look to see if the same or similar information is present on different sites. If the information is credible and accurate, what they read on different sites will be the same or very similar. If they are assessing the trustworthiness of someone they are communicating with, they should determine whether what they say is consistent over time or on other posts they have made.
- **Evaluate.** Conduct a substantive evaluation of the information or person. Is the information being provided consistent with what they already know to be true? Does someone's postings support the conclusion that this person is trustworthy and holds good values?
- **Ask others.** Ask the opinion of others, especially you, friends, and other trusted adults.

Embrace Digital Civility

Foster Positive Relationships in Digital Communities

Unfortunately, sometimes people become hurtful when they are communicating using social media. This is usually called "cyberbullying."

Positively Powerful

The Positively Powerful strategies can empower your child to maintain positive relationships when using social media and to respond if they are treated badly.

- **Think before they post.** Do not post or send any material that others could use against them. Post in a way that builds their positive reputation, establishes positive relationships, and increases their opportunities.
- **Do not follow a hurtful leader.** Do not join in and be hurtful when someone else has started to do so. Do not like or post a comment supporting hurtful material that has been posted.
- **Disagree respectfully.** It is perfectly appropriate for your child to post about and to discuss controversial issues. They should do so in a manner that is respectful to those who hold contrary positions.

- **Focus on the good.** Your child can spread positive energy by being known as the one who consistently posts positive images, stories, and memes and publicly thanks others.
- **Reach out to be kind.** Encourage your child to positively comment on the posts of others every time they use social media. This is a great way to keep their social media community a happy place.
- **Keep their cool and keep their personal power if attacked online.** If someone is hurtful to them when using social media, they must keep their cool. If what this person posted is really bad, they can capture an image and file an abuse report. Your child should keep their hands off the keyboard until they have become calm and have thought things through. Your child could choose to respond. If they do, they should make this a powerfully positive response. They can post a calm and logical response that does not sound at all emotional or angry. In some situations, they may be able to ask kindly about the well-being of the person who posted. They should think about how others will think of them and of this other person when they read the postings. Remember, the vast number of teens really do not like it when they see someone being hurtful. If your child responds in a calm and logical manner, their reputation will be enhanced. They should not continue the conversation if this other person continues to be hurtful.
- **Make a positive connection.** Connect with you, another trusted adult, or good friends to help them Think Things Through to decide what they may need to do. Your child can ask you, the adult, or a friend to provide them with "invisible guidance" to help them carefully craft a message or post that could get the hurtful situation to stop.

Be a Helpful Ally

Being a helpful ally is discussed more in Chapter 10. Young people who witness cyberbullying are in the best position to get this to stop. Realize that other teens really do not like to see this kind of hurtful behavior occurring and truly admire those who step in to help. This is how your child can be a helpful ally in cyberbullying situations.

- **Reach out to be kind.** Your child can reach out privately to the person who has been targeted on social media and tell this person that they have seen what is happening, do not like this, and would like to help. Discuss possible options for response. Your child can also provide "invisible guidance" to help this person make a positively powerful public response.
- **Report abuse.** Capture images of what has been posted for evidence. Then, file an abuse report. Reach out to other mutual friends, tell them what is happening, and ask them to file abuse reports. The more abuse reports that are filed, the faster the hurtful material may come to the attention of the company and be taken down.

- **Tell the hurtful person to stop – with planned back-up.** Your child can also step in publicly to help the person who has been targeted. There is a way they can do this that will reduce the risk of retaliation. They should privately tell their friends that they are going to post a message of support for the targeted person and a request that the person who was hurtful stop being hurtful. Ask their friends to quickly positively comment in agreement on their post. This planned back-up strategy can be very powerful in getting these situations to stop.

- **Report concerns.** Help the person who has been treated badly to connect with a trusted adult. This person could also ask this adult to provide "invisible guidance" or step in to help more visibly, if necessary. If things are really bad and the person being treated badly is concerned about reporting, your child should report to a responsible adult who is in a position to help. This is especially important if the person being targeted is being attacked by many others or is showing signs they are emotionally distressed. If your child tells you, make sure you capture images of what is happening and then share these with the school of the young person who is being cyberbullied or possibly the police.

10

Be a Powerfully Positive Helpful Ally and Leader

Being a Helpful Ally and a Leader for Positive Change

My hopeful objective in writing this book is that the more positively empowered your child becomes, the more they will want to take steps that will help others who are facing challenges or being treated badly. Hopefully, they will also want to work with others to create a positive environment in their school and elsewhere in their community. Not only does reaching out to be kind help your child become happier and feel more empowered, this is also a way for your Thriver child to help others, which will make our world a happier place.

This chapter is focused on how you can empower you child to use the Positively Powerful strategies to be a helpful ally when they witness situations where someone is being treated badly. This chapter also provides guidance on ways you can encourage your child to be a leader and to work with others to better support a positive school community and accomplish other positive change in our society. Those who are truly happy in life are those who have found how to Act in Service to others.

> Life's most persistent and urgent question is, "What are you doing for others?" Martin Luther King Jr.

Positively Powerful Strategies for Empowered Leadership

The Positively Powerful strategies provide a great basis for your child to become a helpful ally and an empowered positive leader.

Make Positive Connections and Reach Out to Be Kind

Encourage your child to establish friendships with other youth and adults who want to make a positive difference and Act in Service in their school or community – and even in the world. It is especially helpful to support your child in expanding friendships to include people who are different from them and may be outside of their typical circle of friends. Encourage your child to also establish relationships with trusted adults who are working for positive change in your community and beyond.

What are your child's passions and desires for their future life directions? How might they want to Act in Service to others? What school or community organizations can your child become involved in that match their passions and future directions? These school or community organizations are places where your child can form friendships and Make Positive Connections with those who Act in Service to others. Acting in service to others through a community organization is a great way for your child to develop positive relationships with adults who could support your child's focus on their future in amazing ways.

When your child consistently reaches out to be kind to many others, this is the foundation for being empowered and engaging in positive leadership. Acting in service to others expands this outreach. You could also talk with the parents of your child's friends to see whether there may be an interest among these friends to work together to Act in Service. If your child is facing challenges, finding a way that they can engage in ongoing acts of service should have a very high priority. This path can help them to shift from "targeted" to "Thriver who is acting in service for others."

Build My Strengths

What are your child's passions and strengths? What are the ways that your child can pursue their passion and build their strengths to create positive benefit for others? Your child's activities in service to others can provide the foundation for future studies and employment.

When your child is on a path to Act in Service to others and be an empowered positive youth leader, it will be important for them to maintain a growth mindset by embracing failure. Taking actions to create positive change will not always yield rapid results. Encourage your child to always keep trying, even when things are tough. Your child must realize that they may work very hard to achieve something and they will not achieve success – yet.

Recall that social scientists from around the world identified and classified the core capacities that lead to goodness in human beings across cultures, nations, and beliefs. These character strengths are the strengths of empowered positive leaders. Encourage your child to focus on how they can build their strengths in their efforts to be a helpful ally and work with others to create a more positive community.

Focus on the Good

An empowered, positive youth leader helps people Focus on the Good and Be Thankful. When they Focus on the Good they can also focus on how they and others are making positive contributions to their school, community, and world.

Keep Your Cool and Keep Your Personal Power

As an empowered positive leader, your child will, from time to time, need to take a stand for actions that are necessary to support positive community. They may need to call the attention of others to concerns that need to be addressed. As a result of their leadership in addressing important concerns, they may come under personal attack. They absolutely need to keep their cool and keep their personal power if this occurs.

Think Things Through

In today's society, we are in need of leaders who can effectively Think Things Through to develop new strategies to address concerns. Part of empowered youth leadership is also engaging in problem solving with others to achieve a common objective. The Think Things Through steps can also be used by a group of young people. This is a translation of the Think Things Through steps for a group:

- Make sure the team has a commonly held understanding of the situation they are seeking to address and their group objectives.
- Obtain data that document the concerns. Having such data is really important. When there is a focus on data and facts, rather than opinions, this will lead to better strategies to address the identified concerns. If it is possible to obtain the same data at a later time, this can be used to assess effectiveness of actions.
- Work as a team to identify, evaluate, and select strategies.
- Create an action plan and make assignments for responsibilities.
- Make sure there is a plan to evaluate the effectiveness of their actions.
- Know that if they do not achieve the results they desired, this is perfectly okay. Just go through the process again using their new insight into what will *not* work to find a strategy that holds more promise of working.

Being a Helpful Ally

When your child witnesses hurtful behavior, they have a choice. They can be a:

- **Helpful ally.** Who steps in to help.
- **Passive observer.** Who ignores what is happening or walks away.
- **Hurtful supporter.** Who joins in or supports the harm.

Helpful allies can help in a variety of ways. They can:

- **Reach out.** Reach Out to Be Kind to the person being hurt or left out. Help others resolve conflict.
- **Say, "Stop."** Publicly or privately tell the person being hurtful to stop.
- **Report concerns.** Tell a responsible adult who can help.

When young people step in to help, they are often very successful in getting hurtful situations to stop.[1] The problem is that too many young people who say they want to help do not take steps to help when hurtful incidents do occur. Research has shown that young people are more willing to step in to help if they believe that others will be supportive of their efforts, if they have sufficient personal power to do so safely, and if they have effective skills. The Positively Powerful strategies can help your child to feel more empowered and to become an effective helpful ally.

Recall the results of my 2015 survey.[2] In this survey, it was found that students truly admire those who are respectful and kind to others, reach out to help someone who has been treated badly, try to include those who have been excluded, tell someone being hurtful to stop, help someone who was hurtful decide to make things right, help other students resolve an argument or conflict, and tell an adult if a situation is serious.

In an open question on this survey, students were asked what words they would use to describe those who step in to help. This is a word cloud of the most frequent words used:

Awesome Brave Amazing Nice Confident Strong Kind Friend Responsible
Caring Respectful Hero Leader Courageous Smart Admirable

Safety Concerns

This is the challenge. If your child sees a hurtful situation and the student who is being hurtful has a high social status and appears to be quite powerful or is a student who is being disruptive and aggressive, your child may not feel as though

---

1 Salmivalli, C. and Voeten, M. (2004). Connections between attitudes, group norms, and behaviors associated with bullying in youth organizations. *International Journal of Behavioral Development* 28: 246–258. Gini, G., Albiero, P., Benelli, B., and Altoe, G. (2007). Does empathy predict adolescents' bullying and defending behavior? *Aggressive Behavior* 33: 467–476. Pöyhönen, V., Juvonen, J., and Salmivalli, C. (2010). What does it take to stand up for the victim of bullying? The interplay between personal and social factors. *Merrill-Palmer Quarterly* 56 (2), Article 4. Menesini, E., Codecasa, E., and Benelli, B. (2003). Enhancing children's responsibility to take action against bullying: evaluation of a befriending intervention in Italian middle youth organizations. *Aggressive Behavior* 29: 10–14. Simona, C.S., Caravits, P.D., and Silmivalli, C. (2008). Unique and interactive effects of empathy and social status on involvement in bullying. *Social Development* 18 (1): 140–163.
2 Willard, N. (2016) Embrace Civility Student Survey. https://www.embracecivility.org/wp-content/uploadsnew/ECSSFullReportfull.pdf (accessed 1 August 2024).

they have sufficient social status or power of their own to publicly challenge this person. Their assessment might be that this would not be something safe for them to do. Your child needs to trust their gut feeling on this. If they do not think publicly intervening would be safe for them, they are likely right.

However, there are some really effective ways they can be a helpful ally and step in to help that do not require them to take any actions in public. These private strategies are safer – and they are also very effective. Those who have been treated badly feel much better if even just one person says to them, "Hey, I saw that and I really did not like it. Is there something I can do to help?" The person who was treated badly will truly appreciate their kind words of support.

Your child can also provide "invisible guidance" to any student who has been treated badly. They can help this student Think Things Through to identify strategies to seek to get the harmful behavior to stop. They can help this student implement any of the strategies that were discussed in Chapter 6.

Knowing strategies and having effective skills to step in to help, both publicly or privately, can increase your child's willingness to do so. There are a lot of different ways your child can be a helpful ally. The following are some of the ways.

Step in to Help

If your child sees someone being treated badly, but is concerned about stepping in to help, they could think of this:

- How they would feel if someone treated them badly and no one reached out to support them?
- How they would feel about themself if they could have reached out to help, but did not do so?

Ways Your Child Can Step in to Help

These are some general ways your child could step in to help:

- Talk to the student being treated badly privately. Tell this student that they did not like what happened and they want to help.
- Text or private message the student who was treated badly to make sure they are okay.
- Smile and say, "hi" when they see this student in the hall or their classroom.
- Ask this student to join them for lunch.
- Offer to go with this student to report to an adult.
- Post an anonymous friendly note on the student's locker.

Discuss these idea with your child. What are some other ways your child thinks they could step in to help?

Step in to Help in Hurtful Situations

If your child sees someone being treated badly, it may be possible for them to safely help the student leave the situation. Helping this student leave the situation is better than trying to resolve or stop this kind of situation. To do this safely, your child should:

- Take a deep breath to keep their cool and hold themselves tall to keep their personal power.
- Ignore the one being hurtful. Go up to the one being treated badly. Start a conversation on something totally unrelated to the hurtful situation.
- Continue to ignore the one who is being hurtful. Encourage the one being treated badly to walk away with them.
- When they are in a place where they can talk, help this student Think Things Through to determine what else needs to be done.

Practice this strategy with your child so that they feel comfortable doing this.

Help a Friend in Difficult Times

If your child's friend is going through difficult times, including if they have been treated badly, are having relationship challenges, or are having other difficulties, your child can encourage them to use the Positively Powerful strategies that have been recommended in this book. These are some other ways your child can help:

- Reach Out to Be Kind by being in frequent contact, both in person and through social media messaging. Send their friend positive memes to let them know they are sending positive thoughts their way.
- Take the time to listen. Help their friend to Think Things Through to decide what to do. Provide "invisible guidance" to their friend to support positive actions to stop the harm.
- Tell their friend they are not alone, that help is available, and that things will get better. Make sure they understand that they, others, and the situation can change and get better.
- Invite their friend to participate in fun activities or in activities where they can Act in Service together.
- Help their friend to Focus on the Good and Focus on Their Future. By focusing on the good things that are happening and what they would like to do in the future, their friend will become happier.
- Help their friend reach out to a trusted adult if things do not get better. Offer to go with their friend to talk with this adult. If their friend appears really distressed, may be at risk, and is afraid to talk to an adult, they should reach out to you or another trusted adult to describe the situation and ask for guidance.

Help Others Resolve Conflict

If your child has some friends who are engaged in a conflict, your child can help them to resolve this conflict by thinking things through. Here is a process:

- Make sure both are calm.
- Ask each person, one at a time, to explain what happened and how this made them feel. The objective is to help both Learn the Story of the other – to help each understand the feelings and reasons for those feelings of the other.
- After the first person makes a comment, reflect back to them saying: "It sounds to me like you are feeling [name feeling], because [identify reason]."
- Repeat until both have had a chance to talk and seem to have come to an understanding of the situation from the perspective of the other. Ask both: "Do you understand how [name of person] is feeling and why?"
- Then, ask them to Think Things Through to find solutions that would allow them both to be happy. Use the Think Things Through process to come up with several strategies that might work. Make sure they think about what might happen if they choose each strategy.
- Help them agree what they will try first – and if this does not work, what they will try next. Make sure they have at least two strategies to try. Make sure they realize that they might need to Embrace Failure if the strategy they select does not work. Your child can help them again.
- Ask them to "shake hands" on their agreement.
- Check back later to see if things are okay.

Say "Stop"

Important Safety Guidelines

Publicly telling someone who is being hurtful to stop can be a risky action, especially if this person has high social status, is powerful in other ways, or has triggered and is being aggressive. It is exceptionally important to always act in a respectful and caring way when telling someone to stop.

There are important steps your child should take if they feel inclined to publicly tell someone who is being hurtful to stop.

- Work with others as a team. If they have friends present, several of them can quickly talk with each other and create a plan on how to intervene. By saying stop as a team together, the individual students will be more safe.
  - It is helpful to have at least three students who are willing to say "stop."
  - It is even easier to work with others as a team when using social media. Your child can private message several friends. They can plan a team approach for one of them to post a "stop" message, which is quickly followed by several more "stop this" messages.

- Strive not to increase attention to the one who is being hurtful. Telling someone to "stop" will either work quickly or not. Your child and their friends should keep their comments short and not say mean things to this person. They should also not get into an argument. They can simply say that their hurtful actions need to stop and, if this does not work, leave.

Ways to Say "Stop"

These are some general ways your child could say "stop." Remind your child that it is very important if they want to say "stop" that they do so in a respectful and calm manner – even if this is not how this hurtful person is behaving. These are some things your child could say:

- "You may not have intended to be hurtful. But it sounded to me that what you said was hurtful. Can you think about this?"
- "Has something bad happened to you? Is that why you are doing this?"
- "This really is not funny. How would you feel if someone did that to you?"
- "We do not do stuff like that here."
- "Please use another word. You may not realize that that word is hurtful."

After making any of these kinds of statements, your child could add: "It would likely help if you told [name of person] you are sorry."

This is how the conversation could unfold with three helpful allies:

Helpful ally 1: "Hey, I just heard what you said. That was not nice. We really don't want students to treat others like that in our school."

Helpful ally 2: "I agree with [name of helpful ally 1]. How would you feel if someone did something like that to you or a friend of yours?"

Helpful ally 3: "I am not sure what challenges you are dealing with, but I think you owe that person an apology."

Help a Hurtful Friend Stop, Own It, and Fix It

Your child may be in a situation where a person they consider to be a friend is the one who is being hurtful. In this kind of a situation, there are two considerations:

- What their friend is doing and the harm this is causing to another.
- What others will think of your child if they know their friend is being hurtful and they continue to support their friend. Your child's reputation and other relationships may be at risk.

Your child can encourage their friend to stop being hurtful, accept personal responsibility, and take steps to make things right – to Stop, Own It, and Fix It. Encourage your child to ask their friend these questions:

- "How would you feel if someone did that to you or to me? What would an adult whose opinion you value think about what you are doing? What do you think other students think about you doing this?"
- "Why do you think what you are doing is okay?" Listen for rationalizations like: "It was just a joke." "Everybody does it." "That person is overreacting, it was not that bad." "That person deserved it." Challenge those rationalizations as excuses for behavior that they know is against positive values.
- If their friend is being hurtful because the other person was hurtful to their friend, encourage their friend to find a more positive way to respond. "How can you respond without retaliating?"
- Encourage their friend to accept personal responsibility. "Are you willing to own it?"
- Encourage their friend to Think Things Through to figure out how to make things right. "How can you fix it?"

Your child will also have to figure out how to respond if their friend refuses to Stop, Own It, and Fix It. What are your child's thoughts on continuing a relationship with someone whose values about how they should treat others may not be in accord with their values and your family's values?

Remind your child that other students do not admire those who are hurtful – and they also do not admire those who support those who are being hurtful. Ask your child to consider how being seen as someone who supports a hurtful friend may harm their reputation, relationships, and opportunities.

Report Concerns

High-risk Warning Signs

It is important for all teens to pay attention to high-risk warning signs. These are the signs that someone may be at higher risk for self-harm, suicide, or causing violent harm to others. It is less likely that younger children will have the insight to be able to do this. The high-risk warning signs are:

- Talking about wanting to die, be dead, hurt themselves, kill themselves, or kill or hurt others.
- Feeling very hopeless and helpless.
- In significant emotional pain, anxious, on edge, or unusually angry.

- Struggling to deal with a big loss or significant challenge in their life.
- Angry and has been showing off or talking about weapons.
- Under serious attack by others, including a social media attack.
- Engaging in risky or self-harm behaviors, such as cutting or burning themselves.
- Being abused or treated badly by an adult or is at risk of getting together with an adult who may be dangerous.
- Experiencing sextortion or being recruited into a hate group.
- Withdrawing from everyone and everything.
- Saying "good-bye" for no apparent reason.

When to Report Concerns

These are the situations that should **always** be reported to a responsible adult:

- Someone your child knows is demonstrating any of the high-risk warning signs.
- It is not safe for your child to do something about a serious situation by themself.
- Their "gut" is telling them something is seriously wrong.

How to Report Concerns

If your child needs to report concerns, they should make sure that they tell the whole story: Who is involved? What has happened? When and where this is happening? Why this is happening, if they know?

Your child should tell a responsible adult who can help. Which adult they should tell will vary based on the situation. If the first adult they tell does not respond in a way that they think is effective, they should tell another adult. They should know to keep telling until someone responds effectively. These are the adults they could tell:

- If they are at school, they should tell a principal or counselor.
- If they are with a youth group, they should tell a staff member.
- If they are on social media, they should capture an image to save the postings and file an abuse report on the site. They should also report and provide the social media evidence to a responsible adult locally. This could be you or someone at school.
- If the situation is potentially really serious and someone could get hurt, they should call 9-1-1.
- If they are not sure, they should talk to you or another other trusted adult.

Please remind your child how important it is to report concerns to a responsible adult who can help. When they do this, they may actually be saving someone's life. The reporting about concerns by young people has been known to prevent school shootings and youth suicide.

Leadership for Kindness and Inclusion

You and your child could suggest to your child's school that they establish a student leadership team to support a positively powerful school climate. To successfully accomplish the objective of improving the school climate for all students requires establishing a diverse group of students to provide leadership to support acts of kindness, respect, and inclusion.

Someone from every social group in your school should be involved with this student leadership team. This includes students with disabilities. Participation in a student leadership team should be open to all students who are interested.

These are just some of the kinds of activities a student leadership team could accomplish:

- **"Welcome to School" display.** Create a display at the entrance of the school that promotes the concepts of kindness, respect, and inclusion of all students.
- **Daily or weekly announcements.** Make a daily or weekly public school announcement related to kindness, respect, and inclusion. Here is an example of what a member of the student leadership team could say:
    - "Hi. I am ___, a member of the [name of group] promoting kindness and inclusion. Here is your quote of the day: 'If I can help somebody as I pass along, if I can cheer somebody with a word or song, if I can show somebody he's traveling wrong, then my living will not be in vain.' It was said by Dr. Martin Luther King Jr. Please take a moment today to reach out to be kind. And remember to say thank you to someone who reaches out to be kind to you."
    - "We are having a meeting of the [name of student leadership team]. Remember, membership on this team is open to anyone who makes a commitment to be kind, respectful, and inclusive and who wants to help our school community live by these values."
- **Random Acts of Kindness campaign.** Launch a campaign to encourage all students to engage in random acts of kindness. The Random Acts of Kindness Foundation site has lots of activities to promote kindness.[3] Conducting an online search on "kindness, schools" will yield additional ideas.
- **Posters, screen savers, bookmarks, or T-shirt design.** Hold a poster, screen saver, or bookmark contest to develop kindness, respect, and inclusion images to spread throughout your school.
- **Quote competition.** Encourage students to find and submit a quote by a famous person that relates to kindness, respect, and inclusion. The quotes could

---

3 https://www.randomactsofkindness.org (accessed 1 August 2024).

be posted in categories. Students could vote on their favorite quotes. These quotes could be turned into posters and the like.

- **School-wide kindness events.** Participate in kindness events that are promoted by other organizations.
  - Beyond Differences. Beyond Differences, provides a number of wonderful activities to help students encourage social inclusion.[4] These are events that take place on one day and include No One Eats Alone, Know Your Classmates, and Call It Out.
  - GLSEN (Gay Lesbian Straight Education Network) No Name Calling Week. GLSEN hosts a No Name Calling Week the third week of January. Their website has excellent resources to support this effort.[5]
- **Calming space or mindful movement.** Set up a space in the school where students can go to meditate or be calm. Set up a mindful movement yoga program for students to participate in during lunch or before school.
- **Wall of Thanks.** Create a bulletin-board area in the school as a "Wall of Thanks." Provide ample note paper and pens nearby. Encourage everyone in the school community – students, staff, and parents – to regularly write personal messages of gratitude to others or for anything they are personally thankful for.
  - To expand on this activity, members of the student leadership team could pick out a few messages each day to read over the intercom in the morning.
- **Celebrating and building strengths.** Encourage the school to have students complete the VIA Character Strengths survey discussed in Chapter 5 and implement strategies to encourage these strengths.
  - Encourage all students to create a name plate for their locker that sets forth their top strengths.
  - Look on the VIA Character Strengths site to find many other activities and approaches that can be used to promote the different strengths. Their team could lead a campaign to focus on one character strength a week.
- **Community service day.** Set up one afternoon a month where students go into the community to provide service to others.
- **Flash dance.** Create a flash dance to perform at the local mall to demonstrate their school's commitment promote kindness and inclusion.[6]

4 https://www.beyonddifferences.org (accessed 1 August 2024).
5 https://www.glsen.org/sites/default/files/2020-06/Organizing%20Your%20First%20No%20
Name-Calling%20Week-%20A%20Comprehensive%20Approach%20.pdf (accessed 1 August 2024).
6 Mitzel, D. (2011) Anti-bullying Flash Mob January 2011. https://www.youtube.com/
watch?v=MhYyAa0VnyY (accessed 1 August 2024);School District of Palm Bech County (2019).
Anti-bullying Flash Mob. https://www.youtube.com/watch?v=FKz3c8POVvo (accessed 1 August 2024).

11

Federal Civil Rights Laws and Free Speech

In the United States there is no federal law that directly addresses bullying. However, discriminatory harassment is covered under federal civil rights laws enforced by the US Department of Education's Office for Civil Rights (OCR).[1] Under these laws, schools are obligated to address the hurtful behavior that is: unwelcome and objectively offensive, such as derogatory language, intimidation, threats, physical contact, or physical violence; is sufficiently serious, persistent, or pervasive so that it interferes with or limits a student's ability to learn and participate in school activities; and is based on a student's race, color, national origin, sex, disability, or religion.[2]

Under the civil rights requirements a more comprehensive intervention is necessary if a hostile environment is found to exist. This holds a much higher potential for success than under state statutes.

This chapter is written in accord with US law. If you are a resident of another country, you will have to investigate how the laws of your country might relate to the insight that is being provided in this chapter. While the legal protections and standards may differ, the approaches to documenting and resolving these situations that are recommended in Chapter 12 are still applicable. The major difference may be related to enforceability.

Civil Rights Laws

The four federal civil rights statutes are:

- Title IX of the Education Amendments of 1972 (Title IX) prohibits discrimination on the basis of sex by an educational program or activity receiving federal

---

1 https://www.stopbullying.gov/resources/laws/federal (accessed 1 August 2024).
2 https://www.stopbullying.gov/resources/laws/federal (accessed 1 August 2024).

Rise Above Bullying: Empower and Advocate for Your Child, First Edition. Nancy E. Willard.
© 2025 John Wiley & Sons, Inc. Published 2025 by John Wiley & Sons, Inc.

funds.[3] This includes discrimination against students who are lesbian, gay, bisexual, transgender, queer, questioning, asexual, intersex, or nonbinary, and individuals who identify their sexual orientation or gender identity in other ways.[4] Under Title IX, discrimination on the basis of sex can include sexual harassment or sexual violence, such as rape, sexual assault, sexual battery, and sexual coercion. Rise Above Bullying is focused only on issues of sexual harassment, not sexual violence. OCR has been developing expanded regulations associated with students who are sexual or gender minorities. Their work generated significant opposition. It is unclear at the time this is being written, summer 2024, how this will proceed.

- Title VI of the Civil Rights Act of 1964 (Title VI) prohibits discrimination on the basis of race, color, or national origin in any educational program or activity receiving federal funds.[5] OCR has taken the position that this includes discrimination based on religion, if grounded in national origin.
- Section 504 of the Rehabilitation Act of 1973 (Section 504) prohibits discrimination on the basis of disability in programs or activities receiving federal financial assistance.[6]
- The Americans with Disabilities Act of 1990 (ADA) prohibits discrimination on the basis of disability.[7]

States also have constitutional provisions and statutes that protect against discrimination, most generally including sex, race, color, religion, and national origin. Some state statutes have been expanded to include other protected classes, including sexual or gender minorities. Charter schools are subject to the same federal civil rights obligations as all other public schools.[8]

The ADA covers private schools as places of public accommodation, which means that the schools must be physically accessible to those with disabilities. But these schools are not required to provide free appropriate education or develop an individualized educational program for students with disabilities. If your child attends a private school, you have very little authority to require that they address the bullying of your child. However, you can learn about the protections that are provided to students in public and private schools under federal civil rights law

---

3 Title IX of the Education Amendments of 1972. 20 USC. §§ 1681–1688.
4 https://www2.ed.gov/about/offices/list/ocr/lgbt.html (accessed 1 August 2024).
5 Title VI of the Civil Rights Act of 1964. 42 USC. §§ 2000d-2000d-7.
6 Section 504 of the Rehabilitation Act of 1973. 29 USC § 794.
7 The Americans with Disabilities Act of 1990. 42 USC. §§ 12131–12134.
8 Office for Civil Rights (OCR) (2014). Dear colleague letter: charter schools. US Department of Education, May 14. http://www.ed.gov/ocr/letters/colleague-201405-charter.pdf (accessed 1 August 2024).

and encourage your child's school to intervene in a way that is in accord with these requirements.

These laws are enforced through agency actions by OCR.[9] If your child's school does not respond effectively to your complaint, filing a complaint with OCR would be the next step. There will be more on this later in this chapter and in Chapter 12. These statutes also provide the basis for litigation against public schools, which will be discussed in this chapter and in Chapter 12.

Unfortunately, only students who are considered to be in protective classes can file a complaint with OCR. However, as you will see below, I have identified a way to accomplish this even if your child is not currently considered to be in a protected class. If as a result of the bullying your child is experiencing, they have developed mental health concerns that are interfering with their ability to learn, your child should qualify for services under Section 504.

It is exceptionally important to note these words: "serious, persistent, or pervasive."

- "Serious" usually applies to incidents that include violence or other truly significant harmful acts.
- "Persistent" is repeated hurtful acts that are more minor. The ongoing nature of these hurtful acts is what causes the harm. Recall the evidence from the PISA survey that was presented in Chapter 3. The PISA 2018 data for the United States indicated that 26% of students reported being bullied at least a few times a month, with 10% reporting frequent bullying of once a week or more. Once a week or more clearly would be considered "persistent."
- "Pervasive" hurtful behavior is hurtful acts that are widespread – directed at many students within a specific protected class. These acts could be serious, but are more likely persistent. As will be discussed in Chapter 12, it is my recommendation that pervasive hurtful situations be addressed by a group of parents and their children filing a complaint with OCR and possibly filing a lawsuit.

As was discussed in Chapter 3, one of the reasons the disciplinary code approach is ineffective is that an investigation under the district policy will focus on whether the accused student engaged in behavior that was significantly serious to warrant a disciplinary response. This generally requires that the student's wrongful actions have created a "substantial disruption." Principals are more likely to consider a serious hurtful act to meet this standard. However, they very often will not consider persistent or pervasive minor hurtful incidents to meet this standard. Students who are hurtful to achieve dominance and social status will rarely engage in violent hurtful actions that could be considered to constitute a

---

9 http://www2.ed.gov/about/offices/list/ocr/index.html (accessed 1 August 2024).

"substantial disruption." Their hurtful acts are almost always persistent or pervasive. This is a very significant reason for why the statutory and disciplinary code approach is woefully inadequate.

Important Documents

You are encouraged to download the following documents. These include regulations, guidance documents, and what are called "Dear Colleague Letters" (DCL), which is guidance provided by the USDOE agencies to schools that dictate their interpretation of regulations.

- OCR 2010 DCL on all aspects of discriminatory harassment of protected-class students.[10] The protections for sexual minority students have increased since this document was issued.
- Office for Special Education and Rehabilitation Services (OSERS) 2013 DCL on Individuals with Disabilities Education Act (IDEA) protections if your child is being bullied.[11] You should obtain this DCL if your child is on an Individual Education Plan (IEP).
- OCR 2014 DCL on Section 504 protections if your child is being bullied.[12] Even if your child is not currently on Section 504, this DCL is important.
- *Parent and Educator Resource Guide to Section 504 in Public Elementary and Secondary Schools.*[13] This document will also be important even if your child is not currently on Section 504.
- In the future, there will be two additional documents to obtain. One is the new regulations for Title IX and the other is new regulations for Section 504. Links to and a discussion of these new regulations will be on the Rise Above Bullying website.
- OCR complaint form.[14]
- It is also necessary that you obtain a document from your district that provides guidance on the process and complaint procedures for students with disabilities in your state under Section 504. Go to your child's school and ask for the procedural

---

10 USDOE, OCR (2010) Dear colleague letter: harassment and bullying. https://www2.ed.gov/about/offices/list/ocr/letters/colleague-201010.html (accessed 1 August 2024).

11 https://sites.ed.gov/idea/files/bullyingdcl-8-20-13.pdf (accessed 1 August 2024).

12 USDOE, OCR (2014). Dear colleague letter: bullying of students with disabilities, at 2. https://www2.ed.gov/about/offices/list/ocr/letters/colleague-bullying-201410.pdf (accessed 1 August 2024).

13 USDOE OCR (2016). Parent and educator resource guide to Section 504 in public elementary and secondary schools. https://www2.ed.gov/about/offices/list/ocr/docs/504-resource-guide-201612.pdf (accessed 1 August 2024). https://www2.ed.gov/about/offices/list/ocr/docs/504-resource-guide-201612.pdf (accessed 1 August 2024).

14 https://www2.ed.gov/about/offices/list/ocr/complaintform.pdf (accessed 1 August 2024).

document for Section 504. This document will contain the grievance procedures that you will need to follow. These will be different in each state and district. These will likely be modified after the issuance of new Section 504 regulations.

- It will also be necessary to contact your state department of education to determine whether there is the ability to file a complaint for discriminatory harassment within your state. This also varies depending on the state. Some state departments of education also provide the ability to file a complaint. In other states, there may be a civil rights agency that is separate from your state department of education.

On my Rise Above Bullying website, there are highlighted and annotated copies of these federal documents. It is my suggestion that you download these documents. Keep them in a three-ring binder. Whenever you are in discussions with your child's school, you can pull out a document that addresses an issue you think is important.

Schools Must Respond

The critical factor to focus on is whether such serious, pervasive, or persistent hurtful behavior has resulted in an interference with or limiting your child's ability to participate in or benefit from the services, activities, or opportunities offered by a school. Schools must respond to situations that they know or reasonably should know about. The focus must be on the interference these hurtful acts are causing to your child's ability to learn.

In Chapter 3, I provided the path on the http://StopBullying.Gov site to learn more about the federal civil rights laws. The page that outlines school responsibilities under federal civil rights laws outlines the following insight.[15]

> ### What Are a School's Obligations Regarding Harassment Based on Protected Classes?
>
> Anyone can report harassing conduct to a school. When a school receives a complaint they must take certain steps to investigate and resolve the situation.
>
> - Take immediate and appropriate action to investigate or otherwise determine what happened.
> - The investigation must be prompt, thorough, and impartial.
> - Interview targeted students, students or staff alleged to have engaged in harassment, and witnesses, and maintain written documentation of investigation.

---

15 https://www.stopbullying.gov/resources/laws/federal (accessed 1 August 2024).

- Communicate with targeted students regarding steps taken to end harassment and check in with targeted students to ensure that harassment has ceased.
- When an investigation reveals that harassment has occurred, a school should take steps reasonably calculated to:
  - End the harassment.
  - Eliminate any hostile environment.
  - Prevent harassment from recurring.
  - As appropriate, remedy the effects of the harassment.
  - Prevent retaliation against the targeted student(s), complainant(s), or witnesses.[16]

The requirements set forth in the 2010 DCL went a bit further. They specifically address that these statutes require more than what is covered under an anti-bullying policy and that a response must be more than just disciplining the hurtful student. As this DCL stated:

> If an investigation reveals that discriminatory harassment has occurred, a school must take prompt and effective steps reasonably calculated to end the harassment, eliminate any Hostile Environment and its effects, and prevent the harassment from recurring. These duties are a school's responsibility even if the misconduct also is covered by an anti-bullying policy, and regardless of whether a student has complained, asked the school to take action, or identified the harassment as a form of discrimination.
>
> ...
>
> When the behavior implicates the civil rights laws, school administrators should look beyond simply disciplining the perpetrators. While disciplining the perpetrators is likely a necessary step, it often is insufficient. A school's responsibility is to eliminate the Hostile Environment created by the harassment, address its effects, and take steps to ensure that harassment does not recur. Put differently, the unique effects of discriminatory harassment may demand a different response than would other types of bullying.[17]

Complying with Federal Civil Rights Regulations

The standards under civil rights regulations apply to all situations where a protected class student is experiencing serious or persistent bullying, or when many students in a protected class are experiencing pervasive hurtful behavior. Failure to take these steps could provide the basis for an OCR agency action or litigation against the district.

---

16 https://www.stopbullying.gov/resources/laws/federal.
17 USDOE, OCR (2010). Dear colleague letter: harassment and bullying, at 3–4.

To reiterate, under civil rights guidance, if a hostile environment is suspected or thought to exist, schools are required to conduct a prompt, thorough, and impartial investigation. If this investigation reveals that a hostile environment exists, the school must intervene by taking prompt and effective steps that are reasonably calculated to:

- **Stop the harassment.** Ensure that the hurtful behavior is stopped. OCR has expressly indicated that this requires more than just punishment.
- **Remedy the harmful effects.** Identify and address the challenges or harms that are being experienced by the student who has been treated badly, including both academic harms and emotional harms.
- **Correct the hostile environment.** Make any necessary corrections to the school environment to address any concerns identified in the investigation. At the top of the list addressing the environment are issues related to how the targeted student is being treated by school staff and how school staff are responding if they witness a hurtful incident or one is reported to them.
- **Monitor to ensure effectiveness.** Schools must engage in ongoing monitoring to ensure that things are better for all involved students.

The StopBullying.gov website does provide insight on what schools must do in situations where there are civil rights harassment concerns in violation of federal law. Unfortunately, the insight provided on this page is hidden away from other pages that are more prominent on the website.[18]

What Should a School Do to Resolve a Harassment Complaint?
- The school must be active in responding to harassment and should take reasonable steps when crafting remedies to minimize burdens on the targeted students.
- Appropriate responses will depend on the facts of each case and may include:
    - Developing, revising, and publicizing:
        o Policy prohibiting harassment and discrimination;
        o Grievance procedure for students to file harassment complaints;
        o Contact information for Title IX coordinators and others responsible for compliance with Section 504 and Title VI.
    - Training staff and administration on how to identify, report, and address harassment.
    - Providing monitors or additional adult supervision in areas where harassment occurs.
    - Determining consequences and services for harassers, including whether discipline is appropriate.

---

18 https://www.stopbullying.gov/resources/laws/federal (accessed 1 August 2024).

- Limiting interactions between harassers and targets.
- Providing targeted student an additional opportunity to obtain a benefit that was denied (e.g. retaking a test/class).
- Providing services to a student who was denied a benefit (e.g. academic support services).
- Schools do not have to wait until behavior creates a hostile environment to act and may respond to misconduct based on a protected class as soon as they learn of it.[19]

The 2010 DCL contained many examples of situations and suggestions for the comprehensive steps that should be considered to address the concerns. The intervention options are multiple and varied – not just a determination regarding whether discipline should occur.[20] The various recommendations have been sorted into like categories. As you will see, these relate to the recommendations presented in Chapter 12.

- **School commitment.** Clearly communicate that the school does not tolerate harassment and will be responsive to any information about such conduct. Reaffirm the school's policy against discrimination and hurtful behavior. Publicize the means by which students may report and to whom.
- **Stop the hurtful conduct.** Provide counseling for the person being hurtful. Take steps to prevent any retaliation against the person who made a complaint or was the subject of the harassment, or against those who provided information as witnesses. Use a progressive disciplinary response. Counsel the perpetrators about the hurtful effect of their conduct. What was left out of these suggestions is holding every identifiable supporter of those who were hurtful also accountable. This is necessary to stop the support for the hurtful behavior.
- **Protection steps.** Separate the accused harasser and the target by removing the hurtful student from a class, team, or group. Ensure more aggressive monitoring by staff of the places where the hurtful behavior has been occurring.
- **Remedy the harm.** Provide counseling for the target. Offer the targeted student tutoring or other academic assistance, as necessary.
- **Correct the environment.** Conduct outreach to involve parents and students in an effort to identify problems and improve the school climate. Provide teachers with training to recognize the various kinds of misconduct and constructively respond to various kinds of hurtful incidents. Host class discussions about harassment and sensitivity to students who may be "different." Educate the entire school community on civil rights and expectations of tolerance.

---

19 https://www.stopbullying.gov/resources/laws/federal.
20 USDOE, OCR (2010). Dear colleague letter: harassment and bullying, at 3–4.

- **Monitoring.** Make sure that the harassed students and their families know how to report any subsequent problems. Conduct follow-up inquiries to see if there have been any new incidents or any instances of retaliation. Respond promptly and appropriately to address continuing or new problems.

A current challenge is that beyond these statements of broad categories under which actions should be taken, there really has been no significant guidance provided to school leaders on how to accomplish these steps in a manner that has a reasonable likelihood of stopping the harassment, remedying the harm to the target, and correcting aspects of the environment that are supporting this harm. In Chapter 12, you will learn the research-based steps that I recommend.

Comprehensive Intervention Settlement

In 2012, OCR and the DOJ entered into a settlement agreement with the Anoka Hennepin School District in Minnesota after a complaint was filed by a group of sexual-minority students.[21] The settlement requirements go even further in what the district was required to do. This is what the district agreed to do:

> (T)he District has agreed, among other things, to: (1) review and improve its policies and procedures concerning harassment to address sex-based harassment, including harassment based on gender stereotypes, by working with an Equity Consultant; (2) hire or appoint a Title IX and Equity Coordinator to ensure proper implementation of the District's harassment policies and procedures; (3) conduct training of all District faculty, staff and students on policies and procedures for reporting and responding to harassment; (4) hire a Mental Health Consultant to assist students who are subject to harassment; (5) create an Anti-Bullying/Anti-Harassment Task Force; (6) administer an Anti-Bullying Survey once per year; (7) identify harassment "hot spots" and assign personnel to monitor these trouble areas; (8) ensure that all of its middle and high schools have a peer leadership program addressing harassment; (9) convene annual meetings between the Superintendent and students at every middle and high school in the District; and (10) provide compliance reports to DOJ and OCR each trimester during the five year term of the Decree.

---

21 Title IX: Sex-based Harassment: Anoka-Hennepin School District (MN) (#05115901). https://www2.ed.gov/about/offices/list/ocr/docs/investigations/05115901.html (accessed 1 August 2024).

There are some critically important aspects of the implementation of this approach that must be emphasized. Note that these requirements are in accord with the recommendations set forth in Chapter 3 for the key three components of a more effective approach to both reduce and respond effectively to hurtful behavior.

- The requirement of an annual survey and the creation of an anti-bullying/anti-harassment task force.
- Significant efforts to establish and support peer leadership programs in secondary schools.
- Ensuring effective interventions by training all district staff in both reporting and responding, district coordination for proper implementation of interventions, and a focus on mental health strategies to remedy the harm to those harassed.

If you proceed in filing a complaint as an individual focusing only on the bullying of your child, it is improbable that you should ask for this kind of a comprehensive intervention. One of the m most powerful times that this can be demanded is if you proceed with a group of parents and students within a protected class, working with the support of an advocacy group.

But My Child Is Not in a Protected Class

The requirements under federal civil rights regulations provide a much more comprehensive intervention approach than under state statutes and disciplinary codes. It is my opinion that these regulations should guide interventions in all instances of serious, persistent, or pervasive hurtful situations targeting any student – whether or not this student is a member of a protected class. Why should a student who is being treated badly in a persistent manner based on their sexual orientation receive a more comprehensive intervention than a student who is being treated badly in a persistent manner based on their weight or the fact that they have acne?

This recommendation is certainly not for the purposes of downplaying in any way the significant importance of schools addressing the increased concerns that students who are in protected classes face. The intent of suggesting that the actions required under the civil rights regulations should also guide the kinds of actions taken for students who are not within a protected class is to ensure consistency and a sufficiently comprehensive approach to also reduce the bullying all students are experiencing – whether or not they are currently considered to be in a protected class.

Based on numerous conversations with school leaders, far too many think that their school district disciplinary code provides the sole basis for their response to all hurtful situations. As was discussed in Chapter 3, one reason for this is the guidance USDOE provided to states in 2010, which was that states and districts include reference to protected-class students in their state statutes and districts policies. Because the district policy in many districts references protected-class students, principals think that their policy covers what they need to do.

This situation raises two interrelated concerns:

- Even if the student who is being treated badly is clearly within a protected class, and thus clearly deserves a more comprehensive resolution, the principal merely follows the disciplinary code – which is highly likely not to result in an effective resolution.
- If principals were to start distinguishing between students within a protected class and those who are not and were to implement a more comprehensive intervention, this would result in what I would consider a discriminatory impact. The situation of a protected-class student would receive a more comprehensive intervention. The situation of a non-protected-class student would be inferior. This simply should not be considered to be acceptable.

So, what is the solution? Make sure that the situations of all students who are being bullied or harassed in a serious or persistent manner that is resulting in an interference in their learning and ability to participate are resolved in the same comprehensive manner.

It is my belief that I have found a way to support parents in insisting upon this. It is highly probable that if your child is being bullied in a serious or persistent manner this has resulted in your child feeling consistently sad (depressed) and scared (anxious). This also very probably has interfered with your child's ability to learn and to participate in school activities. If this is the current situation of your child, then there is a way to have your child designated as having a disability under Section 504. Thus, your child would be considered within a protected class. As an added benefit, the protections under Section 504 are superior to those under Title IX and VI, as will be outlined later in this chapter.

Civil Rights Litigation

In 1999, in the case of *Davis v. Monroe County Board of Education*, the Supreme Court held that schools can be financially liable under Title IX if they are "deliberately indifferent to known acts of student-on-student sexual harassment and the harasser is under the school's authority," so long as the harassment is "so severe, pervasive, and objectionably offensive that it can be said to deprive the victims of access to the educational opportunities or benefits provided by the school."[22]

---

22 *Davis v. Monroe County Board of Education,* 526 US 629, 633, 650 (1999).

Under the decision in this case, the five elements of a case include:

- Student is a member of, or perceived to be a member of, a protected class under federal statutes and the hurtful behavior is associated with the student's protected-class status, or perception thereof.
- The school had actual knowledge of the harassment. ("Should have known" is the standard for agency enforcement.)
- The student or students engaging in the harassment were under the school's authority.
- The harassment was so severe, pervasive, and objectionably offensive that it deprived the student of access to the educational opportunities or benefits provided by the school.
- The school was deliberately indifferent to this harassment.

This liability standard is based on the principle that recipients of federal funds should be held liable only for their own misconduct and not the misconduct of others. Thus, Title IX does not make a school district liable for the conduct of students who are engaged in aggression. Rather, a district is liable only for its own misconduct in being deliberately indifferent in its response to known harassment.

The key element that is frequently in most contention in these cases is whether the school was deliberately indifferent. The most frequently quoted standard on this is from *Vance v. Spencer Cnty. Pub. Sch. Dist.*, a Sixth Circuit case. In interpreting the *Davis* standard, the court stated:

> Where a school district has actual knowledge that its efforts to remediate are ineffective, and it continues to use those same methods to no avail, such district has failed to act reasonably in light of the known circumstances.[23]

The guidance that is provided in Chapter 12 has been developed keeping in mind the possibility of litigation, especially as this relates to the template to document what is happening and the harms. My perspective is that success in litigation is more likely when a group of families collaborate with each other and with an advocacy group to initiate litigation against a district, along with a group complaint to OCR.

---

23 *Vance v. Spencer Cnty. Pub. Sch. Dist.*, 231 F.3d 253, 261 (6th Cir. 2000).

Bullying of Students with Disabilities

You may not consider your child to have a disability. However, if your child is being persistently treated badly, it is an almost certainty that this has negatively impacted their emotional well-being and is interfering with their ability to learn. This impact on their emotional well-being can be considered to have created a "mental health disorder." A "mental health disorder" that is causing an interference with their learning is, under Section 504, considered to be a "disability."

This characterization may make you or your child, feel uncomfortable. Your concern, and possibly theirs, is the use of the terms "mental health disorder" and "disability." If your child is being treated badly in a persistent manner and they are unable to get this to stop, then your child will feel likely be feeling very sad (depressed) and scared (anxious) and have a harder time focusing on their learning. So, yes, they likely have what could be characterized as a "mental health disorder," which can be considered a "disability." However, this "mental health disorder" or "disability" is not their fault. They are sad and scared because of what is happening to them that the school is not taking appropriate actions to stop.

My recommendation (see Chapter 12) is that the situation of all students who are being persistently bullied, which has resulted in their being consistently sad or scared and experiencing challenges in learning or participation in desired school activities, be handled under Section 504. Thus, my recommendation is that you seek to have your child designated as having a "mental health disorder" and a "disability." Doing so will open the ability to insist that the school address the bullying of your child in a way that has the best possible chance for success.

The intervention approach required for students with disabilities under Section 504 is superior to what is required under the two other federal civil rights laws, Title IX and Title VI. Under Section 504, the intervention plan must be developed by the student's Section 504 team and be incorporated into the student's Section 504 plan. The intervention plan to address the bullying the student is experiencing may be the only focus of the Section 504 plan.

When you proceed under Section 504, your child will be entitled to a plan to address the bullying developed by a team of knowledgeable people, which includes both you and your older child. This shifts the situation resolution dramatically away from just a principal making a decision under the disciplinary code. This plan to address the bullying and its harms must be written and incorporated into your child's Section 504 plan. There are valuable procedural safeguards to enforce this Section 504 plan.

If your child is not a member of any protected class, for example, if your child is being bullied because they are overweight, have acne, or any other reason that is not based on membership in a protected class, proceeding under

Section 504 with a mental health disability is the only way to require your child's school to implement a comprehensive intervention in accordance with civil rights regulations.

Even if your child is considered protected under Title IX or Title VI, requesting that your child be placed on Section 504 is advised. This is because of the more comprehensive requirements that the intervention plan be developed by a Section 504 team and the procedural safeguards.

Your child may also be concerned that other students will find out they are on a Section 504 plan, which could lead to more bullying. The fact that your child is on a Section 504 plan is information that your child's school is required to keep private and confidential. Thus, no other students will know unless your child tells them. Further, the reason they are being placed on Section 504 is not because of anything that is "wrong" with them. The reason to pursue a resolution that will be set forth in a Section 504 plan is that this is the most powerful way to get the wrong things that are happening to them stopped.

DCLs Addressing Bullying of Students with Disabilities

The importance of addressing the risks associated with the bullying of students with disabilities was reinforced by the USDOE in two DCLs. The other federal law that protects students with disabilities is the Individuals with Disabilities Act (IDEA).[24] The 2013 Office of Special Education and Rehabilitation Services (OSERS) DCL is specifically related to students who are receiving special education services under IDEA.[25] This DCL indicated that the bullying of or by a student on an IEP must be addressed by their IEP team in an IEP meeting.

A DCL issued in 2014 by OCR made it clear that the concern of a student with disabilities being bullied based on that disability or any other basis be addressed by that student's Section 504 team.[26]

The major concern noted in these documents is that bullying can result in denying a student's right to what is called a Free and Appropriate Public Education (FAPE). The concept of FAPE and the standards by which a hostile environment is considered to be present are the same. Essentially, when the hurtful behavior a student is receiving is interfering with or limiting that student's ability to participate in or benefit from the services, activities, or opportunities offered by a school, this is a both a hostile environment and an interference with FAPE.

---

24 Individuals with Disabilities Act. 20 USC. § 1400 et seq.
25 USDOE, OSERS (2013). Dear colleague letter: keeping students with disabilities safe from bullying.
26 USDOE, OCR (2014). Dear colleague letter: bullying of students with disabilities, at 2.

If Your Child Is on an IEP

As the 2013 OSERS DCL stated:

> Whether or not the bullying is related to the student's disability, any bullying of a student with a disability that results in the student not receiving meaningful educational benefit constitutes a denial of FAPE under the IDEA that must be remedied.[27]

The OSERS DCL placed an express requirement on schools related to any bullied student who is also on an IEP:

> Schools have an obligation to ensure that a student with a disability who is the target of bullying behavior continues to receive FAPE in accordance with his or her IEP. The school should, as part of its appropriate response to the bullying, convene the IEP Team to determine whether, as a result of the effects of the bullying, the student's needs have changed such that the IEP is no longer designed to provide meaningful educational benefit.[28]

While schools may seek to protect students with disabilities who are being bullied by placing them in a more restrictive environment away from the mainstream school community, the DCL specifically warned:

> Schools may not attempt to resolve the bullying situation by unilaterally changing the frequency, duration, intensity, placement, or location of the student's special education and related services.[29]

Further requirements set forth in the OSERS DCL relate to situations when a student with disabilities is found to be engaging in bullying behavior:

> If the student who engaged in the bullying behavior is a student with a disability, the IEP Team should review the student's IEP to determine if additional supports and services are needed to address the inappropriate behavior. In addition, the IEP Team and other school personnel should consider examining the environment in which the bullying occurred to determine if changes to the environment are warranted.[30]

---

27 USDOE OSERS (2013). Dear colleague letter: keeping students with disabilities safe from bullying.
28 USDOE OSERS (2013). Dear colleague letter: keeping students with disabilities safe from bullying, at 2.
29 USDOE OSERS (2013). Dear colleague letter: keeping students with disabilities safe from bullying, at 3.
30 USDOE OSERS (2013). Dear colleague letter: keeping students with disabilities safe from bullying, at 4.

If Your Child Is or Should Be on Section 504

The 2014 OCR DCL directed that if a student is on a Section 504 plan and is experiencing serious or persistent bullying that is interfering with FAPE, these concerns must be addressed in a Section 504 team meeting.

The key statements from this DCL are:

> Today's guidance explains that the bullying of a student with a disability on *any* basis can ... result in a denial of FAPE under Section 504 that must be remedied; it also reiterates schools' obligations to address conduct that may constitute a disability-based harassment violation and explains that a school must also remedy the denial of FAPE resulting from disability-based harassment.[31]
>
> Under Section 504, as part of a school's appropriate response to bullying on any basis, the school should convene the IEP team or the Section 504 team to determine whether, as a result of the effects of the bullying, the student's needs have changed such that the student is no longer receiving FAPE.[32]

Another key statement from this DCL is:

> Building on OSERS's 2013 guidance, today's guidance explains that the bullying of a student with a disability on *any* basis can similarly result in a denial of FAPE under Section 504 that must be remedied; it also reiterates schools' obligations to address conduct that may constitute a disability-based harassment violation and explains that a school must also remedy the denial of FAPE resulting from disability-based harassment.[33]

Several key statements in this document outline the school's responsibility to identify students who are experiencing a disability to ensure that they receive appropriate services.

> Schools also have an obligation under Section 504 to evaluate students who need or are believed to need special education or related services.[34]
>
> The FAPE requirement to evaluate applies to all students who are known or believed to need special education or related services, regardless of the nature or severity of the disability. 34 C.F.R. §§ 104.33, -0.35. For a student

---

31 USDOE, OCR (2014). Dear colleague letter: bullying of students with disabilities, at 2.
32 USDOE, OCR (2014). Dear colleague letter: bullying of students with disabilities, at 6.
33 USDOE, OCR (2014). Dear colleague letter: bullying of students with disabilities, at 2.
34 USDOE, OCR (2014). Dear colleague letter: bullying of students with disabilities, at 3.

who is suspected of having a disability but who is not yet receiving IDEA or Section 504 services, OCR may consider whether the school met its obligation to evaluate the student. 34 C.F.R. § 104.35. For example, if a student suspected of having a disability was missing school to avoid bullying, OCR may consider whether the student's evaluation was unduly delayed (e.g. if the school knew or should have known of the bullying and failed to act) in determining whether there was a denial of FAPE under the circumstances.[35]

These provisions make it clear that if your child has developed a mental health concern that is resulting in an interference with their learning, the school has both an obligation to consider your child for placement on Section 504 and to develop a 504 plan to address the bullying your child is experiencing.

There is language in this DCL that could be confusing. This relates to the distinction between "disability-based harassment" and "bullying on any basis" that is interfering with a student's FAPE. "Disability-based harassment" is harassment that is specifically directed at a student's actual disability; being bullied based on a student's actions associated with autism is an example. This is distinguished from "bullying on any basis" that is interfering with FAPE.

> Similarly, under Section 504, schools have an ongoing obligation to ensure that a qualified student with a disability who receives IDEA FAPE services or Section 504 FAPE services and who is the target of bullying continues to receive FAPE – an obligation that exists regardless of why the student is being bullied. Accordingly, under Section 504, as part of a school's appropriate response to bullying on any basis, the school should convene the IEP team or the Section 504 team to determine whether, as a result of the effects of the bullying, the student's needs have changed such that the student is no longer receiving FAPE.[36]

OCR noted:

> When OCR evaluates complaints involving bullying and students with disabilities, OCR may open an investigation to determine whether there has been a disability-based harassment violation, a FAPE violation, both, or neither, depending on the facts and circumstances of a given complaint.[37]

---

35 USDOE, OCR (2014). Dear colleague letter: bullying of students with disabilities, at 3. 7, n27.
36 USDOE, OCR (2014). Dear colleague letter: bullying of students with disabilities, at 6.
37 USDOE, OCR (2014). Dear colleague letter: bullying of students with disabilities, at 6.

If your child has a disability and is being bullied based on that disability, you may be filing a complaint based both on the disability-based harassment and interference with FAPE. If your child is being bullied on some other basis and this is interfering with their ability to learn and participate, this would solely be a complaint based on interference with FAPE.

This DCL also notes:

> When a student with a disability has engaged in misconduct that is caused by his or her disability, the student's own misconduct would not relieve the school of its legal obligation to determine whether that student's civil rights were violated by the bullying conduct of the other student. For example, if a student, for reasons related to his disability, hits another student and other students then call him "crazy" on a daily basis, the school should, of course, address the conduct of the student with a disability. Nonetheless, the school must also consider whether the student with a disability is being bullied on the basis of disability under Section 504 and Title II.[38]

If, either because of other disabilities or in response to being bullied, your child triggered and also engaged in hurtful behavior, this misconduct of your child should be addressed in addition to addressing the bullying of your child. The fact that your child has also been hurtful does not negate the requirement to address how your child is being treated.

Like the 2010 DCL, this DCL provided excellent insight into the many strategies that the school should consider implementing to address these concerns.

> OCR could require, for example, that the district (1) ensure that FAPE is provided to the student by convening the Section 504 team to determine if the student needs different or additional services (including compensatory services) and, if so, providing them; (2) offer counseling to the student to remedy the harm that the school allowed to persist; (3) monitor whether bullying persists for the student and take corrective action to ensure the bullying ceases; (4) develop and implement a school-wide bullying prevention strategy based on positive behavior supports; (5) devise a voluntary school climate survey for students and parents to assess the presence and effect of bullying based on disability and to respond to issues that arise in the survey; (6) revise the district's anti-bullying policies to develop staff protocols in order to improve the district's response to bullying; (7) train

---

38 USDOE, OCR (2014). Dear colleague letter: bullying of students with disabilities, at 5, n20.

staff and parent volunteers, such as those who monitor lunch and recess or chaperone field trips, on the district's anti-bullying policies, including how to recognize and report instances of bullying on any basis; and (8) provide continuing education to students on the district's anti-bullying policies, including where to get help if a student either witnesses or experiences bullying conduct of any kind.[39]

As absolutely clear as the requirements set forth in these two DCLs are, what I have found is that its requirements are not being implemented by schools throughout the country.

As noted above, OCR will be releasing new regulations for Section 504. I have reviewed the comments submitted by major education organizations related to these new regulations. There was not a strong focus on bullying in these comments. I also wrote to OCR to ask them. OCR could not, of course, tell me what was going to be in the regulations. I did ask specifically about the 2014 DCL. This was their response:

> Thank you for your support for OCR's 2014 Dear Colleague Letter concerning the bullying of students with disabilities and the effects of that bullying on their education, including on the special education and related services to which they are entitled. As you are aware, that guidance states that schools have an obligation under Section 504 to evaluate students who need or are believed to need special education or related services, and that bullying on any basis of a student with a disability who is receiving Section 504 FAPE services can result in the denial of FAPE that must be remedied under Section 504. If a parent disagrees with any decisions regarding the identification, evaluation, or educational placement of his or her child, the parent may seek an impartial hearing. 34 C.F.R. 104.36. You may find it helpful to refer to an additional OCR guidance, *Parent and Educator Resource Guide to Section 504 in Public Elementary and Secondary Schools*, which discusses these and other issues.

My reading of this response is that OCR still strongly supports this DCL. I had specifically asked about situations where students had developed mental health concerns that were interfering with FAPE because they were being bullied. This would fall within the "are believed to need" situations. Their response provides an endorsement for the approach I am recommending.

---

39 USDOE, OCR (2014). Dear colleague letter: bullying of students with disabilities, at 10.

Parent and Educator Resource Guide

In 2016, USDOE OCR issued an excellent guide, the *Parent and Educator Resource Guide to Section 504 in Public Elementary and Secondary Schools.*[40] You will find on the Rise Above Bullying website a highlighted and annotated version of this document. As you will see in Chapter 12, in persistent hurtful situations that have caused your child to be experiencing mental health concerns and that are interfering with their learning or participation, you are encouraged to request that your child both be placed on a Section 504 plan and that the bullying of your child be addressed by the Section 504 team, with this plan incorporated into your child's Section 504 plan. In fact, the plan to address the bullying may be the only component of your child's Section 504 plan.

To accomplish this, it will be helpful for you to know the basics of Section 504 and how you can take steps to ensure your child's school complies with its requirements. The following are the key provisions and protections for students.

Eligibility

Under Section 504, schools must identify and locate all students who are disabled and are not receiving FAPE.[41] Schools must also notify these students and their parents of the district's responsibility under Section 504.[42]

The Section 504 definition of impairment includes any mental or psychological disorder that substantially limits a major life activity.[43] Major life activities include learning, concentrating, and thinking. The ability to fully participate in learning and other activities at school is considered a major life activity for any student. A student can qualify for Section 504 even if they are successfully maintaining good grades due to their significant efforts.

Thus, if your child has developed mental health concerns as a result of being bullied in a serious or persistent manner, which has created a substantial limitation on their ability to learn, concentrate, think, and fully participate in classroom and school activities, your child should be considered eligible for services under Section 504.

---

40 USDOE OCR (2016). Parent and educator resource guide to Section 504 in public elementary and secondary schools.
41 34 CFR §104.32(a).
42 34 CFR §104.32(b).
43 34 C.F.R. §104.3(j)(2)(i).

Aids and Services

What needs to be included in a Section 504 plan are the aids and services that the school will provide to better support the student. Often, these aids and services are called "accommodations." Sometimes, a Section 504 plan is called a "504 Accommodations Plan."

Unless your child has other challenges, they will not need any aids and services other than a comprehensive plan to address the bullying. Even if your child does not need other kinds of services more typically provided to students with disabilities, your child is fully protected from disability-based discrimination under Section 504's general non-discrimination requirements and the bullying of your child must be addressed in a Section 504 plan.[44]

For a student who is experiencing bullying, the aids and services incorporated into the plan must include all of the actions the school will take to address the bullying concerns that your child is experiencing. This includes how the school will stop the hurtful behavior, remedy the academic and emotional harm to your child, correct the hostile environment, and monitor to ensure effectiveness. More on these strategies in Chapter 12.

Evaluation/Investigation

Under Section 504, school districts must conduct an evaluation in a timely manner of any student who needs or is believed to need special education or related services because of a disability. Under all civil rights regulations, if the school suspects that a hostile environment exists, it is required to conduct a prompt, unbiased, and comprehensive "investigation." The terms "evaluation" under Section 504 and "investigation" under civil rights regulations mean the same process. However, under Section 504 regulations, schools do not have a specific time frame within which they need to engage in this evaluation. This is likely to change with the new regulations. Under civil rights regulations, the investigation must be "prompt."

School districts must have standards and procedures to evaluate students who may have a disability and need Section 504 services. The evaluation of a student, however, must be individualized and conducted by a "knowledgeable person."

The person who conducts an evaluation of your child's situation must have an in-depth understanding of bullying and civil rights regulations. You will need to specifically inquire about this. My inquiries of Section 504 coordinators have yielded insight that they generally are ill prepared to know how to do this.

---

44 34 C.F.R. §§ 104.4(b), 104.21-23, 104.37, 104.61 (incorporating 34 C.F.R. § 100.7(e)).

Under IDEA, a parent has the right to an Independent Educational Evaluation (IEE) paid for by the district if the parent disagrees with an evaluation provided by the school district.[45] An IEE means an evaluation conducted by a qualified examiner who is not employed by the school district. If a parent requests an IEE, the school district must provide information to parents about their criteria for an IEE. The current criteria of most districts does not focus on what kind of an evaluation would be necessary to address bullying and hostile environment concerns. However, the school district must also provide parents with an opportunity to demonstrate that unique circumstances justify an IEE that does not meet the district's current criteria. If a parent requests an IEE, the school district must, without unnecessary delay, either ensure that an IEE is provided or initiate a due process hearing to show that its evaluation is appropriate.

While IDEA regulations specifically provide for an IEE at public expense, Section 504 regulations are not as robust on the need for districts to pay for an IEE. However, the Parents and Educator's Guide does provide some insight that could be helpful in requesting this. It reads in part:

("Recipients must also pay for psychological services and those medical services necessary for diagnostic and evaluative purposes."); ... If a school district does not have the appropriate personnel on staff to conduct a medical assessment for diagnostic and evaluative purposes, the district must make arrangements for the medical assessment at no cost to the parent.[46]

A strong argument can be made that, if the district does not have a knowledgeable person on staff who has excellent insight into both bullying and the requirements under Section 504 to address these concerns, then the parent should have the right to request an IEE. As noted, at the time of writing of this book, OCR is developing new regulations for Section 504. It is probable they will provide greater clarification over when school districts must make arrangements to provide an assessment at no cost to the parent. Updated information will be provided on the Rise Above Bullying website, along with a template letter to request an IEE if the regulations expand this opportunity and if you think this is necessary.

An online course that is on the Rise Above Bullying website will provide professionals in the community with the insight they need to effectively conduct this kind of IEE.

---

45 20 USC 1415(b)(1) and (d)(2)(A)); 34 CFR 300.502(a)(1).
46 USDOE OCR (2016). Parent and educator resource guide to Section 504 in public elementary and secondary schools, at 13, n51.

Section 504 Team

The Section 504 team must consist of "knowledgeable people." This may include school nurses, teachers, counselors, psychologists, school administrators, social workers, doctors, and so on. This Section 504 team must interpret the evaluation/investigation and determine what aids and supports are needed. I suggest asking your child to identify a school staff member who they trust to be on this team. In addition, if your child participates in any after school programs or extracurricular activities where bullying is also occurring, a representative from this program or activity should be included on the team.

You and your older child are the most knowledgeable people about what is happening to your child, the harm, the environment, and what is necessary to support your child. Under the current Section 504 regulations, the school does not have a legal requirement to include you or your child on the Section 504 team. Most all schools do. If your child's school has other parents and students participate in Section 504 teams, they absolutely must allow you and your child to do so. This is also an issue that may change with the new regulations. It will be necessary to exclude you from any discussions related specifically to how the school will address the students who are being hurtful. But the Section 504 plan should include the general approach the school will be using to accomplish this.

Bullying and Harassment

The *Parent and Educator Resource Guide to Section 504* also provides a section on bullying and harassment that reads in part:

> Section 504 prohibits disability-based harassment by peers that is sufficiently serious to deny or limit a student's ability to participate in or benefit from the school's education programs and activities (in other words, creates a hostile environment). When a school district knows or reasonably should know of possible disability-based harassment, it must take immediate and appropriate steps to investigate or otherwise determine what occurred. If an investigation reveals that the harassment created a hostile environment, the recipient must take prompt and effective steps reasonably calculated to end the harassment, eliminate the hostile environment, prevent the harassment from recurring, and, as appropriate, remedy its effects.
>
> Bullying and harassment of a student by his or her peers, based on disability, may deny a student equal educational opportunities. Note, however, that the label used to describe an incident (for example, bullying, hazing, teasing) does not determine how a school is obligated to respond. Rather, the nature of the conduct itself must be assessed for civil rights implications.

...

Schools also have responsibilities under Section 504's FAPE requirements when a student with a disability is harassed or bullied on any basis (for example, bullied based on disability, or national origin, or homelessness, or appearance). This is because the bullying or harassment can result in a denial of FAPE under Section 504 and, if that occurs, it must be remedied. FAPE may be denied to a student when, for example, the effects of the bullying include adverse changes in the student's academic performance or behavior.[47]

Note the earlier discussion on the timeline for which an evaluation must be conducted. In a situation of bullying, OCR directs that this investigation must be "immediate." Note the reference to the prompt and effective steps reasonably calculated to end the harassment, eliminate the hostile environment, prevent the harassment from recurring, and, as appropriate, remedy its effects. Note that your child's school may not remove your child from a class or activity if your child is being bullied. If removal from a class or activity is deemed necessary, the student who is engaging in bullying must be removed.

Note the statement "on any basis." Based on this statement and the requirements set forth in the 2014 DCL, if your child is being bullied on any basis, and this has resulted in your child experiencing mental health concerns and an interference with their ability to learn and participate, your child both qualifies for Section 504 and the appropriate prompt and effective steps to address this concern. This means that if your child is not within a protected class under civil rights laws or receives protection under other civil rights laws, your child is entitled to protection under Section 504.[48]

Procedural Safeguards

Under Section 504 conflicts between parents and the school about Section 504 issues are to be resolved through due process or through the school district's grievance procedures. School districts are required to establish and implement a system of procedural safeguards for parents to appeal district actions regarding the identification, evaluation, or educational placement of students with disabilities

---

47 USDOE OCR (2016). Parent and educator resource guide to Section 504 in public elementary and secondary schools, at 32, 34.

48 This section also references situations where a school staff member is being hurtful: USDOE OCR (2016). Parent and educator resource guide to Section 504 in public elementary and secondary schools, at 32, n121.

who need or are believed to need special education or related services. This obligation is more commonly known as "due process."

The grievance procedures for your child's school will be outlined in the document you should obtain from your child's district. This most often is a document created by your state's education agency. Template letters you can use or draw from are on the Rise Above Bullying website.

Generally, you have five options if you are in disagreement with your child's school:

- **Option 1: Negotiation.** If you are having challenges with your child's school, contact the district and ask for the name of the district's 504 coordinator. Send an email or letter to this person outlining the concerns, what has happened, and the outcome you desire.
- **Option 2: Alternative dispute resolution.** "Alternative dispute resolution" is a term that refers to different ways to resolve a conflict. This could include a process called mediation, when you and the school try to reach an agreement with the help of a neutral third person. Some, but not all, states and school districts offer alternative dispute resolution for 504 plans. Alternative dispute resolution can be a very effective approach. However, you will need to be prepared to educate the mediator.
- **Option 3: Impartial hearing.** You can request to resolve a dispute through an impartial hearing. You will need to file a request for an impartial hearing in a letter to your district. An impartial hearing will provide you with an opportunity to present your side of the story to a neutral person who decides the case. This person is usually called a hearing officer. If you do not like the decision, you can appeal. Your district's document will inform you how you can appeal. The rules on these hearings vary from state to state and can be complicated. You might consider hiring a special education advocate or lawyer before you ask for a hearing. You will need to be prepared to educate the hearings officer.
- **Option 4: Office for Civil Rights complaint.** You can file a complaint with OCR. You must file the complaint within 180 days of the violation. An OCR complaint may lead to an investigation of the school. Details of how to file a discrimination complaint with the Office for Civil Rights appear on the OCR website.[49]
- **Option 5: Litigation.** If you believe the school is discriminating against your child and the harm has been significant, you can also file a lawsuit. A huge challenge is that these lawsuits can be very expensive and will require retaining a lawyer. Most frequently, these lawsuits proceed on a contingency basis. This means you will have to pay for costs, but the attorney agrees to pursue the case based on an agreement with you to share in the proceeds. The attorney will have to spend a lot of time doing this, which is a cost to them, so an attorney is going

---

49 https://www2.ed.gov/about/offices/list/ocr/docs/howto.html?src=rt (accessed 1 August 2024).

to want to have a strong feeling they will be able to prevail. You can frequently get a free or low-cost consultation with an attorney. If your child is among a group of students of the same identity group, a lawsuit filed on behalf of the group is likely stronger. You may be able to obtain legal services through an advocacy group that supports this identity group.

Family Educational Rights and Privacy Act

The Family Educational Rights and Privacy Act (FERPA) is a federal law that protects the privacy of student education records.[50] The law applies to all schools that receive funds under an applicable program of the US Department of Education.

It is absolutely imperative that no one outside of the staff members on the Section 504 team know that you and your child filed a complaint. If the student who was hurtful is told that you or your child filed this complaint, retaliation is possible. If any staff member discloses that your child filed the complaint, this news could get to this hurtful student. Any reference to a complaint should relate that it was filed by a "witness." Your child is a witness to what has been happening.

Additionally, because of the huge battles going on in our society related to minority identity groups, it is essential that you insist that the fact that you and your child filed a complaint be kept confidential. FERPA gives you the right to file a complaint with the district if any of this information is shared.

Free Speech

Bullying behavior can be physical. More often, bullying is verbal or relational aggression. Given that the concern is hurtful speech, the free speech rights of students are an important issue to consider. Currently, there are huge controversies related to speech rights of students at the university level. This has heightened the concerns about who gets to speak on campus and when does the line between speech that some might disapprove of cross over to hurtful speech that should give rise to some limitations or punishment.

It is helpful to frame this discussion with an analysis of the historical underpinnings of the free speech provision in the First Amendment. There is considerable disagreement about exactly what the framers of the Bill of Rights were thinking.[51]

---

50 20 USC § 1232g; 34 CFR Part 99. https://www2.ed.gov/policy/gen/guid/fpco/ferpa/index. html#:~:text=The%20Family%20Educational%20Rights%20and,the%20U.S.%20Department%20 of%20Education (accessed 1 August 2024).
51 Levy, L. (1985). The Emergence of Free Press. Oxford University Press.

However, the natural rights philosophy advocated by John Locke, who was revered by many early leaders, was likely influential. The natural law perspective was expressed as follows:

> Without Freedom of Thought, there can be no such Thing as Wisdom; and no such Thing as Publick Liberty, without Freedom of Speech: Which is the Right of every Man, as far as by it he does not hurt and control the Right of another; and this is the only Check which it ought to suffer, the only Bounds which it ought to know.[52]

An excellent contemporary discussion of these issues from the perspective of schools was set forth in a document entitled "Harassment, Bullying and Free Expression: Guidelines for Free and Safe Public Schools":

> It is important to distinguish between speech that expresses an idea, including religious or political viewpoints – even ideas some find offensive – and speech that is intended to cause, or school administrators demonstrate is likely to cause, emotional or psychological harm to the listener. Words that convey ideas are one thing; words that are used as assault weapons quite another.[53]

Note the great similarity between this statement and the prior statement by Locke. Essentially, the line at which students' free-speech rights cross over to speech that can be restricted in school is when such speech intrudes with other important student rights that schools must also protect, specifically the right to receive an education.

There have been five Supreme Court cases addressing student free-speech rights. Four of these relate to situations that could be involved when considering student speech that disparages other students. These are: *Tinker v. Des Moines Ind. Comm. Sch. Dist.*, *Bethel School District v. Fraser*, *Morse v. Frederick*, and *Mahanoy v. Area School District v. B.L.*[54]

---

52 Trenchard, J. and Gordon, T. (1720). Cato's Letters, letter 15, February 4 (6th ed., 1755), 1:96 (emphasis added).

53 American Jewish Committee and Religious Freedom Education Project/First Amendment Center (2012). Harassment, bullying and free expression: guidelines for free and safe public schools. https://www.christianlegalsociety.org/wp-content/uploads/2023/01/FAC-Harassment-Free-Expression-BROCHURE.pdf (emphasis added) (accessed 1 August 2024).

54 *Tinker v. Des Moines Ind. Comm. Sch. Dist.*, 393 US 503 (1969); *Bethel School District v. Fraser*, 478 US 675 (1986); *Morse v. Frederick*, 551 US 393 (2007); *Mahanoy Area School District v. B.L* 141 S. Ct. 2038 (2021).

The *Tinker* case involved the right of students to wear black armbands to protest the war in Vietnam. The Court made strong statements related to the protection of students' free-speech rights, but also indicated schools may restrict student speech if there are reasons to believe it could cause a substantial disruption or a significant interference with other students. This case provided the foundational basis for when school officials could discipline students for on-campus speech.

The next Supreme Court case addressing student free speech was *Fraser*, which involved student speech presented during an assembly that included an explicit sexual metaphor. The Court determined that school administrators could respond to student speech that was "lewd, vulgar, plainly offensive, and contrary to the school's educational mission."

The case of *Morse* involved student display of a sign that read "Bong Hits 4 Jesus" at what the court considered to be a school event, where students were watching the Olympic torch passing the school. The manner in which the Supreme Court approached its analysis in *Morse* focused on student safety – related in this case to drug abuse. As such, this decision is directly applicable to the situation involving speech that could harm other students, including situations involving bullying. Essentially, the court held that if the issue is student safety, the school has more latitude to restrict student speech.

In the *Mahanoy* case, the Court ruled that a public high school student's off-campus social media postings in which she used vulgar language and disparaged school programs constituted protected speech. However, the Court noted that schools can intervene in situations of student off-campus speech if such speech has or reasonably could create a substantial disruption at school or interference with the rights of other students. This could include situations involving serious or severe bullying or harassment targeting particular individuals.

At the lower court level, the courts have varied in their analysis. Most of the cases addressing the authority of schools to restrict disparaging speech have been in situations involving student dress codes. These cases have not specifically focused on situations involving bullying or harassment. In most, but not all, cases the courts have upheld schools' decisions to prohibit the Confederate flag at school, under *Tinker*. Past racially charged violent incidents allowed the officials to predict that the display of the Confederate flag foreseeably could substantially disrupt the schools.[55]

In cases where the issue has been anti-homosexual speech based on religious objections or anti-Islamic speech, the decisions have been more varied. In *Nixon*

---

55 *Nixon v. Northern Local School District Board of Education*, 83 F. Supp. 2d 956 (S.D. Ohio 2005); *West v. Derby Unified Sch. Dist.*, 206 F.3d 1358 (10th Cir. 2000).

v. Northern Local School District Board of Education, a Federal District Court upheld the right of a student to wear a T-shirt that stated: "Homosexuality is a sin! Islam is a lie! Abortion is murder! Some issues are just black and white!"[56] In *Zamecnik v. Indian Prairie School Dist. #204*, the Seventh Circuit upheld the right of students to wear a T-shirt stating: "Be Happy, Not Gay."[57] In *Harper v. Poway*, the Ninth Circuit upheld the school's right to restrict Harper's anti-homosexuality speech, but this decision was vacated on appeal by the Supreme Court.[58] In *Sapp v. Alachua*, a Federal District Court supported the decision of a school in a suit brought by students who were prohibited from wearing T-shirts stating: "Islam is of the Devil."[59]

A close reading of these cases reveals that the reasons for the differences appear to be mostly related to the sufficiency of the evidence presented by the school that the speech had or could reasonably be predicted to cause a substantial disruption or interference with the rights of other students to feel secure.

What is happening now on college campuses appears to be different from the prior situations involved in the case law. At this point in time, there is the presentation of speech that is controversial and potentially offensive to some done in a manner that is either respectful, such as a speech at a law school, or in protest, such as student protests regarding Gaza, that is received in a manner of protest or expressions of fear. Given the current societal divides, it can be anticipated that issues related to the boundaries of student speech in situations of controversial speech regarding identity groups will continue to be a source of significant controversy.

Recognize that the current state of legal analysis on these free-speech concerns will create significant challenges for your principal. There is no clear guidance on how they should handle these situations. The best way for you to proceed if you are independently filing a complaint with the school on the basis of the concerns presented to your child is that you not focus on general hurtful speech within the school, but on the hurtful speech directed at your child. If you are working with a group of parents and students and there are indicators of hurtful speech that are more generally focused on the identity of the students in your group, examples of this hurtful speech should be documented. This way OCR can be the ones who direct the district to place limits on such speech.

---

56 *Nixon v. Northern Local School District Board of Education,* 83 F. Supp. 2d 956 (S.D. Ohio 2005).

57 *Zamecnik v. Indian Prairie School Dist. #204,* 636 F.3d 874 (7th Cir. 2011).

58 *Harper v. Poway Unified School District,* 445 F.3d 1166 (9th Cir. 2006).

59 *Sapp v. School Bd of Alachua Cnty No. 09-242* (N.D. Fla. Sept. 30, 2011).

12

Stop the Harm

Insist That Your Child's School Stop the Harm

Having provided substantial guidance on how to empower your child to better handle bullying situations, we now come to the advocacy chapter – how to insist that your child's school take the proper steps to stop and remedy the harm that is occurring to your child. As was discussed in Chapter 3, the current approach most schools are using, under the dictates of their state statutes, is not working.

This chapter will outline how to document what is happening and how to proceed either individually or with a group of parents of similarly treated students to insist your child's school take the steps that are reasonably calculated to stop the hurtful behavior, remedy the harm to your child or a group of students, correct aspects of the environment that are supporting such hurtful behavior, and monitor to ensure that these steps have been effective.

Empower – Advocate

There are two key words in the title of this book: "empower" and "advocate." Chapters 4 through 10 have provided extensive insight into strategies to better empower your child to be able to maintain positive relationships and respond effectively when hurtful incidents or situations occur. If you and your child follow this guidance, the concerns about hurtful behavior directed at your child may be effectively managed.

Hopefully, this empowerment guidance will result in a decrease in the hurtful treatment your child is experiencing. Unfortunately, this may not have happened. This chapter will provide you with guidance on how to advocate for your child at their school to insist that the school take the steps to ensure that the hurtful treatment your child is experiencing is stopped.

Rise Above Bullying: Empower and Advocate for Your Child, First Edition. Nancy E. Willard.
© 2025 John Wiley & Sons, Inc. Published 2025 by John Wiley & Sons, Inc.

Individually or as a Group

You might proceed in filing a complaint only on behalf of your child. The other alternative is to work with a group of parents of students who are in the same identity group.

When proceeding as a group of parents of students in the same identity group, it is advised that the group reach out to a local, state, or national advocacy group that can provide legal guidance and support you in filing a complaint with OCR. The group can also support parents and students in filing a lawsuit. This would add some strength to the OCR complaint. A list of possible advocacy groups who support different minority identity groups is on the Rise Above Bullying website.

In this situation, all parents and students should complete the Documentation Guide set forth below. When proceeding as a group, you have the opportunity to accomplish a much more extensive analysis of the school environment issues that need to be addressed to ensure greater kindness, respect, and inclusion for all students. This is an advantage of proceeding as a group.

Addressing Concerns of Staff Hurtful Behavior

If a staff member is being hurtful to your child, this is a challenging situation to handle. The staff member is very likely to object to any insinuation that they are being hurtful. If, as a result of your complaint, the staff member brings in union representation the situation could get even more nasty.

It is my recommendation to initially raise these concerns very carefully within the context of the need to make corrections to the school environment that appear to be influencing students to be hurtful. If any staff member has been making hurtful comments directed at your child, initially you may refer to these comments as unintentional statements that are hurtful or that appear to demonstrate bias or prejudice. The statements of school staff may be very clearly intentional or knowingly biased or prejudiced. However, if you initially present this as concerns about unintentional aggression, the corrections may be more effective with this staff person.

It is my further recommendation not to initially pressure for any disciplinary action against a staff member. Provide your documentation of how the staff member is treating your child, as is outlined in the Documentation Guide below. Ask that this be corrected within the context of corrections to the school environment, together with the need to address how staff are responding if students are hurtful to your child in their presence. If a staff member continues to be hurtful to your child after this correction plan has been developed, that will be the time to raise this as a direct complaint.

If you do have absolutely verified examples of intentional hurtful behavior of staff, with other witnesses willing to talk, you might decide to proceed more directly to address this concern. Having an advocate or even an attorney to support you in these kinds of situations would be advised.

Documentation Guide

Below is a Documentation Guide for how to document what has been happening to your child and the harmful impact. This form is available on the Rise Above Bullying website in a word-processing document so that you can easily add your responses.

Note my guidance that you obtain a three-ring binder in which to store the civil rights documents suggested in Chapter 11. This binder is also a place to keep all of the documents you obtain from the school or district or otherwise. You should also create a folder on your computer with all of these documents.

Every communication you have with the school or district must be saved. If you have a meeting with a school or district staff person about this concern, take notes during the meeting. These notes go into your binder. Also, as quickly as possible, send an email to the person you met with. Write up your description of what was discussed and decided. At the end of this e-mail, type: "This email sets forth what we discussed and decided. If your recollection is different in any way, please promptly communicate this to me." This is in order to make sure everyone has the same understanding of what was discussed and decided.

This Documentation Guide uses student voice. The reason for this is that it is necessary to fully engage your child in the documentation of what is happening to them and the resolution. This will provide your child with a greater feeling of control over the situation – which is important for their feelings of empowerment. A document written from the perspective of "this is what is happening to me and how this is making me feel" will likely be more powerful in achieving a positive resolution than a document where parents or a professional set forth what is happening to a young person.

In completing this documentation, it will be helpful for you to have a calendar and to obtain the attendance records of your child from the school. These attendance records may be helpful in identifying the days when your child was treated badly if your child asked to go home or wanted to be absent the following day.

Documentation of What Has Been Happening

Protected Class

- Establish whether you are in a protected class. Students who are treated differently based on race, color, religion, sex, sexual orientation or identity, national origin, or disability are within a protected class. You are considered to be in a protected class if you are a member of that class – or are perceived to be. So if you are being bullied based on a perception that you are a sexual minority, even if you are not, you are considered to be in a protected class. You can also be in more than one protected class.

- Are you in a protected class? Alternatively, are you perceived to be in a protected class? If so, what protected class or classes?
- How are the hurtful acts relate to your protected class status? Demonstrate this based on what has been said, written, or other acts. This especially should include any name-calling based on membership or perceived membership in one or more of these classes.
- If you do not think you are in a protected class or are perceived to be, it will be necessary to establish that you are now suffering from mental health concerns that are associated with what has been happening and this is negatively impacting your learning and participation at school. The evidence from the questions below related to Harmful Emotional Impact and Harmful Interference with Learning and Participation will be helpful in establishing this.

Treated Badly by Students at School

- Describe how you have been treated badly by other students while at school. Assuming there are frequent hurtful acts, describe as many of these recent incidents as you can remember. Especially describe the more serious incidents, incidents where staff were present, incidents that were reported, and incidents where there were witnesses. These should be labeled by number: Incident 1, Incident 2, and so on. This way you can reference individual incidents in relation to the later questions.
  - What has happened? Where and how did this happen? Who was being hurtful? What other students were supporting the hurtful acts?
  - Identify other students who were present who might be willing to describe what happened.
  - Describe the possible motivations of the student being hurtful. Does this student or students appear from your perspective to have any kinds of challenges like easily triggering and becoming disruptive? Is this student or students being hurtful in a way you think may be to attract attention and gain social status? Have you had past interactions with this student or students that may be related to what is happening? Is this student seeking dominance, social status, and popularity? Has this student been hurtful to you in relation to some goal they have which is related to school activities? Does this student treat you badly because you do not follow the social norms of the school,

because you are considered "different" or a "misfit?" Are several students being hurtful to you because they all are participating in a friend group? Are issues related to dating partners involved? Does the student being hurtful appear to be doing this for their own entertainment and the entertainment of their followers?

Staff Response When Treated Badly by Students at School

• Further describe or identify from above any hurtful incidents that occurred in front of staff members or that you reported to a staff member. Describe how that staff member responded.
  – What staff member was present? How did the staff member respond? What staff member did you tell? What happened after this? Did things get better, stay the same, or get worse?

Treated Badly by Students Using Social Media

• Describe how you have been treated badly by other students from this school or other schools in the district when using social media, either while at school or outside of school. Describe how these hurtful social media acts are related to what is happening in school. Hopefully, you have saved or can find some examples of what has been posted or sent.
  – What has happened? Where and how has this happened? Who was being hurtful? What other students were supporting the hurtful acts?
  – Are there ways in which the hurtful online acts are related to what is happening at school? Describe this relationship.
    o Save and print out all social media communications, posts, or comments.

Treated Badly by School Staff

• Describe any situations where a school staff member has insulted, denigrated, bullied, harassed, or sexually harassed you. This includes brief statements or actions that communicate negative thoughts about you or other students who may be in the same protected class.
  – What has happened? Where and how has this happened? How frequently? Was this in the presence of other students?
  – Were any other staff members close by? If so, specifically describe how any other staff member reacted.
  – Identify other students who were present who might be willing to describe what happened.

Response If Reported to School

- Describe what happened if any of the above incidents or situations were reported to the school by you, by your parent, or by anyone else.
  - If you reported that students were hurtful to you at school or online, describe who you reported to, what happened in response, and what happened after this. Did things get better, stay the same, or get worse? Did you feel as though your concerns were heard and responded to effectively?
  - Did you experience retaliation in any way from the student who was hurtful, other students, or staff? If so, describe in full.
  - If you reported to the school that you were treated badly and a staff member saw this and did nothing in response, describe who you reported to, what happened in response, and what happened after this. Did things get better, stay the same, or get worse? Did you feel as though your concerns were heard and responded to effectively?
  - Did you experience retaliation after reporting? If so, describe in full.
  - If you reported to the school that you were treated badly by a staff member, describe who you reported to, what happened in response, and what happened after this. Did things get better, stay the same, or get worse? Did you feel as though your concerns were heard and responded to effectively?
  - Did you experience retaliation? If so, describe in full.
  - If you decided not to report in any of the above incidents or situations, why did you make the decision not to report?

Harmful Emotional Impact

- Describe how you are feeling as a result of these hurtful acts. This can be after each act or in general. Describe these concerns in as much detail as possible.
  - Do you find that you are frequently thinking about what has been happening to you? Are you having upsetting memories of what has been happening? Do these memories occur at times when you are not at school? Do you have dreams where people are hurtful to you? Do you feel distressed just thinking about going to school? If so, describe.
  - Do you find that you are avoiding or trying to avoid thinking about things that can bring up memories of how you are being treated? Are you avoiding or trying to avoid people, places, or activities that relate to how you are being treated? If so, describe.
  - Are you feeling anxious, sad, angry? Do you have negative thoughts about yourself, other people, school, the world? Do you sometimes blame yourself? Are you avoiding activities that you used to like to do? Do you feel disconnected from others? Do you have difficulties feeling positive emotions like being happy and joyful? If so, describe.

- Do you find that sometimes you are upset or become aggressive? Are you engaging in impulsive or self-harming behavior?
- Especially when you are at school, do you feel like you constantly have to be on guard because someone might be hurtful to you? Do you sometimes startle when people come up to you?
- Do you have difficulties concentrating? Do you have problems sleeping?
- Are you having headaches or stomach pain or other unexplained feelings of physical discomfort?

Harmful Interference on Your Learning or Participation

- Describe how, as a result what is happening to you, you have been unable to concentrate, learn, and/or participate in school activities. This also can be after each act or in general. Describe this in as much detail as possible.
  - Have you skipped school one or more days, skipped a class one or more times, or were late to school because you were upset and did not feel safe or welcome?
  - Have you had difficulties concentrating in class, found it hard to complete assignments, received lower grades, or not felt comfortable participating in class discussions?
  - Have you avoided riding the bus, going to certain areas of the school building, using the bathroom, using the locker room, or going into the cafeteria?
  - Have you avoided participating in school clubs, participating on a school sports team, or attending school activities?

Aspects of the School Environment That May Be Contributing

- Describe any aspects of the school environment that appear to be contributing to or reinforcing the way you are being treated badly by others. Hurtful statements made by staff or staff ignoring or not responding well when they have witnessed you being treated badly should be described. This may also include behavior management practices that have acted to denigrate or exclude you and any other aspects of the environment you think may be contributing to the concern.
  - Describe how staff behavior, such as statements made to or about you, how you are treated in class, how staff members respond if they witness you being bullied or you have reported this to them is contributing to how you are being treated or feel after you have been bullied.
  - Describe how behavior management practices used by the school, such as rewards, fun events for only some students, or a requirement that you carry a behavior card, appears to be contributing to how students are treating you.
  - Describe any other ways that your school is doing things that make you feel unwelcome or uncomfortable.

Hurtful Response by You

- Describe any incidents or situations where you responded badly because of how you were being treated, engaged in some form of retaliation, or fought back. Be sure to accept personal responsibility for your actions.
  - Specifically describe how you were treated right before you responded badly.
  - Was this reported? Were you punished? Did you try to explain the entire situation? What was the result?
  - Describe what has happened in the past that relates to this. This might include recent incidents when school staff saw you being treated badly and did nothing or just laughed, and prior incidents that were reported and nothing was done or what was done was not effective or made things worse.

Letter from Pediatrician and Counselor

After you and your child complete this documentation, it would be exceptionally helpful to obtain a letter from your pediatrician and counselor to include when you submit your complaint. Obtaining these services can be a challenge in some parts of the country and for some families. If this will be a financial challenge for you to obtain, there is specific reference in the *Parent and Educator Resource Guide to Section 504* for the requirement that the district will pay for such services. Footnote 51 in this document provides:

> Recipients must also pay for psychological services and those medical services necessary for diagnostic and evaluative purposes. ... If a school district does not have the appropriate personnel on staff to conduct a medical assessment for diagnostic and evaluative purposes, the district must make arrangements for the medical assessment at no cost to the parent.[1]

In another document on the USDOE OCR website is the following statement:

> A school district must conduct or arrange for an individual evaluation at no cost to the parents before any action is taken with respect to the initial placement of a child who has a disability, or before any significant change in that placement.[2]

---

1 USDOE OCR (2016). Parent and educator resource guide to Section 504 in public elementary and secondary schools. https://www2.ed.gov/about/offices/list/ocr/docs/504-resource-guide-201612.pdf (accessed 1 August 2024). https://www2.ed.gov/about/offices/list/ocr/docs/504-resource-guide-201612.pdf, p. 13, n51 (accessed 1 August 2024).
2 https://www2.ed.gov/about/offices/list/ocr/docs/edlite-FAPE504.html (accessed 1 August 2024).

On the Rise Above Bullying website, there is a template of what the pediatrician or counselor could say in this letter. The following recommended text should be adapted related to your child's current situation:

> A patient/client of mine is being bullied at [name of school]. I have discussed this situation with my patient/client and have found the following.
>
> Based on reports from my patient/client and their parent, it appears that they are experiencing both serious and persistent bullying from their peers. [Add staff if appropriate.] The kinds of hurtful actions that appear to be occurring include: [describe some reported situations].
>
> This bullying appears to be related to their identity within a community that receives protection under federal and state civil rights laws [or the perception thereof].
>
> It is my professional opinion that my patient/client is now experiencing: [input mental health diagnosis].
>
> It appears that as a result of this bullying, there has been a significant interference in the ability of my patient/client to learn and participate in school activities. This includes: [describe some interferences – especially focusing on times your patient/client stayed home with what were likely psychosomatic illnesses].
>
> It is my understanding that if a student of yours is experiencing a mental health condition and this is interfering with their receipt of a Free Appropriate Public Education, they should be evaluated for placement on a Section 504 plan.
>
> It is my further understanding that if a student who is receiving or is entitled to receive services under Section 504 is being bullied on any basis, this must be addressed by a Section 504 team in a team meeting and a plan of action must be developed that will be included in their Section 504 plan. While [name of your child] appears to not currently be receiving services under Section 504, this letter should notice you that it is my professional opinion that they are now experiencing mental health concerns and that there is an interference with their ability to learn and participate fully in school activities.
>
> It is my further understanding that this plan of action must include prompt and effective steps that your 504 team has reasonably calculated that will end the hurtful behavior, prevent it from recurring, remedy its harmful effects on my patient/client, correct the hostile environment to reduce the potential the hurtful acts will continue, and monitor to ensure effectiveness.
>
> I would be happy to assist with these efforts.

An important reason for these letters, especially from a pediatrician, is that you and your child are now engaged in a power dynamics relationship with your child's school. School principals are the "boss" of their school. District leaders are even more powerful "bosses." They have to act like "bosses" because they are responsible for the safety of many. Parents and students are on the lower levels in this hierarchy of power. Sometimes, this can result in the school leader presenting a position that they know what they should do. In society, pediatricians are in a significant position of power. A letter from a pediatrician will help you and your child to gain "power points" that will hopefully increase the willingness of the school leadership to take your concerns seriously.

Bullying Reports or Surveys

There are additional reports you should obtain, if possible. If you are living in a state that requires schools and districts to file annual bullying incident reports with your state department of education, make a public records request for the last five years of reports. Also go onto the OCR website that provides the data on the national reports of bullying of protected-class students at https://civilrightsdata.ed.gov and get the data for your district and school.

In addition, request copies of the results of any student wellness and school climate surveys that have been used in your child's school. If you are proceeding as a group, request all survey results from the district.

When you are able to get both surveys and reports, you will be able to compare. If 10% of your school's or district's students say they are being treated badly once a week or more, and there are very few reports on your school's or district's annual bullying reports and on the OCR website, this will be powerful example to the school and district leaders that what they are doing to address bullying is not working. Students are not reporting or, if they are, these situations are not being addressed.

Preparing the Complaint

Once you have the documentation, it is time to prepare a complaint to be submitted to the school. It is best that this complaint is written using the parent's voice. The following template is for use when you are requesting your child be placed on Section 504 and a resolution plan be incorporated into your child's Section 504 plan. A complaint template is also available on the Rise Above Bullying website in word-processing format. You will be able to pick out the language you want to use and cut the unnecessary language. If your child is receiving services on an IEP, the language will be different. An alternative version of this complaint form is on the Rise Above Bullying website.

If your child is in secondary school, the person who should receive this complaint likely will be the assistant principal. These are the school leaders who most often deal with disciplinary matters. You should also provide this documentation to your child's school counselor and to the school's Section 504 coordinator so that they are fully engaged in this process from the start.

> The attached report describes how my child is being bullied at [name of school] by students from this school while at school, by students from this school using social media, by staff members. I am submitting this report and this complaint, along with letters from my child's pediatrician and counselor. [If you cannot obtain a medical and psychological assessment, ask for this to be provided and paid for by the district.]
>
> As is documented in this report, my child is experiencing persistent, sometimes serious, bullying by their peers both at school and while using social media. My child is also being treated badly by [staff member] in ways that appear to be encouraging other students to be hurtful. I do not know if this staff hurtful behavior is intentional, based on bias, or is grounded in some other challenges. However, this also needs to be addressed. My documentation also describes situations where my child was treated badly in front of staff members and the inadequate response by those staff members. This also needs to be addressed.
>
> My child is considered a member of [name of protected class]. My child is being bullied based on the perspective they are a member of [protected class]. As is documented in the report, and validated by the letters from my child's pediatrician or counselor, my child is now experiencing a mental health disorder. This is causing an interference in their ability to learn, concentrate, think, and communicate in school. It is my understanding that this is considered to be an interference with FAPE.
>
> I request that my child be placed on Section 504. As has been directed by the US Department of Education's Office for Civil Rights [see attached – provide 2014 DCL], my child has a right to have this concern addressed by the Section 504 team, with a Section 504 plan that contains the aids and supports necessary to address these concerns.
>
> In addition to the documentation I have provided to you, I understand that you are required to engage in a prompt, unbiased, and comprehensive investigation. This investigation must be accomplished by a "knowledgeable person." In this case, a "knowledgeable person" must have a full understanding of the concerns of bullying and the requirements under federal civil rights, especially Section 504, for schools to respond. Prior to this investigation being launched, I request notice of who will be conducting this investigation. I also request insight into the recent trainings or professional development this

person has received recently to ensure that they are "knowledgeable." [There may be an additional strategy you could use, which is to ask for the district to pay for an Independent Educational Evaluator to conduct this investigation. This will depend on the new regulations for Section 504. More information will be on the Rise Above Bullying website.]

The Section 504 plan for my child should include how the school intends to take reasonable steps to stop the bullying, remedy the academic and emotional harm to my child, correct aspects of the environment that appear to be contributing to this problem, and monitor to ensure the hurtful behavior has stopped.

Both I and my child will participate on this 504 team. We do understand that if the team needs to specifically address how possible disciplinary actions might be taken against a student who is bullying my child, it would be inappropriate for us to participate in these discussions.

It is well known that if a student reports being bullied to the school, other students, including the one who has been hurtful, often engage in retaliation. In today's society, others in the community could also become hurtful to my child or our family because we have filed this complaint.

Therefore, I want to make this demand very clear. The fact that my child and I are filing this complaint must be treated as confidential by the school. All information about this complaint should be considered private and protected under the Family Educational Rights and Privacy Act. All staff members should be made aware of this, so that they do not disclose any information further. Information about this complaint should be restricted to only those staff members who have a specific need to know.

At such time that the student(s) who are being hurtful are informed or may become aware of this complaint, it is imperative that they not be told that my child and I are the ones who filed the complaint. These students should be told that a witness reported this concern, which was then further investigated. My child was a witness, in addition to also being the target.

Any violation of my child's privacy rights will immediately result in action against the school under FERPA.

Desired Outcome

Your desired outcome and the appropriate response by the school should be:

- Designate your child as receiving Section 504 services due to a mental health disability and interference with their ability to learn and participate in school activities, thus an interference with your child's FAPE.
  - If your child is already on an IEP or is receiving services under Section 504 for other challenges, this step is not necessary.

- If your child is also considered protected based on other identities, such as being a racial or religious minority or a sexual or gender minority, this Section 504 designation should be in addition to these protections. This is because the Section 504 protections provide for greater procedural safeguards and a team-based approach to resolution.
- Prompt, unbiased, and comprehensive investigation of the situation by a knowledgeable professional who will review your documentation and conduct further investigation.
  - This person must have knowledge of bullying and discriminatory harassment under civil rights laws and be unbiased.
- Hold a Section 504 team meeting.
  - This team should include you and your child, if older – and any other person who you think could provide assistance. However, you and your child should not be present when the team discusses issues specifically related to discipline or supports to be provided to the student who is being hurtful and their supporters – to protect their privacy.
- Develop a plan of action that is included in the Section 504 plan as aids and supports that is reasonably calculated to stop the hurtful behavior, remedy the harm to your child, correct the hostile environment, and monitor.

Possible Inappropriate Response by School

It is, unfortunately, quite possible that your principal does not know the difference between the district's disciplinary code and a requirement to respond under federal civil rights laws, especially how to respond under Section 504, based on the 2014 DCL. My assessment is that many school leaders have not received professional development on these issues.

If the principal responds that they will handle this situation under your district's disciplinary policy, respond as follows:

> I am not filing this complaint as a violation of the school's anti-bullying policy. Please review the attached 2014 Dear Colleague Letter from the USDOE Office for Civil Rights. I am requesting that my child be evaluated for designation as receiving Section 504 services, that an evaluation and investigation be promptly accomplished by an unbiased, knowledgeable professional who has expertise in bullying and civil rights regulations, followed by a Section 504 team meeting to address these concerns. It is my understanding that the Section 504 team, which will include me and my child, will agree to steps that are reasonably calculated to stop the harmful conduct, remedy the harm to my child, correct the hostile environment, and monitor the situation to ensure the hurtful conduct is stopped. These steps will be included in my child's Section 504 plan.

If the district does not have an unbiased, knowledgeable professional who has expertise in bullying and civil rights regulations to conduct this investigation, then I request that the district pay for an independent evaluator. (More insight into how the new Section 504 regulations might impact this request is on the Rise Above Bullying website.)

If the principal does not immediately proceed in response to your request, ask for information on your child's due process rights under Section 504 and follow the due process or grievance procedure as outlined by your district. A statement you can make in filing a due process hearing is:

Based on the directives provided by USDOE's Office for Civil Rights, that are attached, I have requested that my child be designated as appropriate for receiving Section 504 services, because as a result of being treated badly in a serious or persistent manner, my child has developed a mental health condition and this is interfering with their ability to learn and participate in school activities.

I have requested that a comprehensive evaluation and investigation be promptly conducted by an unbiased, knowledgeable professional who has expertise in bullying and civil rights regulations. If the district does not have an unbiased, knowledgeable professional who has expertise in civil rights regulations to conduct this investigation, then I request that the district pay for an independent evaluator. I further request a Section 504 team of knowledgeable people, including my child and I, be convened to develop a plan of action with steps that are reasonably calculated to stop the hurtful behavior, remedy the harm to my child, correct aspects of the environment, and a process for monitoring to ensure the hurtful behavior has stopped to be included in my child's Section 504 plan.

If you are denied a due process hearing, or the due process hearing decision is not supportive of your child's right to receive Section 504 services, or the Section 504 team does not create a plan of action that you and your child think will achieve the desired results, or, after the plan of action was agreed to, it is not appropriately or effectively implemented, then file a complaint with OCR. You may also have rights in some states to file a complaint at the state level – do both and they will connect and coordinate.

Investigation

A comprehensive evaluation and investigation is a necessary first step to create a plan of action. This investigation must address the concerns in a sufficient manner to accomplish an effective plan of action – how the school will take steps to respond in accord with the requirements.

The evaluation and investigation must be comprehensive, prompt, and unbiased. The investigator must have had recent training in both bullying and federal civil rights regulations. You should have the right to question this expertise and to request the district pay for an independent evaluator, although this is uncertain at this time. See the Rise Above Bullying website for updated information on how to request this.

It is exceptionally important that you insist that no one who the investigator interviews is told or is able to figure out that you or your child filed this complaint. The investigator should always use the phrase, "This based on a witness report that we are investigating."

The evaluation and investigation should address:

- The dynamics of the hurtful incidents.
  - This should set forth a comprehensive understanding of where, who, how, and when these incidents occurred and a general assessment of the perceived motivations and any challenges of student(s) being hurtful and their supporters. Some of this information may be considered to be protected under federal privacy laws; however, you should receive sufficient information to allow you to ascertain that the school has taken the time to consider these issues and incorporate this insight into their efforts to stop the hurtful behavior.
- Protections and support needed for your child.
  - This should be a complete evaluation of the common occurrences to allow the identification of steps that need to be taken to ensure the protection of your child.
  - The harm to your child, both in terms of emotional distress and harm to your child's academic progress, should be outlined so that plans can be developed to remedy these concerns.
  - If your child has any challenges in maintaining personal relationships, these should be identified so they can be addressed as positive relationship objectives in your child's Section 504 plan or IEP.
- Aspects of the environment that may be implicated and must be corrected.
  - Assess whether any staff members are treating your child in a disrespectful manner or not responding effectively if they witness your child being treated badly. This will allow for plans to correct staff behavior and improve the skills of staff in responding to the hurtful incidents they witness.
  - Other aspects of the school environment should be evaluated related to the objective of addressing environmental concerns that are specific to your child, especially behavior management practices that may be disparaging to students and the school's efforts to increase inclusion and belonging of all students.

- Recommendations on the following:
  - The strategies to support unmet needs and challenges of any student(s) being hurtful. This will need to be kept private from you.
  - The general strategies the school will use to ensure the hurtful student(s) and their supporters accept personal responsibility and will take steps to remedy the harm to your child.
  - The steps necessary to better protect your child and to ensure that these students will abide by any requirements related to such protections.
  - The requirements to be placed on these students to avoiding any further hurtful behavior directed at your child.
  - Strategies to better support and empower your child.
  - Positive relationship objectives for your child to address any identified concerns in their personal relationship skills.
  - Changes necessary in the school environment that will address any concerns of how your child is being treated by staff and to support staff in responding in an appropriate manner if they witness or are told about any hurtful incidents involving your child and any other aspects of the school environment that impact how your child is treated.
  - How this situation will be monitored and addressed if challenges continue.

Comprehensive Intervention

The following is my guidance on the components that should be included in a comprehensive intervention plan.

Positive Action Plan

The Positive Action Plan for your child should be shaped based on the concerns faced by your child, with the objective of remedying the harm caused by the bullying, improving their personal relationship skills, and building their resilience and empowerment. These actions are grounded in the insight provide in Chapter 5, with the further guidance provided in Chapter 6.

What is most important is that this plan is developed collaboratively, with your child. Your job will to make sure your child's voice is being heard and their concerns are truly being addressed. Seek to avoid having the staff generate their "solutions." Remember that your child's personal power has been taken from them because of the way they have been treated. The best way to empower your child is to ensure they are fully engaged and collaborating in creating this Positive Action Plan.

Components of the Positive Action Plan might:

- **Designate staff allies.** Prior to a Section 504 team meeting or an IEP meeting, ask your child to identify two staff members who they trust and think would support them. It will be helpful if these staff members will serve on your child's Section 504 team and also agree to be appointed as staff allies for your child. At the meeting, make plans for how often and when your child will check in with their staff allies.

- **Determine need for a daily positive action check-in.** A daily positive action check-in may be helpful, especially coming out of this meeting when this new plan is going into effect. The daily check-in may be with the principal, a counselor, or a staff ally. During the daily positive action check in, the staff member should:
  - Focus on positive developments in your child's life and relationships. Ask the four Positively Powerful Happiness Thinking Questions: Who did you have a positive connection with today? How were you kind to someone else? What did you do that you are proud of? What happened today that made you happy?
  - Determine whether your child is consistently using the reach out to be kind, transition calming, and hold themselves tall strategies at transition times and encourage this approach.
  - Discuss any times during the day when your child felt distressed or had to keep their cool to handle a challenging situation and how this worked. Celebrate successes or discuss strategies that could improve effectiveness.
  - Ask questions about any new hurtful incidents and the effectiveness of the current "safe passages plan," if this has been established. See below.
- **Remedy of harm to academic success.** Your child may have suffered harm to their academic progress. The Positive Action Plan should incorporate the steps the school will take to assist your child in getting onto a path to academic success. This may require tutoring or other forms of academic support, preferred enrollment in any important classes, the ability to improve grades by doing an extra credit assignment, and the like.
- **Remedy of harm to involvement in student activities.** If the bullying has resulted in your child dropping out of participation in school activities that the hurtful student and their followers are still participating in, the Positive Action Plan should address how this will be handled. Ideally, your child should have the ability to participate in these activities. If this is a concern, the Accountability Agreement entered into by these students may address this. As these students may be popular and known for their involvement with these activities – for example, a top-level athlete – pressure to remove them from participation is not advised. The retaliation your child would suffer could be intense. However, these students should know that any further hurtful acts directed at your child would be a violation of the Accountability Agreement they have entered into and they would face removal.
- **Address challenges your child might have related to relationship skills, as well as their strengths.** Determine whether your child's lack of effective personal relationship skills may be contributing to the challenges they are facing. This may include how your child is presenting themselves, your child's effectiveness in reading social clues, and how your child responds when treated badly. This must be done in a way that does not blame your child for how they

are being treated. Establish a regular time for your child to work with a school counselor to focus on improving these relationship skills.

- If your child does have some behavior or relationship challenges, a helpful tool to more clearly identify these challenges is the Collaborative Problem Solving Thinking Skills Inventory, which focuses both on identifying your child's strengths and effective strategies, along with their challenges.[3]

- In Chapter 5, I encouraged you to have your older child complete the character strengths inventory at the VIA Character Institute or the brief version that is included as an appendix on the Rise Above Bullying website. Encourage your child to share the results of this character strengths inventory with the team. This way everyone can have a common understanding of your child's strengths and will support your child in using their strengths.

- Collaboratively, you, your child, and the team could identify strategies to assist your child in moderating any disturbing behaviors they engage in to lessen the potential of their being targeted.

- **Develop and practice an incident response plan of action**. This is likely best accomplished in a collaboration between your child and a school counselor. The counselor can collaboratively work with your child to develop effective incident responses in situations where someone is hurtful. These should rely on the Positively Powerful strategies, especially Keep My Cool, Keep My Personal Power, and Think Things Through. With the counselor, your child can practice specific strategies to use whenever someone says or does something hurtful.

  - After getting away from any hurtful situation, your child should know to talk with one of their staff allies or a counselor to gain emotional support and to discuss how to respond further, if deemed necessary. If this hurtful act was done by a student who is currently under an Accountability Agreement, discussed below, this should be reported. This should be considered a violation of that agreement.

- **Address digital and social media activities.** Managing your child's social media activities will be your responsibility. It may be appropriate to discuss ways to lessen the possibility that your child's social media activities may be contributing to concerns. A specific focus on your child's possible addictive access to check on social media posts may be an important issue to address. Shifting your child's focus to engaging extracurricular activities, fun activities in

---

3 ThinkKids. (2016). Collaborative problem solving thinking skills inventory. http://www. thinkkids.org/wp-content/uploads/2016/05/Electronic-CPS-Assessment-and-Planning-Tool-LIKERT-05-2016.pdf (accessed 1 August 2024).

the community like an arts class or martial arts, and finding ways for your child to Act in Service to others can help shift your child's attention away from how many "likes" or comments they have received on their post.

- **Identify strategies to strengthen your child's friendships.** Consider the current status of your child's friendships. The team can determine whether there are any school activities or organizations your child could participate in that would increase their friendships. You may be encouraged to support your child's involvement in out-of-school activities to increase their friendships.
- **Identify strategies to increase advancement and act in service.** Identify expanded ways that your child could be more actively involved to Be Proud and focus on the future in pursuing their specific interests while at school. The team may also be able to identify and support your child in exploring their special interests through involvement in acts of service in the community that are in line with your child's interests.

Protection Plan

A Protection Plan may be necessary. This plan should be developed collaboratively with your child. The plan should address the following:

- **Place of refuge and calming.** Identify several places in the school where your child feels most safe. The school library, counseling office, or calming room might be the places where your child may feel more safe. Arrangements should be made for your child to have the ability to go to one of these places if there is a potential someone may be hurtful or they are feeling distressed. A "permission pass" may be necessary.
- **Safe passages.** Identify any physical areas of the school, to or from school, or any involvement with school activities that present greater concerns. Set forth arrangements to increase safety in these areas. This may include increased staff supervision or a requirement that the student who was hurtful avoid this location.
- **No contact order or other requests.** If your child has specific reasonable requests of the student who was hurtful for "no contact," this should be honored. If a no contact order will be necessary, the provisions should be incorporated into the Accountability Agreement for hurtful student and possibly the Accountability Agreements of the hurtful supporters.
- **No change in your child's schedule or activities.** What the protection plan should *not* contain is any requirement that your child change classes or disengage in school activities, unless truly desired by your child. If any change is necessary to ensure the protection of your child, the hurtful student and supporters must make those changes.

Holding Hurtful Students and Supporters Accountable

Motivations and Actions

The investigation should identify the perceived motivations of the hurtful student and history of the relationship interactions. This will lay the groundwork that will hopefully form the basis for an approach by the school to assist the holding the hurtful student and their supporters accountable.

The investigation should also include an assessment of whether the hurtful behavior appeared to be reactive or proactive. In other words, does it appear that the hurtful student has challenges in maintaining their own behavior and were their actions impulsively hurtful? Or does it appear that the hurtful behavior is proactive behavior of a hurtful student or students who have the ability to maintain control of their own actions and are being hurtful to achieve dominance and social status.

All students who have engaged in hurtful behavior absolutely need to be held accountable for the harm caused by their actions. Students who are hurtful and who have other challenges need to also receive additional support services from the school to better address how they are being treated and other concerns related to the trauma they have experienced.

If it is determined that the student is being hurtful in what is perceived to be actions directed at achieving attention from other students and to demonstrate their dominance and social status, the intervention approach will require actions to support this student in stopping such hurtful behavior and identifying more positive ways that they can exert their leadership interests.

It is also important to identify any students who are consistently being hurtful supporters of the student who is being hurtful. The reason this is important is that these students should be considered as participants in causing the harm and should be held accountable for such remedying harm.

The hurtful student and supporters have privacy protections that would limit the provision of this information to you. However, you should ascertain that these issues were investigated and will be addressed.

Accountability Process and Agreement

An approach called an Accountability Process and Accountability Agreement can be used with the hurtful students and supporters.

The Accountability Process could be considered a restorative diversionary intervention – with any disciplinary consequence held in abeyance. Schools have been strongly encouraged to use restorative practices. This Accountability Process also incorporates other research to best influence students to engage in positive behavior. One reason to call this a restorative disciplinary diversion is that it may be possible for the school to avoid having to report this incident to the state or to OCR as a "bullying" incident. This really should not matter. But as your child's school's principal absolutely wants to avoid any such reporting, possibly this will help.

In addition to the identified hurtful student, any students who were clearly identified as being hurtful supporters – who took actions that were clearly indicated as being supportive of the hurtful behavior of the hurtful student – should also be engaged in this Accountability Process.

The Accountability Process is designed to lead a hurtful student and supporters to acknowledge their wrongdoing, understand the negative impact on the student they bullied, accept personal responsibility, create a plan to remedy the harm to this student and to the school community, and commit to avoiding any further harm. If necessary, this should also include their agreement to abide by provisions in your child's protection plan, such as a "no contact" order.

If a student successfully abides by the terms of the Accountability Agreement, they should be able to avoid a disciplinary record. They should learn a very valuable lesson that will support success in the future. This approach should alleviate the concerns about a permanent disciplinary record, which will hopefully generate greater parent support for responsible behavior and compliance.

This Accountability Agreement should be a signed statement by the hurtful student that describes what they did that was hurtful, and states that they accept personal responsibility for their wrongdoing, they will agree to the protection steps asked for by the targeted student, and their commitment that they will not engage in any further hurtful actions. It would be nice if this agreement also included an apology. However, a fake apology is not of significant value. Acceptance of personal responsibility and their commitment that they will not engage in further hurtful actions should be the objective.

The hurtful student and supporters, and their parents, should be asked to agree to allow a portion of the Accountability Agreement to be shared with your child. A signed waiver of the student's possible privacy rights under FERPA has been included in the Accountability Agreement.

One of the reasons I suggest that your child receive copies of these agreements from both hurtful students and their supporters relates to the issue of personal power. The hurtful student and their supporters were seeking to take personal power from your child. The fact that your child has been provided with a written document from those who were hurtful indicating that they acknowledge that they were hurtful and this was inappropriate, as well as their commitment to stop being hurtful, is a process that will help to return personal power to your child. It will be very important that your child not use these agreements in a way that is hurtful to these students.

Some of the questions included in the Accountability Process for the student who was primarily hurtful include:

- What did you do and how was this hurtful to [your child's name]?
- What were you trying to accomplish?

- Why did you think what you did was okay? What are your family's values about how you should treat others and how were your actions in accord with or not in accord with your family's values?
- Are you willing to accept personal responsibility for your hurtful actions and agree to remedy the harm to both [name of your child] and to the school community?
- Will you make a commitment that you will not continue to be hurtful?

The questions for hurtful supporters are similar. Guidance for school leaders on how to conduct this Accountability Process and create Accountability Agreements with hurtful students and their supporters is on the Rise Above Bullying website.

Correct the Hostile Environment

A hostile environment corrections plan should be developed to ensure any necessary corrections to the school environment that appear to be supporting hurtful behavior of your child.

- **Correct any hurtful staff behavior.** Your documentation and the more expanded investigation may have identified concerns related to how your child is being treated by school staff members. If any staff member has been treating your child with disrespect, this is unacceptable modeling to other students. Such staff behavior must be changed. Some aspects of enforcing such a change will be considered confidential, as this relates to the staff member's employment. However, your child's Section 504 plan or IEP should outline *that* this correction will occur and the specific steps you and your child should take if any such inappropriate staff behavior continues to occur. As noted earlier, as a first step it is likely best to characterize this hurtful behavior as unintentional hurtful behavior that need to be addressed, unless you or the investigator have been able to provide absolutely verified examples of intentional hurtful behavior, with other witnesses willing to talk.
- **Correct how staff respond.** Your documentation and the investigation may have identified concerns related to how staff are responding in situations when your child is treated badly in their presence or has reported concerns to them. If there are any concerns associated with this, your child's Section 504 plan or IEP should outline the school's commitment to agreed-upon standards for how staff will respond, insight into how staff will receive training, and the precise steps you and your child should take if there are any future hurtful incidents where the staff member's response is not effective.
- **Assess and address other concerns.** Determine whether there are any other concerns, especially any behavior management approaches used by the school that may model the denigration and exclusion of your child. For example, does

your child have some behavior concerns and have they been forced to carry a "behavior card" with them through the day? These behavior cards alert to other students which students are considered "problem students" by school staff. Does your child's school give rewards to the compliant students who do not have challenges and does your child more often not receive any rewards? The rewards approach used in schools essentially designates to all students which students the staff think are "good" and which they think are "bad." What activities is the school engaged in to establish student leadership in efforts to encourage kindness and respect? Do these need to be established or expanded? Determine whether there are specific activities the school could implement to correct the environment as this relates to your child and others.

Monitoring and Compliance

Your child's Section 504 plan or IEP should set forth how this situation will be monitored and addressed if hurtful behavior continues. Your child and you should know how to report concerns and have the expectation that a prompt response will occur. Information on how to report such concerns should be incorporated into your child's Section 504 plan or IEP. Remember that provisions that are incorporated into a Section 504 plan or IEP are enforceable. You can file a complaint with the district if the school fails to abide by the commitments set forth in this plan.

Proceeding as a Group

If you are proceeding as a group of parents and students, it will be helpful for all parents and students to complete the Documentation Guide. In a larger discussion of the group, both parents and students should focus on more comprehensive analysis of aspects of the school environment that appear to be supporting the hurtful behavior of some students. It is strongly advised that your group work with a local, regional, or national advocacy group.

Your group could start with a complaint at the school level or proceed direct to OCR and file a group complaint with them. The most important benefit of proceeding as a group of parents and students to file an OCR complaint against the district is the potential to pressure the district and all of your children's schools to make more comprehensive changes to support a more positive school climate with greater kindness, respect, and inclusion of all students. Recall the description of the comprehensive hostile environment correction actions that were included in the Anoka Hennepin settlement that were presented in Chapter 11. These are the kinds of corrections that a group of parents and students can accomplish.

Likelihood of Success

The development of this school environment correction plan must be implemented in a continuous improvement manner that assures the greatest likelihood of success. Using approaches that have a reasonable likelihood of success is essential because, as discussed in Chapter 3, there are no proven-to-be-effective bullying prevention approaches.

Decades ago, there was a federal funding program called the Safe and Drug-Free Schools and Communities Act (SDFSCA). This program provided block-grant funding to states and schools to support safe and drug-free schools. The program required the use of evidence-based programs, which are programs that have demonstrated in research implementations to be effective in achieving desired outcomes.[4] There are no evidence-based programs to support reduction of bullying.

Under SDFSCA a waiver from the requirement for evidence-based programs allowed for the use of innovative programs that demonstrated a likelihood of success to address new concerns.[5] The requirements that were considered necessary under SDFSCA to support obtaining such a waiver are the same requirements I suggest be incorporated into a school environment correction plan. These requirements were:

- A needs assessment based on local objective data that described the problems currently faced by the school.
- A description of the measurable performance objectives the program or activity would address.
- The rationale for the program or activity. This should include how this was designed and why, based on research insight, it was expected to be successful in accomplishing the improvements described in the performance objectives.
- A discussion of the most significant risk and protective factors the program or activity was designed to target.
- A detailed implementation plan, including a description of how the program or activity would be carried out, the personnel to be involved, the intended audience or target population, and the time frame for conducting the program or activity.

---

4 USDOE, Safe and Drug-free Schools and Communities Act (SDFSCA) Title IV, Part A, Subpart 1, Elementary and Secondary Education Act, as amended by the No Child Left Behind Act of 2001, Section 4155(a)(1).

5 §4115(a)(3) WAIVER: A local educational agency may apply to the State for a waiver of the scientifically based requirement to allow innovative activities or programs that demonstrate substantial Likelihood of Success. §4115(a)(1)(C) Programs or activities funded under Title IVA (SDFSCA) must be based on scientifically based research that provides evidence that the program to be used will reduce violence and illegal drug use. §4114(d)(8) A waiver request will be available for public review.

- An evaluation plan that addressed: the methods used to assess progress toward attaining goals and objectives; the personnel who would conduct the evaluation; the way the results of the evaluation would be used to refine, improve, and strengthen the district's comprehensive plan; and the way progress toward attaining objectives would be publicly reported.
- Evidence to support that the program or activity has a "substantial likelihood of success." This was required to include: a description of the prevention research and principles the program was based upon; a description of the results achieved from previous implementation of the activity or program in a setting similar to the one the district was proposing or, if the program has not yet been rigorously evaluated, a description of the plan and timeline for doing so.

The Every Student Succeeds Act (ESSA), enacted in 2015, requires that schools implement programs that are "evidence based." Fortunately, the concept of "evidence based" has been set forth in a manner that supports implementation of newly developed approaches that are logically grounded in research, when the implementation also includes an evaluation component.[6] These approaches fall under what is considered to be Level 4 "Demonstrates a Rationale." Note that the concept of "demonstrated a rationale" is the same as "substantial likelihood of success." To demonstrate a rationale, the intervention should be based on high-quality research findings or positive evaluation that such activity, strategy, or intervention is likely to improve student outcomes or other relevant outcomes; and includes ongoing efforts to examine the effects of such activity, strategy, or intervention.[7]

Continuous Improvement Planning Approach

The following guidance translates these requirements into what should be considered a continuous improvement approach to address the concerns that your child and other students are experiencing bullying by other students and also possibly by staff. As you can see, these closely mirror what was required under the Anoka Hennepin settlement agreement.[8]

- **Establish task forces with representative leadership.** Establish both district and school task forces that include administrative and staff representatives, as well as student and parent representatives. These representatives

---

6 Section 8101(21)(A) of the ESSA.
7 USDOE (2016) Non-regulatory guidance: using evidence to strengthen education investments. https://www2.ed.gov/policy/elsec/leg/essa/guidanceuseseinvestment.pdf (accessed 1 August 2024).
8 Title IX: Sex-Based Harassment: Anoka-Hennepin School District (MN) (#05115901). https://www2.ed.gov/about/offices/list/ocr/docs/investigations/05115901.html (accessed 1 August 2024).

should be reporting back to and obtaining feedback from their respective communities.

- **Gather and analyze data.** All available data related to bullying, student well-being, and school climate should be gathered and effectively analyzed. This includes the comprehensive school climate survey or student wellness surveys that schools are using.
  - Districts should focus on school data that provides evidence of how safe, welcomed, and respected students feel in school. This should include absences data – because excess unexcused absences and excess absences for psychosomatic illness, such as headaches or stomach aches, are an indication of concerns.
  - Most student well-being surveys, like the Youth Risk Behavior Survey, ask questions that are in three categories:
    o Student demographics, including minority identity groups and socioeconomic status.
    o Relationship and school climate issues such as experiencing bullying, relationships with school staff, and feelings of safety while at school.
    o Outcomes data, which includes mental health, suicidal behavior, avoiding school because of fears of safety, bringing weapons to school, and the like.
  - What is important with these surveys is to do further disaggregated analysis of the data. The data must be disaggregated based on demographics and relationships and then disaggregated further based on the responses to the outcomes questions. What percentage of students with disabilities or who are sexual minorities are experiencing bullying, do not think any staff member really cares about them, or do not feel safe? For those students with disabilities or who are sexual minorities who are being bullied, what percentage of them are reporting mental health concerns, suicidal behavior, and so on?
  - It is also essential to consider data on discipline rates and absences.
- **Develop objectives.** Based on an assessment of the data, the positive school climate committee should generate measurable objectives for improvement. These objectives must be grounded in actual data. If the data show that 9% of students report being treated badly by peers once a week or more, an objective may be to see this reduced in the following year to 4%. If only 72% students think that a staff member really cares about them, next year the objective would be that 85% will report that they think a staff member cares about them.
- **Develop an action plan.** The task forces should identify research-based strategies to address the concerns identified in the data and achieve the objectives and develop an implementation plan for these strategies.
- **Provide professional development.** The overall effectiveness of school staff in detecting, intervening in, and reporting incidents should be assessed and action plans should be put into effect to remedy any identified concerns. These

plans should include directives to staff, as well as professional development on strategies for staff to more effectively intervene. The professional development plans may also require a focus on assisting the staff in gaining greater cultural competence, specifically in relation to the identity groups of students who are frequently treated badly. Issues of implicit bias must be effectively addressed as the bias of staff many be implicated in their behaviors that are modeling disrespect to students in these identity groups.

- **Develop an evaluation plan.** The administration of surveys and assessment of data the following year will provide the opportunity for evaluation of effectiveness and revision of objectives and strategies. This is critical. All members of the school community should know of these objectives – and that their school community's success in meeting these objectives will be measured by the next delivery of the survey.
- **Provide the plan to the community.** The draft plan should be provided to the community for review and feedback. Based on this feedback, the plan may need to be modified.

This continuous improvement planning approach has been specifically developed to avoid the tendency of districts to look at the data and do nothing to further analyze the concerns, develop and implement strategies to address the identified concerns, and evaluate their effectiveness with subsequent data.

Blessings and Forward

It is my hope that the insight and guidance I have provided in *Rise Above Bullying* will truly have a positive impact on your child and all children and teens. Additional resources are available on the Rise Above Bullying website.

Index

a

Academic definition, of
  bullying 11
Accountability process and
  agreement approach
  266–268
Active consent 174
Active parenting 183
Acute trauma 33
ADL. *See* Anti-Defamation League
Adults 104–106
  character strengths for
  113–114
  connecting with 106
  importance of 104
  standards for 106
American Educational Research
  Association 32
American Psychiatric
  Association 33
American Psychological
  Association 181
Amygdala-threat response
  center 75

Animal aggression 43
Anterior cingulate cortex 73
Anti-bias training 26
Anti-bullying approach
  58–61
  effectiveness of prevention
  programs 58
  effectiveness of "tell an adult"
  59–61
  student perspectives of staff
  effectiveness 58–59
Anti-Defamation League (ADL)
  20–21
Asian American, identity-
  based bullying 20
Assert-with-care communication
  155–158
  digital communication to
  hurtful staff member
  157–158
  digital communication to
  hurtful student
  156–157
  reasons for 156

Rise Above Bullying: Empower and Advocate for Your Child, First Edition. Nancy E. Willard.
© 2025 John Wiley & Sons, Inc. Published 2025 by John Wiley & Sons, Inc.